THE ADOPTION RESOURCE BOOK

THE
ADOPTION
RESOURCE BOOK

LOIS GILMAN

1817

HARPER & ROW, PUBLISHERS, New York
Cambridge, Philadelphia, San Francisco, London
Mexico City, São Paulo, Singapore, Sydney

Excerpt from *The Chosen Baby* by Valentina P. Wasson. Illustrated by Glo Coalson. Copyright 1939, 1977 by J. B. Lippincott Company. Reprinted by permission of Harper & Row, Publishers, Inc.

FIRST EDITION

Designer: Sidney Feinberg

Library of Congress Cataloging in Publication Data

Gilman, Lois.
The adoption resource book.

Bibliography: p.
Includes index.
1. Adoption—United States. 2. Intercountry adoption—United States. 3. Adoption—United States—Directories. I. Title.
HV881.G55 1984   362.7′34   84-47622
ISBN 0-06-015340-7   85 86 87 88 10 9 8 7 6 5 4 3 2
ISBN 0-06-091160-3 (pbk.)   85 86 87 88 10 9 8 7 6 5 4 3 2

To Ernest, Seth, and Eve

Contents

Preface

"Why are you writing a book about adoption?" This question came up in nearly every interview. Was I a social worker passing on her long experience in the field? Was I a psychologist who counseled children and parents and wanted to promote family health? Was I a lawyer who had handled many a tricky adoption?

No. The answer is really very simple. I'm the mother of two children who are adopted. I am also a historian and a professional researcher. From the time my husband and I made our first inquiries about adoption, I found myself putting my researching talents to work. As I made my calls and built up my own "adoption file," I wondered: What do others do? How do they get the information they need? When I looked at books on adoption, I was surprised at how much was missing. I began to feel that there ought to be a clear, accurate guide that would anticipate many of the questions and present much of the information that *I*—a prospective adoptive parent and now an adoptive parent—had to learn from others piece by piece. I felt that poor information (and sometimes misinformation) too often stood as a barrier between prospective parents and children who needed homes. So I wrote *The Adoption Resource Book*.

Although writing a book ultimately comes down to the rela-

tionship between the author and the typewriter, its creation
depends upon the help of many people. My thanks to them all.

Dozens of adoptive parents took the time to talk with me at
length about their pre- and postadoption experiences. Their
stories shaped the questions that I have tried to answer and the
scope of the book. Since their stories were told in confidence,
I have changed their names and avoided identifying details.

This book has profited from the activities of adoptive-parent
groups around the country. The 1982 North American Conference on Adoptable Children introduced me to many people
and issues, as did the 1983 Project Orphans Abroad conference.
I found the fifty or so parent-group newsletters to which I sub-
scribed invaluable. My special thanks go to the groups that
responded to my request for a complimentary subscription:
OURS In Ky.; the Sonoma County chapter of OURS; the Missis-
sippi Council on Adoptable Children; the Illinois COAC; the
Council of Adoptive Parents; Adoptive Single Parents of New
Jersey; Families for the Future; Kids in Need; Knoxville COAC;
Alabama Friends of Adoption; the Oklahoma COAC; Colorado
Parents for Adoption; the Delaware Coalition for Children;
Families for Children; Oregon Chapter of OURS; the Open
Door Society of Long Island; and Gathering International Fami-
lies Together.

Many people and organizations extended help when it was
requested. Among them, Cheryl Markson of FCVN; Karen
Clarke; Nancy Boucneau, International Mission of Hope; Nancy
Carey, North American Council on Adoptable Children; Toni
Oliver, National Adoption Exchange; Nancy Greene, Interna-
tional Social Service/American Branch; Peggy Soule, The CAP
Book, Inc.; Rosemary Stowe, Spence-Chapin Services to Fami-
lies and Children; Maris Blechner, Lutheran Community Ser-
vices; Donna Haanen, Catholic Social Services, Diocese of
Green Bay; Paul Dubroff, Jewish Family and Children's Service;
Reuben Pannor, Vista Del Mar Child-Care Services; Lois
Melina, *Adopted Child*; Roselle Shubin; Joyce Kaser, Marlene

Ross, Family Building Associates, Inc.; Terry Allor; Patricia McCormick, Deborah Burke, Massachusetts Adoption Resource Exchange; Kenneth J. Hermann, State University of New York, College at Brockport; Vicki Vidak, Partners for Adoption; Hope Marindin, Committee for Single Adoptive Parents; and Virginia Brackett.

Blanche Gelber, Sara-Jane Hardman, Pat Shirley, Ellen Fritz, Susan Pignato, Wilfred Hamm, Barbara Tremitiere, Marlene Piasecki, and Betty Laning read portions of the manuscript and offered insightful comments. Connie Anderson, the editor of *OURS* Magazine, kindly read a draft of the entire manuscript and served as a much-needed sounding board for ideas.

Family and friends offered invaluable support. Lotte Prager pitched in to verify the telephone numbers and addresses of the U.S. agencies. Dan Carlinsky, David Heim, Katherine Foran, Eleanor Prescott, Nick Garaufis, Jeanne and Clem Heymann, Susan and Brian McCarthy, and Susan Stone Wong were always a telephone call away, willing to listen to my latest idea or draft of a paragraph. Deirdre Laughton provided a special service, keeping my children happy. My agent, Victoria Pryor, offered help in innumerable ways. My editor, Janet Goldstein, lent her enthusiasm and gently guided me to the best way to tell the story.

This book has been dedicated to three special people in my life. It is hard now to remember a time when I wasn't Seth's and Eve's mommy with my various entitlements. Since the day Ernest Gilman first served as my editor on the *Columbia Daily Spectator*, he has been my most ardent supporter and my toughest critic. While many husbands have given only lip service to equality in a marriage, he has always shared in the household responsibilities and in the care of our two children. He has given me the best perspective I could bring to this work: "For love, all love of other sights controls."

THE ADOPTION RESOURCE BOOK

1

Learning About Adoption

Once upon a time there lived a man and woman named James and Martha Brown. They had been married for a long time and were very happy together. Only one thing was missing in their lives. They had no babies of their own, and they had always wanted children to share their home.

So begins *The Chosen Baby,* Valentina P. Wasson's adoption classic for parents to read with their young children. James and Martha, so the story goes, meet with Mrs. White at the adoption agency. She asks them many questions and then visits their home to see where the child would sleep and play. A little baby named Peter is eventually placed in their home. When Mrs. White introduces them to Peter, she says, "Now go into the next room and see the baby. If you find that he is not *just the right baby for you,* tell me, and we will try to find another." But Peter is. An adoptive family is created.

The Chosen Baby, published in 1939 and reissued over the years in updated versions, has been read to three generations of adopted children. A story written about adoption in 1984 might be quite different:

• Linda and Edward Tuttle contact Mrs. Andrews at the adoption agency. She tells them that her agency places infants;

however, the birth mother selects the future parents of her child. Helen Doe reads Linda and Edward Tuttle's application and chooses them as Peter's adoptive parents.

- Linda and Edward Tuttle have three children—two boys (ages ten and eight) and a girl (age fourteen). They have always wanted many children to share their home. They contact Mrs. Andrews at the adoption agency to tell her that they would like to adopt two teenagers. They find John and Suzanne, twelve and eleven, in a photograph book distributed by their state that describes children needing permanent homes.

- Linda and Edward Tuttle have no babies of their own and they want children to share their home. So they place an advertisement in a newspaper in their state: "ADOPTION: Happily married couple wish to adopt white infant." Helen Doe calls them up about her baby.

- Linda and Edward Tuttle contact Mrs. Andrews at the adoption agency. Her agency places children from Latin America. After she studies their home, she sends their application to an agency in Colombia. A year later Linda and Edward Tuttle travel to Colombia to pick up their infant son, Pedro.

- Linda and Edward Tuttle have been nine-year-old Peter's foster parents for the past three years. They contact Mrs. Andrews at the adoption agency to ask whether they might adopt him.

- Linda Tuttle has always wanted children. But she's forty and single. She contacts Mrs. Andrews about the possibilities of adoption. She adopts eight-year-old Peter, who has cerebral palsy.

- Linda and Edward Tuttle contact Mrs. Andrews at the adoption agency. She tells them that her agency will not take any applications. Five years later Linda and Edward Tuttle are still waiting.

The story of adoptive families is changing. Childless couples are still adopting, but so are couples with birth children, and so are singles. Agencies are still placing babies, but they are also placing older children, sibling groups, and children with physical and mental handicaps. People are still coming to agencies for help in becoming parents, but they are also seeking to adopt on their own. They are also forming families by adopting children born abroad. It's difficult to draw a composite portrait of adoption today.

It would be nice if we could start by citing some current statistics about adoption. They don't exist. Says a government statistician: "The federal government has been out of the business of keeping track of adoptions for almost ten years now. We know how many hogs (6,450,000 in 1981) are in Illinois, but we don't know how many children are adopted. We have no idea of the total number of adoptions in the United States today." The U.S. government used to collect statistics from the states, but today it does not. Some of the states' departments of social services know (1,549 nonrelative adoptions in Minnesota in 1982; 633 in Iowa; 986 in Arizona). Others do not. An official from Oklahoma reported in 1983: "There are no reliable statistics on the total number of adoptions which took place in the State of Oklahoma."[1]

What do we know? We know that the majority of adoptions involve the adoption of a child by a relative (e.g., a stepparent). These adoptions predominated in the early 1970s when the U.S. government had good data. Current data provided by states show a similar trend. For 1974 a government expert estimated the total number of adoptions at 149,000, with 36 percent (59,000) involving adoption by a person not related to the child. Scattered reports from a variety of states suggest that there has not been a major change in the number of nonrelative adoptions. Nonrelative, nonagency adoptions (often referred to as "independent" or "private" adoptions) have been estimated to account for upwards of 20 percent of adoptions. In 1983 the National Committee for Adoption claimed that there "are not more than 40,000 healthy infants placed for adoption each year," while the Children's Bureau has established that in December 1982 about 17,000 children were being adopted out of the public foster-care system annually. The State Department can tell us that in fiscal year 1983, 7,350 children abroad were issued visas in connection with an adoptive placement.[2] Until the federal government gets back into the adoption statistics collection and analysis business, we're left with scattered pieces of information that don't quite add up.

It's equally complex to try to explain what adoption is today. The dictionary definition of *adoption* is very simple—to take a child of other parents voluntarily as one's own—but what that may mean in practice is not. Adoption has traditionally been seen as an event that culminates when the new parents go to court and vow before a judge to receive a child as their new son or daughter. At that time the bonds between the child and his/her birth parents are legally terminated. The child's past history—the documents that record how the child moved from his or her relationship with the birth family into the relationship with the adoptive parents—is sealed away. The adoptive parents raise the child as their own, following the model of the family created by birth. To take a child as one's own has meant to cut the child off from his or her genetic past.

Now that view has come under attack. The veil of secrecy that has traditionally surrounded adoption is being lifted. Adults who were adopted as infants are telling us that growing up as an adopted child is different. They have come back to the agencies and the courts that hold their records and demanded the right to know about those other parents. They have challenged us to look at adoption as a lifelong event, with the court hearing marking the beginning rather than the end. They have told us that we can't obliterate their other parents. Birth parents, in turn, are voicing the desire to take part in the adoption process and even to maintain some contact with the child and the adoptive parents after the placement has been made. Some adoption professionals are now talking about adoption as an experience in "shared parenthood." The story of the chosen baby is being rewritten. In its place we have the "adoption triangle"—the birth parent, the adoptive parent, and the adoptee, all with needs and rights that have to be acknowledged.

New agency practices are emerging. Among them, parent preparation for adoption in group meetings; continued agency involvement with families after the finalization of adoption; disclosure of detailed information to adult adoptees about their past; contact between birth parents and adoptive parents through letters or direct meetings.

The Adoption Resource Book tries to answer both the older and the newer questions that adoptive parents have about creating and raising a family. Like most adoption handbooks, it begins with information about how to build a family. As Chapters 2 to 9 make clear, however, there are now many keys that will unlock the door to parenthood. Chapters 10, 11, and 12 try to sketch out the needs of parents and children—the preparations parents should make; the weeks, months, and years that go into family building; the issues involved in raising a family created through adoption. These chapters seek to point out what parents will need to consider rather than to provide definitive answers. Finally, there are state-by-state directories of U.S. and intercountry adoption agencies and a reading list.

Underlying this book are a few basic premises:

- Children have a right to grow up in permanent families. Adoption offers them this opportunity.
- Adoption is a way of building a family. It is no better or worse than any other way. It is different, however. That difference must be acknowledged and dealt with.
- Prospective parents need good, basic, accurate information about adoption.

- Adoptive families need support from others—support that begins when parents think about creating their families and that continues throughout the life of the family.
- Adoptive parents must focus on the needs of their children as well as their own needs. Communication and openness are important.

Approaching Parenthood

Adopting a child will involve making many decisions. What kind of child? Do you want to adopt through an agency? If not, what other means will you use to make it happen? First, though, you should look at yourself. Is adoptive parenthood, or even parenthood itself, what you really want? Your own feelings will help determine what type of child you seek to adopt and have a direct impact on the child that you raise. Since adoption involves deliberate family planning, as you get started, ask yourself these basic questions:

- How important is it for you to be a parent?
- Are you satisfied that you can provide a healthy family life for a child?
- Have you explored adequately other avenues than adoption for parenting?
- How do you feel about parenting a child who is not biologically related?

Coming to Terms with Your Infertility

According to a study released by the National Center for Health Statistics in 1983, some 3 million American women would like to have babies but are unable to conceive. If your inability to produce a child has led you to think about adoption, you will want to be sure that you have dealt with your infertility *before you adopt a child.*

What do you know about infertility?

Infertility specialists estimate that some 50 to 70 percent of all fertility problems can be resolved medically. In the past ten years, many breakthroughs have been made in the treatment of infertility. Microsurgery can often repair damaged tubes in women, while another surgical procedure that ties off a varicose vein in a testicle seems to improve fertility in men. Drugs such as Clomid and Pergonal can induce or regulate ovulation in women. Endometriosis may yield to drug therapy or surgery. For women whose tubes are damaged beyond repair or have been removed, *in vitro* fertilization, an experimental and costly procedure, offers a 15–20 percent chance of pregnancy.

Do some basic reading about infertility. Dr. Sherman Silber states: "Even for those who have no hope of pregnancy, at least a clear understanding of how their bodies work can prevent needless anxiety about whether or not they have gone far enough in their search."[3] Following are some excellent books that you can consult:

Lori B. Andrews, *New Conceptions* (New York: St. Martin's Press, 1984).
Robert H. Glass and Ronald J. Ericsson, *Getting Pregnant in the 1980s* (Berkeley: University of California Press, 1982).
Barbara Eck Menning, *Infertility: A Guide for the Childless Couple* (Englewood Cliffs, N.J.: Prentice-Hall, 1977).
Sherman J. Silber, *How to Get Pregnant* (New York: Scribner's, 1980).

If you have lost a child through miscarriage, ectopic pregnancy, or stillbirth, you will want to look at Rochelle Friedman and Bonnie Gradstein, *Surviving Pregnancy Loss* (Boston: Little, Brown, 1982).

Understanding human reproduction and infertility gives you the tools to ask the questions and find the answers that you will need to come to terms with your medical condition.

If you adopt a child, will you get pregnant?

Robert H. Glass and Ronald J. Ericsson are clear on this point: "Careful studies have shown that the pregnancy rate is identical for infertile couples who adopt as for those who do not adopt."[4] Adoption cannot replace damaged tubes or undo the effects of endometriosis.

What medical advice and support have you sought?

Both of you will need a full medical work-up by a specialist. For the man, that means a physical examination as well as a semen analysis. Almost half the time, infertility can be traced to the man. Often both the man and the woman contribute to the problem. Sometimes small changes in both may result in a pregnancy.

Your regular family physician or your gynecologist may be a fine doctor, but he or she is not necessarily the person most qualified to analyze a fertility problem. Some gynecologists, urologists, and reproductive endocrinologists have developed specialties in infertility. The **American Fertility Society** (1608 13th Avenue South, Suite 101, Birmingham, Alabama 35256; 205-933-7222) can refer you to qualified specialists in your area. The self-help group **Resolve** (P.O. Box 474, Belmont, Massachusetts 02178; 617-484-2424), which has local chapters throughout the United States, also provides infertility counseling and referral services. Support groups give you a chance to talk about your feelings.

If you have a choice of several specialists, try to learn a little about them before you make your decision. Does the doctor have a subspecialty within the field? Does he work with a team of other specialists? Does he have an infertility counselor (a therapist who will talk with you) on his staff? Be sure to choose a doctor with whom you feel comfortable and who will permit you to ask questions. Your physician has many infertile patients to consider; you have only one—yourself.

Even after you have found your doctor, you may want to talk with another specialist to confirm a recommended course of treatment, to get a second opinion before surgery, or to help you decide whether it might be time to give up altogether. Before your visit, check with the specialist to be sure your doctor has forwarded your medical records. It can also be helpful for you to prepare your own medical résumé for the consultant, a summary of your past history, surgery, and drug therapy. Preparing this résumé will force you to evaluate where you are.

What have you asked your doctor?

Ask *all* the questions that you want answers for, and don't be shy about bringing in a list. You'll want a full explanation of any procedures your doctor is advocating, including their risks and success rates. Try to pin him or her down as to the expected length of any course of treatment. You have a right to know the game plan. If possible, have your spouse present to give you moral support and to be sure that all issues that concern you are raised.

Have you acknowledged to yourself and to others how being infertile makes you feel?

If you have been struggling to become pregnant, you've probably felt depressed, overwhelmed, guilty, and cheated. There may be tension in your marriage. You may have harbored thoughts of divorce so that your spouse can find a more fertile partner. You've probably found it painful to be around friends with children. You may find that your sleep is disturbed; that you have nightmares; that you awaken feeling distressed. One woman remembers the day when she, a nondrinker, "got royally stewed" on a whole bottle of Kahlúa because she was so

devastated at having her period again, despite yet another
month of drug therapy. Says infertility counselor Roselle Shubin: "As a medical problem, infertility is rather unique. You
can't get adjusted to it. Every month the question arises—will
ovulation occur and will the husband perform sexually? Infertile couples are in an almost constant state of crisis."[5]

Resolving this crisis means not only getting the medical answers that will satisfy you but also coming to terms emotionally
with your infertility. The failure to produce a biological child is
a major loss and blow to your self-esteem. There are strong
feelings that must be acknowledged. Two couples speak:

> No one understands what a tragedy this is. It's a real loss—like the
> death of a child through illness.

> There is the loss of control of your body, the loss of your biological
> future, and the loss of the child you want to have.[6]

To work through your infertility, you must face it openly. Says
Shubin, "Coming out of the closet is critical." You must talk to
your spouse and others. Express your feelings. Support groups
like Resolve can help you. Since infertility involves loss, you
must grieve for the child you never had, for the child who might
have been, for your inability to create life. You'll feel angry,
upset, guilty, and finally you'll be able to let go. Says Reuben
Pannor, director of community services of Vista Del Mar Child-
Care Services:

> First and foremost, the couple must work through the feelings of
> guilt and loss arising from the infertility of their marriage and come
> to a mature understanding and acceptance of it as a fact of life that
> cannot be altered by adopting a child or by any other means. Until
> this kind of emotional resolution is achieved, the couple really is not
> ready to adopt. It is worth noting that counseling can be very helpful
> in achieving this aim.[7]

Pannor, who has written a major book about adoption, believes
that trouble in adoptive families starts when "adoption is used
to avoid resolving the sense of loss infertility brings."

To move beyond infertility means to give up the role of the

patient and the never-ending search for the medical solution. It takes time. Roselle Shubin says, "Sometimes I'll say to a patient, can you give me your thermometer?" (Thermometers are a basic tool in most infertility treatments.) Coming to grips with your infertility may mean giving up the quest and accepting yourself and your family as you are.

BioOptions

Each year more than 10,000 babies are conceived through artificial insemination by donor (AID), a process in which a couple or a single woman seeking to start a family "adopt sperm." In a doctor's office, the sperm of an anonymous donor is inserted into a woman's vagina near the cervix. Pregnancy is now a viable possibility for families in which the husband's infertility has previously made it difficult. The couple signs a special consent form acknowledging the children produced by artificial insemination as legitimate.

Be aware that in many states the legal status of AID children is not clear. According to Lori B. Andrews, a specialist in medical law with the American Bar Foundation, twenty-four states have passed laws that make the husband the legal father. In some states where there are no statutes, the infertility specialist may refer the couple, after a successful insemination, to an obstetrician who is not told about the procedure. Says Andrews: "In a divorce case in states without statutes, there could be the question as to who gets custody and who is the father. The majority of the states don't have any protection for all the parties—the child's right to inherit from the couple, the donor's right not to be expected to support the child." Whether parents tell their offspring about AID is also not clear, nor is it certain how this knowledge (or a sudden later discovery) may affect an individual's emotional development. Nor do we know what the emotional burden is for parents who keep this secret.

If "sperm adoption" through AID is now a routine procedure, "egg adoption" may not be far behind. In November 1983, the world's first "donor egg" baby was born in Australia. A woman donated an unfertilized egg, which was then fertilized in a petri dish with the sperm of another woman's husband. After the egg had cleaved into two cells, it was placed in the uterus of the second woman. The embryo implanted in the recipient's uterus and she carried the pregnancy to term. A different procedure for embryo transfer has been developed in California (first birth, January 1984). A fertile woman is artificially inseminated with the sperm from the husband of an infertile woman. About five days after fertilization, doctors remove the egg by flushing out the woman's uterus. If a fertilized egg is found, the embryo is deposited in the uterus of the infertile woman and the recipient carries the baby to term. Similar questions as raised for AID come up here.

A third possibility involves the use of surrogate mothers. A couple contracts with a willing, fertile woman who agrees to be artificially inseminated with the husband's sperm, to carry the pregnancy, and after delivery to relinquish all parental rights to the biological father and his wife. The surrogate mother must go to court to release the child; the father must legally acknowledge the child; the wife must adopt the child. The costs can be extraordinary—upwards of $20,000. Be aware that the legal situation is in a snarl, with some experts declaring surrogate parenthood illegal and others drawing parallels with artificial insemination. In several states legislation has been introduced to give surrogate parenting a legal footing.

For a full discussion of these options, including a thorough discussion of emotional and legal issues, see Lori B. Andrews' *New Conceptions*.

Getting Information About Adoption

As you contemplate adoption, you will need to explore both resources that will help you build your family and resources that you can turn to for continuing information and support in the years ahead. Your initial steps will take you in three directions: (1) making contact with adoptive families and parent groups, (2) checking with social-service agencies for general information as well as for details about specific adoption programs, and (3) reading.

Making Contact with Adoptive Families and Parent Groups

Getting to know other adoptive families is a first step in adoption and one you should continue to take as the years pass by. You may know people who have adopted and who will share their experiences with you. Spend time with their families and observe their children. If you are thinking about an intercountry adoption, talk to people about their experiences and observe their children. If you are contemplating an older-child adoption, spend some time around older children. Ask parents what it's like to start your family with a ten-year-old.

There are now several hundred parent groups in the United States. Local groups can give you basic information about adoption. **The Open Door Society** of Massachusetts (25 West Street, Boston, Massachusetts; 617-527-5660), for example, is a statewide organization with a membership of several hundred families. Its philosophy is: "If there are people who want to be parents and there are children needing homes, they should be brought together as quickly as possible. Parents and adoption agencies, working together, can create a future in which there are parents for every child." People interested in adopting can call to request fact sheets that describe the types of children available for adoption and list the agencies to contact (there are fact sheets for both U.S. and intercountry adoptions). Members also serve as adoption-information aides for the state adoption service—the Massachusetts Adoption Resource Exchange—answering questions for people who inquire about adoption. There are sixteen chapters that hold monthly meetings. The

Open Door Society publishes a newsletter, sells books, and holds an annual New England Adoption Conference. Some sample sessions: "Adopting Sibling Groups"; "Explaining Adoption to Your Child"; "How to Pick an Adoption Agency." The 1984 conference even had a panel discussion led by older teenagers for other youths about the common issues in being an adoptee.

Some parent groups have created adoption information courses. **Families Adopting Children Everywhere (FACE)** (P.O. Box 28058, Northwood Station, Baltimore, MD 21939; 301-799-2100) offers a six-week course at various locations throughout Maryland and northern Virginia. The course— "Family Building Thru Adoption"—uses parents and experts to cover such issues as accepting infertility, adoption in the U.S., intercountry adoption, how to adopt, adjustments, telling a child, and dealing with prejudice. The FACE course (its course booklet can be ordered for $3) has served as the prototype of many adoption-information courses around the country. Peggy Phillips, an adoptive parent who developed a continuing-education course for the Northampton County Area Community College in Pennsylvania, says, "It is much easier to walk out of a class than an adoption agency. This way, you can learn the pros and cons and ask questions you might feel hesitant to broach at an agency for fear you might say something out of line."

To find parent groups in your area, contact the **North American Council on Adoptable Children (NACAC)** (810 18th Street N.W., Washington, D.C. 20006; 202-466-7570). NACAC is a nonprofit coalition of individuals and organizations working for the rights of children in the areas of foster care and adoption. As a major national adoption organization, it functions in part as a clearinghouse for adoptive parent support groups around the country. NACAC has a computerized list of parent groups nationwide, so you can ask them about groups in your area as well as request basic information about adoption. NACAC's state representatives (listed in the "Domestic Adoption Directory") will inform you about local parent groups and local

agencies, and will be glad to answer many of your basic questions about your state's adoption practices. As an adoption
advocacy group, NACAC monitors federal child-welfare legislation, pushes for better access to adoption services, sponsors
an annual national adoption week as well as a biannual national
conference, and publishes a newsletter. NACAC also distributes books about adoption (contact them for a list).

Another major parent group is **OURS, Inc.** (3307 Highway
100 North, Suite 203, Minneapolis, Minnesota 55422; 612-535-
4829), with over 7,000 members around the country. Membership ($13 annually) includes a subscription to an excellent bi-
monthly magazine featuring personal accounts by which
adoptive families "reach out" to others. The magazine also lists
books and other items that families can purchase from OURS.
Some 100 parent groups across the country are affiliated with
OURS.

The **Committee for Single Adoptive Parents** (P.O. Box 15084,
Chevy Chase, Maryland 20815) serves as a clearinghouse for
singles seeking information. Membership ($10) entitles you to
a list of agencies and other contacts (with updates) that singles
will want to approach about adoption. The committee can also
provide you with the names of single-parent groups as well as
other single parents to talk to. *The Handbook for Single Adoptive Parents* ($6, available from the committee) is an excellent
introductory guide to single parenthood, offering help on such
topics as "managing single parenthood."

Checking with Social-Service Agencies

Seeking out a parent group is a beginning; so is contacting your public agencies. Your state department of public welfare may be able to supply you with useful information: brochures describing state adoption programs; subsidy programs
(see Chapter 10), fact sheets describing intercountry adoption
procedures. A few states now have toll-free telephone numbers
that you can call to request information about adoption. (If you

write, don't be surprised if it takes two or more months to get a reply.) You'll also want to start by getting in touch with local agencies, both public and private, to learn about their specific programs. The next chapter, "Exploring Adoption through an Agency," provides a basic orientation to agencies and how they work. The directories at the back of the book list agencies state by state. Even if you ultimately decide to pursue an independent U.S. or intercountry adoption, touching base initially with agencies gives you a better grasp of adoption in the U.S. and in your state today.

Reading

As a prospective parent, you will probably read books that focus on child care and child development. As a prospective adoptive parent, you will also want to read books that touch on some specialized topics related to adoption. References to these works are placed at the appropriate points in the text. The annotated bibliography at the back of the book surveys current books about adoption. You may want to read some of these now; others may be more relevant in the years ahead.

As you start making your adoption plans, you might want to read some personal accounts. Some special books are:

Barbara J. Berg, *Nothing to Cry About* (New York: Bantam Books, 1983). An autobiography that talks about miscarriage, birth, and adoption.

Joseph Blank, *Nineteen Steps Up the Mountain: The Story of the DeBolt Family* (Philadelphia: Lippincott, 1976). The story of a family and their adoption of special-needs children.

Jill Krementz, *How It Feels to be Adopted* (New York: Knopf, 1982). Nineteen boys and girls share their thoughts.

Doris Lund, *Patchwork Clan: How the Sweeny Family Grew* (Boston: Little, Brown, 1982). Chronicles the formation of a family that grew to include seventeen children.

Each of these captures family life and feelings.

The Children Needing Placement in the U.S.

Despite rumors you may have heard on television or from a neighbor about the lack of infants for adoption, you'll find that infants are still placed for adoption. Indeed, statistics reveal that as many as 80 percent of adoptions may be infant adoptions. Since many people want to adopt infants, many agencies will tell families that they should expect to wait, often for several years, for white infants (there is often not a wait for black infants). However, there is another way that infants enter adoptive families: In all but six states, birth parents may bypass agencies and choose to place their babies directly with adoptive parents. (See Chapter 7 for a full discussion of independent adoption.)

When you inquire at an agency about adoption, you're likely to be told that the children currently waiting for homes are older, or black, or of other minority-group parentage. They may be part of a sibling group. Some may have physical handicaps such as cerebral palsy, hydrocephalus, spina bifida, or Down's syndrome. Others have emotional handicaps or are developmentally delayed. Some of the older children are physically healthy (though they may have emotional problems) but they wait nonetheless because of their ages. Marlene Piasecki, director of the National Adoption Exchange, says that the relatively healthy white children *waiting* for adoption are usually twelve years old or more. The younger the child is, the more severe the disabilities are likely to be. Most agencies occasionally place healthy white toddlers and young school-age children, but they will have waiting lists for these children. The profile of the black children waiting for adoption, however, is different. There are black children of all ages waiting for homes. Black sibling groups are particularly common. If you are white and thinking about adoption, be aware, however, that many agencies will not place children transracially. (For a full discussion, see Chapter 8.)

The Children's Bureau estimates that at any given moment there are some 30,000 children *waiting* for adoptive homes. The children who need adoptive families but have not found them might be:

Mike, age twelve, white. Four foster-care placements and one group home since he entered care at age six.

Mia and Marilyn, five-year-old twin girls, white. Born with Down's syndrome.

William, Arthur, and John, brothers who are eight, six, and four years old, black. Living for the past three years in a foster home.

Jimmy and Joanna, four and three years old, brother and sister, Hispanic. Born with congenital cataracts. Developmentally delayed.

Donald, nine years old, black.

Children who have been waiting for adoptive families for a period of time are often referred to as "waiting children." Children who have disabilities are often referred to as "special-needs children." For a good description of special-needs children—who they are and how to assess your potential for parenting them—see Joan McNamara's *Adopting the Child with Special Needs* (Washington, D.C.: North American Council on Adoptable Children, 1982). In some states you may also find that children who are members of a minority group or who are older are referred to as "special-needs children."

Chapter 4 discusses the children in other countries who wait for homes and those who have been placed in American adoptive homes.

Making Your Adoption Plan

The chapters that follow survey how you can go about building your adoptive family: working through an agency; working independently; searching for an infant or an older child in the United States; searching for an infant or an older child abroad.

As the next chapter on agencies makes clear, not all agencies are alike—their philosophies may differ radically. How they approach adoption may directly influence how you view adoption and how you create your family. Sometimes it is possible for you to make choices; sometimes not.

Your basic goal now, as you ferret out information, is to seek out supports and build your own adoption network. The friends that you make, the groups that you join, the services that you uncover will stay with you in the years ahead. You're beginning an experience that has no end.

2

Exploring Adoption
Through an Agency

Whatever kind of adoption you're thinking about, your road to parenthood will probably take you through, or at least past, an agency. There are different types of agencies that you can contact. Each state has a public agency charged with the care of children in the state. The state agency—frequently identified as the Bureau of Family and Children's Services, the Division of Social Services, or the Department of Public Welfare—oversees the provision of services to children, including foster care and adoption. The state agency usually has local—often county—branches around the state. Cities may have their own departments of social services for children in their care.

Although public agencies serve the people of a state, your public agency may not be able to work with you. If you want to adopt a white infant, for example, and the agency does not have many children to place, it may offer to put your name on a waiting list. You may be told that you will have to wait several months or years before the agency is ready to take a formal application and evaluate your family as a resource for a child. A public agency may also be so understaffed that it may tell you that you must wait before it can work with you. If you wish to adopt a child from overseas, many state agencies will decline to study your family; their main priority will be to help find permanent homes for children currently in their care. Check with your local public agency or your state adoption unit about adoption policies in your state.

States also license private child-placing agencies. These agencies, often called "voluntary agencies," will have children in their care needing homes. They can also study your family for an intercountry adoption or for the adoption of a waiting child. Some agencies, like Bethany Christian Services, serve a specific sectarian population; others, like the Children's Home Society, do not. Some of the voluntary agencies are also branches of a national religious or church-sponsored organization.

Keep in mind that a private agency with a name like Presbyterian Children's Home and Service Agency does not necessarily restrict services to Presbyterians. Nor does it place only Presbyterian children. Some agencies may have a current religious requirement for service; others may not. Often an agency's name reflects its past practices (some agencies may have been placing children for fifty years or more). Some agencies do have a religious standard for service, but it may be broader than a particular denomination (e.g., you may find agencies that only work with Christian families or with "practicing Christians"). Other agencies are strictly nondenominational. Don't eliminate any agency from consideration on the basis of its name.

Certain agencies have developed specialties. The Family Builder agencies, such as Children Unlimited in Columbia, South Carolina, are a network of nonprofit adoption agencies located around the United States that place older, handicapped, and minority children. Since these agencies serve waiting children, they charge no fees to adoptive parents and collaborate with other agencies in accepting referrals of children needing families. Downey Side in Springfield, Massachusetts, is a licensed adoption agency exclusively for adolescents (usually fourteen to eighteen years old). Downey Side has been working primarily in New England. Still other agencies focus solely on finding homes for children through intercountry adoption.

Homes for Black Children, in Detroit, Michigan, recruits black families and has placed over 900 children since it began. Homes for Black Children has streamlined the adoption process for black families, doing away with long waiting periods, complicated application forms, and fees. Their recruitment literature sets the tone: "There is only one thing you need to adopt a child through Homes for Black Children—the ability to love and raise that child as your own." The agency has been setting up programs in other cities around the United States. Contact them to learn about their programs and for information about other U.S. agencies that have worked with them to create outreach programs for black families.

There are even some agencies that specialize in infant adoption. The Edna Gladney Home is a nationally recognized maternity home in Fort Worth, Texas. In 1982 it placed 358 babies in several states. The Golden Cradle Home in Pennsylvania has also attracted national attention for its aggressive recruitment techniques ("Call collect in confidence 215-289-BABY") and its services to birth mothers.

Requirements

As you learn about agencies, you will discover that all agencies have some requirements for prospective adopters. Some have just the minimum required by state law. Others have developed criteria in addition to those mandated by state law.

Be aware that there are no uniform laws of adoption; each state has its own laws and requirements. State regulations are made "in the best interests of the child" and seek to protect everyone's rights.

SOME COMMON REQUIREMENTS

Age
- You should be between eighteen and sixty years old.
- An agency will be concerned that you be young enough to see your child grow to maturity.
- An agency may specify a minimum number of years (often no less than fifteen) or a maximum number of years (often no more than forty) that can separate parents and children.

Marital Status
- Couples may have to be married a certain number of years before they can apply.
- Some agencies may be more concerned about the stability of the relationship than the length of the marriage.
- Previous divorce is often acceptable.
- Singles may not be acceptable.

Income
- Some agencies may require that you meet a specific financial standard.
- Some agencies will ask that you show that you can manage effectively on your income.

Health
- Agencies usually require medical exams.
- Some agencies, if you are applying for a younger child, will require that you provide a fertility report.
- If you are significantly overweight, an agency may question your health and life expectancy.

Religion
- Some states may require that the child be placed in a home of the same religious background as the biological parents.
- Some agencies will require that you have a religious affiliation and may ask for a recommendation from a pastor.

Family Size
- Some agencies may specify that only childless couples can have an infant placed with them.

- When placing an infant, some agencies may state that there may be no more than one other child in the home.
- Some agencies may discriminate against large families.

Residency
- Some agencies may serve only a specific geographic region.

You may discover that an agency, when placing infants, will accept applications only from couples married for several years who can show medical evidence of infertility. The agency may also set an age limit, often specifying that the applicants be no more than thirty-five or forty years old. The Barker Foundation in Washington, D.C., tells its applicants that it "attempts, in good faith, to select as adoptive parents those couples from the potential candidates who present the least risk considering the numerous factors such as candidates' health, medical history, economics, emotional and marital stability."

Agencies that specialize in placing handicapped or older children often have more flexible requirements. Peirce-Warwick Adoption Service in Washington, D.C., a Family Builder agency, tells its applicants:

> We want to hear from all who feel they have love and understanding to share. Single women or men can adopt. The size of your home or whether or not you own it doesn't matter. You can live in an apartment. . . . Mothers can work. . . . Your lifestyle may be different. . . . You can be an older person and adopt. . . . Adoptive parents can themselves be handicapped. What DOES count is that you are interested in providing a loving and supporting home for a child who waits.

An agency like Peirce-Warwick may view singles as the "placement of choice" for particular children. But many agencies are still wary of singles. If you are a single seeking to adopt, be prepared to find barriers thrown up in your path. "Adoption agencies are the last bastion of the two-parent family," grumbled one single adoptive parent. "I tried any number of agencies. What hurt most was when the local department of human services hung up on me, saying flat out, 'Sorry, no singles.' I'm a taxpayer and a homeowner, but simply because I'm single, I couldn't use the public agency."[1] Singles often find that agencies will not place infants or younger children with them. An agency may try to encourage them to take special-needs children for whom the agency has had difficulty finding homes. Some singles complain that they are treated as the "dumping ground" for such children and that agencies have told them flat out that they are reserving certain children for two-parent families.

You may have to bend over backward to show an agency your ability to adopt. One single father who has adopted several handicapped children complained that "my biggest hassles haven't been with my kids but with agencies. Each adoption has been an adversary proceeding, with the agency trying to show why I shouldn't have a child and my having to prove myself."[2] In 1983 the Committee for Single Adoptive Parents, an adoption advocacy group, reported that it had become upset by letters it had received "from prospective single parents that document years of professional and volunteer activities" as well as demonstrate people's stability and experience with children and that then "describe the unwillingness of agencies in their areas to talk with them about the placement of a U.S.-born child." As a result, some single parents have turned to intercountry adoption.

People with chronic medical problems or physical handicaps must also be prepared to convince an agency that their condition will not affect their ability to parent. Likewise, if you are the parent of several children, don't be surprised if an agency tries to discourage you from adopting or turns you down. Again you may even be told that you are eligible to apply only for specific children. The agency worker may question how you can have room for one (or many more) and may even suggest that you are running a group home rather than parenting individual children. You may have to search for the right agency to work with you in your quest. Or you may need to adopt independently or explore adoption abroad.

Diane Nason's autobiography *The Celebration Family* (Nashville: Thomas Nelson, 1983) touches on the difficulties that people with large families may encounter. After the Nasons had completed several adoptions, they were told by the state agency that it would not approve them for additional children. So they turned to a private agency. Their social worker at this agency, however, decided she could not approve a family with more than eight children.[3] The Nasons appealed to the board of directors of the agency and the social worker's recommendation was overruled.

David Frater also had to fight to adopt a child. He is a homosexual. In January 1983, the *New York Times* reported that Frater had successfully adopted a seventeen-year-old boy in California who had entered his home as a foster child. He had spent two years battling for the finalization of his son's adoption. Gay applicants who are honest about their life-style are likely to encounter resistance when they try to adopt. To explore the possibilities of adoption as well as how to approach an agency, talk first with other homosexuals who have successfully adopted. Contact the **National Committee on Gay and Lesbian Issues of the National Association of Social Workers** (7981 Eastern Avenue, Silver Spring, Maryland 20910; 301-565-0333). If you have identified a specific child whom you wish to adopt, the **Lamda Legal Defense and Education Fund** (132 West 43 Street, New York, New York 10036; 212-944-9488) can help if you need legal advice.

Fees

Public agencies usually charge no fee, although a few do charge a fee for services. Private agencies usually charge fees, although they may reduce or waive fees when families adopt waiting children. Some private agencies have a set fee (which might be as high as $4,000 for an infant adoption). Many agencies use a sliding scale, based on a family's income, to determine the fee. Sliding-scale fees usually have a set maximum. You may find that the fees range from $1,000 to $4,000, although this will vary by state. Some states may set ceilings on the fees that agencies can charge; others may not.

Open Adoption

Agencies have traditionally strived to protect the rights of birth parents, adoptees, and adoptive parents by maintaining confidentiality through the practice of closed adoption. In recent years adult adoptees have challenged this practice, returning to the agencies and demanding to learn more about their birth parents. Some birth parents have also come to agencies asking for an update about their surrendered children. Thus the secrecy that underlies agency policy has come under attack. Kathleen Silber, director of the San Antonio office of Lutheran Social Service of Texas, describes how her agency took a step forward. "After writing a letter to the adoptive parents of her child, a practice we had been allowing (not encouraging) for several years, a determined birth mother asked the unthinkable question, 'Will you ask them to write back? I want to know what they think about my baby.' "[4]

Silber's response to that question was the first step in the creation of a different policy for her agency—open adoption, which involves contact between birth parents, adoptees, and adoptive parents. This led her to a different definition of *adoption*—"the process of accepting the responsibility of raising an individual who has two sets of parents,"[5] and to a call for different practices: sharing names, sharing letters, sharing photographs, meeting face-to-face.[6]

Catholic Social Services in Green Bay, Wisconsin, is another agency whose adoption program has changed. When the agency first looked at its practices, social worker Donna Haanen says, "openness was thought to be providing information for adoptive parents about their child's origins." By 1983, however, the agency's practices had evolved to the point where adoptive parents and birth parents were meeting at the time of the child's relinquishment and sharing information about each other.

Michael, Joan, Ralph, and Wanda are all participating in an open adoption that occurred with the help of Catholic Social Services.[7] Joan, seventeen years old, unmarried and living at home with her parents, released her infant son, Michael, at birth. She picked out his adoptive parents by reading applicants' autobiographies and selecting the family that she felt matched her own. She saw her son at the foster home prior to his placement, met with his adoptive parents, and has continued to visit him and his adoptive parents. She says, "I told my counselor that I wouldn't give up my child without knowing the parents. I wanted to know who he was throughout his life." Joan wanted an open adoption because she feared that she would "be wondering every time that I see a child on the street whether he's my son."[8]

Ralph and Wanda are Michael's parents. When Wanda first met Joan and her parents, they talked with each other about their families. Wanda describes the conversation, which lasted several hours, as "just like sitting and talking about old friends." The families shared a myriad of details about their lives—what Joan's interests were, what her ethnic heritage was, even what Michael's chances were of going bald. They got a chance to look each other over. Wanda feels that by meeting Joan and now continuing to hear from her, "we will be able to give Michael an idea about his mother and also why she gave him up." Although Wanda sometimes thinks about what it will be like when Michael is older if Joan continues to visit, she's prepared to face that challenge.

This is Wanda's second adoption through Catholic Social Services and she likes to point out the changes. With her other son's adoption two years earlier, they were given his birth mother's name, address, phone number, and a simple autobiography. The birth mother did not receive any identifying information about them. With Michael's adoption, they had to provide their names and phone numbers at the start and be prepared to meet with the birth parents.

Agencies that encourage open adoptions do so because they believe that it is in the best interest of the child. They believe that a child is a fuller, more secure individual when he knows both sets of parents. They also feel that the contact between birth parents and adoptive parents helps to alleviate the fears and fantasies that each has about the other.

Catholic Social Services is in the forefront of the open-adoption movement with its policy of establishing direct contact between birth parents, adoptive parents, and adoptees. Other agencies are not so bold in their approach. They may encourage communication only through the buffer of the agency itself, which passes on letters and photos but not names and addresses.

The adoption of older children may also be more open in effect, since older children often have lived with their birth families or another relative (perhaps a grandparent or an aunt) before their placement in a foster or adoptive home. Children may have brothers or sisters still residing with their birth parents or with another foster family. Before placement, an agency may indicate that there must be, or might be, ongoing contact among the adopting family, the child, and members of the birth family, whether in the form of letters, cards, telephone calls, or visits.

Some older children adopted from abroad may also remain in touch with family members. "Mia started writing to her Korean grandparents when she arrived," states the mother of a ten-year-old. "We write every Christmas and send them photographs." Amerasian children often have been relinquished by family members who could not care for them but believed there would be some continued contact.

Although most agencies still practice closed adoptions, the number of agencies that institute some form of an open adoption is likely to grow in the years ahead. If you're interested in learning more about the practice of open adoption, you'll find the following books stimulating reading:

Catholic Social Services, *A View of Open Adoption* (booklet, P.O. Box 38, Green Bay, Wisconsin 54305).

Kathleen Silber and Phylis Speedlin, *Dear Birthmother* (San Antonio, Texas: Corona, 1983).

Arthur D. Sorosky, Annette Baran, and Reuben Pannor, *The Adoption Triangle* (Garden City, N.Y.: Anchor Books, 1979). This book explores the potential for more open communication.

Identified Adoption

Ron and Jane live in Massachusetts. They heard about a pregnant woman who was interested in arranging an independent adoption. Independent-placement adoptions are illegal, however, in Massachusetts, so Ron and Jane contacted various agencies and presented their predicament. "We called around and were treated rather shabbily," Ron recalls. Finally they were referred to Jewish Family and Children's Service in Boston, one of several agencies in Massachusetts that have a special program called "identified adoption." In identified adoption, couples who have "identified" a link to a birth parent approach an agency for services. ("Identified adoption" is a misnomer since adoptive parents and birth parents usually don't actually know each other's identity; rather, it describes the link between the birth parents and the prospective adoptive parents.)

"If the agency accepts the referral as a valid one," says Paul Dubroff, director of children's services, "then we extend services to all parties—birth parents, infant, and prospective adoptive parents." The birth mother agrees to work with the agency and receive counseling. The agency does a home study of the adoptive parents. When the child is born, its medical condition is evaluated by the agency's pediatrician; the agency secures the parental releases and then places the child with the "identified" adoptive parents.

Ron and Jane also agreed in writing to pay for the mother's medical services even if the mother decided to keep her baby or if they themselves later decided against the adoption. (This is Jewish Family and Children's Service policy. Other agencies have very different policies as to what costs the couple is always responsible for in an identified adoption.) Says Dubroff: "We don't represent the adoptive parents' interest. We represent the interests of the birth mother and the baby." Things went smoothly for Ron and Jane, and several months later they brought their baby home.

There are, however, some drawbacks to the identified-adoption approach. The costs can be high. Since adoptive parents pay agency service fees, medical expenses, and possibly living expenses for the birth mother during the pregnancy, they can incur costs at Jewish Family and Children's Service that range from $8,000 to $15,000. (At this agency the basic costs break down as follows: $3,500 for physician and hospital bills if there are no complications; $1,500–$3,000 legal fees; $3,000–$4,000 agency fees. At the discretion of the agency, reasonable living expenses such as rent, food, clothing, and transportation are considered.) Other drawbacks are that identified adoption also has the risks—both financial and emotional—that independent-placement adoption incurs. In traditional agency infant adoptions, families are usually contacted when a child is ready to be placed. In an identified adoption, families are aware of a potential child several months in advance and experience an agonizing wait. Says Ron: "It was torturous. It was like a pregnancy of sorts and the bonding began before birth."

If you live in a state where independent adoptions are not permitted (or where third-party nonagency involvement is prohibited), identified adoption may be a viable alternative for you.

However, be prepared to find that most agencies are not aware of the practice, and you may be rebuffed.

If you want to learn more about identified adoption, the Open Door Society of Massachusetts can tell you about several local agencies' programs. Check also with your state department of social services or a local agency about their willingness to develop this type of service.

Legal-Risk Adoption

To move children into permanent homes faster, some agencies employ a new kind of placement—legal-risk adoption, sometimes called "foster/adoption." A family agrees to take a child—one whose permanent plan is expected to be adoption —into their home as a foster child while the legal process goes on to free the child.

Hillary was placed with her adoptive parents when she was two months old, but her adoption was not finalized until she was nearly four years old. Explains her adoptive mother:

> Hillary's mother was a patient at a mental institution. The mother's condition had been caused by a childhood fall and she had been admitted to the institution by her mother, who had many children and who couldn't handle her daughter's injury. She'd been there for eighteen years and had become pregnant. The agency did not know who the father was. They had to track down the mother's relatives to notify them about the grandchild and to get their release. Even if the agency failed to find the relatives (they had not visited her in the eighteen years), it would still take time.

There was a lot of red tape involved in Hillary's adoption. The agency went through a long search for the mother's family, and over the years there was also a switch in social workers. Although Hillary's mother knew from the day Hillary arrived that she was likely to stay, "every once in a while we'd see a report on television where a family had to give a child back. And we'd get very nervous."

Legal-risk adoptions often involve the placement of younger children, even infants and toddlers, in adoptive families. Children have the chance to get into their permanent homes faster; parents, the chance to raise their children from infancy or toddlerhood. But legal-risk adoption brings with it emotional strain. Said one parent about the legal-risk experience: "It's living on an emotional roller coaster. One day you're high— she's ours. The next day, reality—another court delay. How do you cope with that reality?"

Since legal-risk placements begin as foster-care arrangements, birth parents have the right to visit their children in their new homes. There is the real risk that the birth parents will decide not to relinquish the child. It can and does happen.

Bonnie became the mother of a two-year-old boy through a legal-risk placement. His mother had brought him to the agency saying that she wanted to voluntarily relinquish her parental rights since she had been separated from his father and the father had recently been killed in an auto accident. Recalls Bonnie: "He fit right into our lives. Days and weeks passed. His birth mother never asked to visit him and she remained firm in her decision." After four months of counseling, his mother set a date with the agency to sign the relinquishment papers. That day arrived, but his mother didn't keep her appointment. "A little later in the day," Bonnie remembers, "she called the social worker and said that she wanted to see her son. She was beginning to doubt whether she could follow through on her decision to surrender him." The visits began, and over the next few weeks she visited frequently. Finally his birth mother took him home. "Having him leave was devastating for us and we missed him tremendously," says Bonnie. "I think about him often and wonder how they are doing." Bonnie and her husband went on to adopt four other children, but the pain of forming an attachment to, and then losing, one child is still there.

If you are willing to consider this type of adoptive placement, you will need to find an agency that uses this practice. If your agency offers you a legal-risk placement, be sure to demand as much information as possible. What is the known situation of the birth parents or the immediate family? How many releases have been signed? When is the legal case likely to be presented to the court? Risks can be of varying degrees (some agencies will rank them low to high). You need to assess how much risk you feel you can assume. Even with a low-risk situation, the court case can drag on for years—or something unexpected can happen. Are you willing to live in a state of limbo? Legal-risk adoption is not for everyone.

Foster-Parent Adoption

Foster parents can adopt their foster children, particularly if the child has been living in the foster home for an extended period of time. Agencies will often ask foster parents if they would like to adopt their foster child when he or she is freed for adoption. But foster parents may also be forced to persuade the agency to let them adopt a child, or they may have to push an agency to make a permanent plan for their foster child.

If you are interested in adopting a foster child in your care, talk first with the agency responsible for your child. If they are unwilling, or uncertain as to how to proceed, contact a local adoptive-parent group or a local foster-parent group. Another resource is the **National Foster Parent Association,** National Office, P.O. Box 257, King George, Virginia 22485 (804-775-7410).

The Interstate Compact

Sometimes families will identify a child in another state whom they would like to adopt. Or they may wish to apply to an agency in another state that has an intercountry adoption program. These adoptions are carried out under the Interstate Compact on the Placement of Children. The compact is a uniform law enacted by the majority of the states. It establishes orderly procedures for the transfer of children and fixes specific responsibilities for those involved in the placement of the children. At each step of the adoption process, your documents, and a prospective child's, are passed through ICPC personnel. The interstate compact is designed to protect children and parents and to make sure that everyone knows what is happening.

Contacting an Agency About a U.S. Adoption

Learning about agencies involves evaluating them and exploring the types of programs they offer. Ideally, you should be able to find several local agencies that provide different kinds of services, and then select the agency that most closely fits your needs. But that is not the reality of adoption. The type of child that you seek to adopt may involve your waiting a long time with a local agency. Finding an agency that meets your needs and is able to work with you may take some searching. If you live in a state like Alaska, your choice of an agency to work with will be limited to the public agency and a handful of private agencies. If you live in a state like New York, however, your choices are much greater. The state-by-state listing of agencies at the back of this book can help you get started. The North American Council on Adoptable Children (NACAC) and OURS, in addition to the directory, can give you up-to-date information. You can also check with the **Child Welfare League** (67 Irving Place, New York, New York; 212-254-7410) if you have any questions about agencies and their practices.

Your first telephone call may very likely start and end with the comments "Sorry, we're not taking any applications right now" and "Sorry, we don't have any children to place." There *are* children who need homes, so persevere. Don't be put off by an agency's perfunctory first responses.

If you are interested in adopting an infant, particularly a white infant, you may very likely be told that the agency is not taking applications or that they have a long waiting list. Don't give up. Ask questions. When will the agency's waiting list be open? Can you fill out an application now? If not, when? Recalled one adoptive parent who successfully adopted an infant through an agency: "They said to me, 'Don't bother.' I called my agency seven times and they said, 'No babies.' The eighth time they said that they had opened the 'list.' You can't be frightened by the agencies. They are hoping that you'll walk away from them. You have to be persistent to become an adoptive parent."

Agencies may even discourage people who are considering an older child. One hot line for an adoptive-parents group got calls from people who had been told by a local public agency that there were no older children available for adoption. This agency did not refer callers to the state photolisting book, which included descriptions and photos of waiting children. If you are interested in an older child, insist to the agency that you come in, talk with them, and look at the state's, not the agency's, list of waiting children. Don't let an agency automatically tell you that there are no children.

Be sure that you pin down an agency about their waiting list. How do they determine whom to call in to file an application? Is the waiting list for a child placement or for a home study? As will become clear in later chapters, having a completed home study opens doors to finding children. Unless you are specifically waiting for one of this agency's children, make it clear that you have a strong interest in a home study. It may serve as your passport.

Orientation Meetings

Many agencies begin the adoption process with an orientation meeting. In New York City, agencies hold orientations once a month, but that policy is not standard throughout the United States. An agency may hold orientations once a year, when it has several applicants, or when it has social workers free to do home studies. Orientation meetings are a chance for the agency to provide you with information about adoption, about its policies, and about the whole process. The orientation meeting is also a notorious part of the self-selection process in adoption: People may attend a meeting, walk away discouraged, and decide that they can't adopt.

Consider the very different experiences that one prospective adoptive parent had at two well-known New York City agencies. The group that met at one agency was rather diverse—a few white couples, some Hispanic women, some older black women, and some young black couples. Two social workers from the agency welcomed the group and began listing the agency's requirements. Although New York State had very few requirements for adoption, this agency had many. They had rules about the age gap between parents and children. They had rules that "you cannot share a room with the child if it is over a year old" and that "children of opposite sexes may not share a room," whatever their ages. The social worker did not make clear to the group that these were her agency's rules only —that the same rules might not exist at another agency.

The worker declared that "infants are a rare breed." She then talked about the children available for adoption through the agency. Although New York State expects the agency to show prospective adopters a copy of the New York State photolisting books, this worker announced: "I didn't bring the New York State blue books because it becomes very confusing. I brought a sampling of the children listed. These children happen to be ours." So the group saw photos of perhaps thirty children, not the several hundred typically featured in the state's book.

After the meeting, the group examined the photographs and profiles of the children that the agency currently had available for adoption. A young black couple was dismayed to hear "no infants." A Hispanic woman who really wanted a school-age girl was concerned that most of the children pictured were boys. If these were all the children available for adoption, she was out of luck. Another woman commented that there were photographs of only thirty children and there were at least thirty people in the room. There clearly were not enough children to go around. A single black woman in her fifties, who had a grown son, had concluded that adopting an eight-year-old was impossible since the worker had told her that there should be no more than a forty-year age span between parent and child. So most of the group left, convinced that the kind of adoption they wanted was out of the question.

Sound familiar? Perhaps you've had the same experience. What would have happened if you had stepped into the orientation session of another local agency, which prides itself on its outreach program? This social worker, herself an adoptive parent, informed this group that the agency had a small number of children to place but that she considered all of New York State's waiting children hers. To prove her point, she had circulated the photo books before the meeting began. She told the group: "You go through the blue books and ask to have your home study sent out." She promised that every time families pursuing an adoption met with their social worker, they'd look at the photo books because "every two weeks there are thirty new kids" in the state's photolisting book. There might be 600 new kids featured in the next year.

She tackled the question of infants head on: "What does it mean that you want a baby? Do you want a newborn? A child in diapers?" By her second definition, a three-year-old could still be a baby. She asked another caseworker, the mother of a recently adopted teenager, to talk. The mother said, "My son needs to be the baby. This is a fifteen-year-old who needs to be cuddled and who likes to sit on my lap. He's Swiss cheese, all full of holes that need to be filled up." So much for babyhood and diapers. "Expand your horizons," both workers urged.

During this orientation, prospective parents learned about adoption today. But they also learned much more about the spirit they would need to go on with the search, whether with this agency or elsewhere. "If you definitely want to adopt," the social worker told them, "you'll find the way. There's a push. If you want it, you'll do it." Many of the people who attended this meeting would not work with this agency—some wanted infants (and would probably pursue an independent adoption); some wanted to consider an intercountry adoption (and were referred to other local agencies with special programs); others were not ready. But all left with a much clearer understanding of the adoption process.

Agencies are not all alike. You must choose them with great care. Pat Shirley, who has served as president of the parent group FACE, cautions that "the agency that can do your home study the soonest may not be the best choice." Examine the agency and its practices carefully before you commit yourself. Inquire about the agency. Is it affiliated with some national organization? Check with a local parent group. Talk with others who have adopted through the agency. Your research not only will help you determine whether the agency is right for you, but may help the home-study process that follows go more smoothly. Be sure to check out the agency's reputation. If you are planning to use this agency as a springboard to working with another agency elsewhere, be sure this agency hasn't been blacklisted by any other agency. If you can, determine a particular agency's credibility locally and nationally.

If you have the opportunity, you may want to attend the orientations of several agencies. You may also want to place your name on the waiting list of several agencies if they are appropriate to your needs.

Contacting U.S. Agencies About Intercountry Adoption

Some fifty agencies in the United States have developed intercountry adoption programs. Some agencies place children only with families who reside within a certain geographic area,

BASIC QUESTIONS TO ASK AN AGENCY

Agencies will ask you many questions during the adoption process. Before you commit yourself to any agency, you, too, should ask each agency some basic questions:

- What are your requirements for adoptive parents?
- Do you have fertility restrictions?
- Do you have religious restrictions?
- Do you have a minimum income requirement?
- What is the maximum number of children a family may have prior to adoption?
- Will you place a child older than the oldest in the family? Same age as another in the family?
- What are your fees? Any reductions for sibling groups?
- What are your medical requirements for applicants? If a family is applying for an infant, must they present evidence of a fertility problem?
- How many and what kinds of legally free children are in your agency's case load?
- How many children did you place for adoption last year? What were the characteristics of the children placed?
- Does the agency place children in prospective adoptive homes as foster children?
- How many children from outside the county, or outside the state, were placed with families studied by the agency?

while others have developed programs that accept applicants from throughout the United States (for a full discussion, see Chapter 4). Holt International Children's Services in Eugene, Oregon, for example, places children from Thailand and has accepted applications from people throughout the United States. When the applicant lives in Massachusetts, for example, a local agency does the home study (and later follows the family after the child's placement) and then forwards the home-study report to Holt. The local agency approves the applicant for adoption; but it is Holt that, after reading the home study and other supporting documents, then forwards the documents to

- Are you presently accepting applications for healthy infants?
- Could you briefly describe your home-study process? Do you offer group home studies? (See Chapter 3 for a full discussion of home studies.)
- What is the estimated wait between application and start of home study for the waiting child? For the healthy infant?
- How long will it probably take to complete a home study?
- Will you do a home study for an intercountry adoption?
- Will you do a home study for single applicants? Have you placed children with singles? Will you? What types of children will you place with singles?
- Will you forward copies of a home study to another agency? How often?
- May I see a copy of the completed home study?
- How long will it probably take your agency to assign a child after the home study is approved? (Ask this if the agency expects to place its children with you.)
- What type of contact does your agency encourage between birth parents, adoptees, and adoptive parents?
- What types of pre- and postplacement services do you provide?
- Do you offer classes in infant care or discussions about child care to prospective adopters?
- What types of support groups are available for adoptive parents?
- Do you offer any services to families after the adoption is finalized?[9]

the placing agency abroad. Each of the three agencies involved —the local, Holt, and the foreign agency—must evaluate and accept the family.

An agency may have developed intercountry adoption programs for several different countries. Each program may also have different requirements. Korea, for example, requires that the agency placing the child do both the pre- and postplacement supervision. While an agency like Holt can place children from Thailand in many states by accepting referrals from a local agency, it can place Korean children only in states where it is licensed. As you learn about agency programs, you are likely to discover that you are ineligible for some agency programs but not others. Korea in 1984, for example, did not accept applications from singles. Thus, if you are single and the local agency that has an intercountry program places only Korean children, you won't be able to apply to them. (It's still worthwhile checking to be sure that policies or programs have not changed.) That does not mean that you, a single person, should not think about an intercountry adoption; it just means that you will need to contact an agency outside of your immediate area, one that accepts applications from singles and will make a referral to you through a local agency.

The Intercountry Adoption Directory at the back of this book lists U.S. agencies that have active intercountry adoption programs. Since these programs are constantly changing, you will want to contact parent groups for the most current information. The *Report on Foreign Adoption* (available for $10 from the International Concerns Committee for Children, 911 Cypress Drive, Boulder, Colorado 80303) is a compendium of intercountry adoption information; it lists adoption programs country by country and tries to keep people informed of programs through its annual volume and nine updates.

Whether you write or call an agency, be sure to request information about all its programs. Agency workers sometimes frown on phone calls—they say talking takes their time away from working on their programs. But many people feel they learn more from the telephone contact. (If you call, keep in mind the agency's location and be aware of time zones.) Ask for an application. If you are told that the agency is not taking applications, ask when intake will be open. Remember that the situation in intercountry adoption can change quickly, so try again within a few months. An agency may open a new program or expand its waiting list. If you are willing to be a pioneer in a new program, indicate your interest. If you are willing to consider a special-needs child (see Chapter 4 for a discussion of special-needs children abroad), say so and ask for information.

If you are going to write an agency to inquire about inter-country adoption, make your letter brief and send a self-addressed stamped envelope. Include in your letter some basic biographical information, but leave your letter open enough so that the agency sends you as much information as possible. The more specific you are about yourself and your wishes, the more likely that you will inadvertently shut doors. (For a letter to an agency abroad, you will want to use a different approach; see Chapter 9.) One family wrote to a U.S. agency and stated that the wife had a job. The agency wrote back saying that the couple was ineligible to apply because the wife worked. This agency made a decision before the family ever filed an application, a decision based not on what the wife would do when the child arrived but on what she was doing more than a year before any child would be expected. It would have been better to explain her working in a longer letter at the time of application and in the home study.

Since many adoption agencies have only recently developed intercountry adoption programs, you may want to check about their programs—how long they have been operating and how many children they have placed. You can check with a state's adoption unit or its attorney general's office. Adoptive-parent groups can also help you learn about a program's reputation and an agency's track record. Be sure that you look into program fees carefully as these can vary widely in intercountry adoptions. *Be aware also that a licensed agency in the United States may not necessarily be working with a licensed agency in the foreign country; some agencies work with attorneys, social workers, or doctors.* If their foreign counterpart concerns you, be sure to ask about sources. There have been some recent accounts of foreign attorneys under investigation.

In most states, whether or not you choose to work with an agency that has an intercountry adoption program, you will need to work with an agency in order to complete an intercountry adoption. The United States Immigration and Naturalization Service requires that all individuals who bring a child into the country for the purpose of adoption submit a home study. In some states you may be able to have a certified social worker do your study, but in most you will need to have an agency undertake it. When you approach an agency, be sure to explain that you are seeking an intercountry adoption. Often an agency that has a religious requirement for placing its own children (e.g., a Catholic agency, which usually serves Catholic families) can waive this requirement if you make it clear that you need their help in completing an intercountry adoption. Some agencies, however, may have restrictions about the types of foreign sources they will work with, or may require that the agency that will be placing the child make a formal request for their assistance.

3

The Home Study

For all agency adoptions and for all intercountry adoptions, you will need a preadoptive home study. For all intercountry adoptions, the Immigration and Naturalization Service requires a home study before it will grant a child permission to enter the United States for the purpose of adoption.

The home study has traditionally involved a series of meetings between the applicants and an adoption-agency worker. While the applicants explore their feelings about adoption, the worker sizes them up as potential adoptive parents. Agencies placing healthy infants for adoption often see the home-study process as a time for the worker to screen out financially or psychologically unsuitable applicants. Consider The Cradle Society's description of its process:

> The social worker will use this period to get to know you, to become familiar with your home environment and to determine what type of family life you can offer an adopted child. During this time your application for adoption is under continuous study and review by the staff's Adoption Committee.

After a period ranging from weeks to months, the worker writes up a report on the family (the home-study document itself), which becomes the basis for the agency's decision as to whether or not to place a child in the family.

Some agencies use a group process as part of the home study. They may require that people interested in adoption take an adoption-information course sponsored by a local parent group. Others hold group meetings with prospective clients before the social worker meets with people individually. Still others conduct the whole home study in a group setting. With the group process, the agency's focus in the home study tends to shift from judging people to helping them prepare for their role as adoptive parents.

The home-study process has evolved in this way partly because of the increased interest in placing special-needs children. Observes Thomas D. Morton, director of the National Child Welfare Leadership Center in Chapel Hill, North Carolina:

> When adopting an older child, families found that issues of adolescence were immediate, not abstractions encountered in twelve or so years. Families needed information to help them make realistic decisions about whether or not adoption was appropriate for them. The process had to make maximum use of the family's role in decision-making and it could only do so if the worker's role changed from that of investigator to educator, from judge to enabler.[1]

Agencies and families are working together to reach a mutual decision regarding a family's interest in adoption. Says Barbara Tremitiere, director of the adoption program at Tressler-Lutheran Service Associates, an agency that pioneered this approach: "You don't have to be Barbie and Ken. You can have real lives and have real struggles. You watch people relax. They are in the driver's seat. They are the ones who decide to adopt and when."

The written home-study document is also changing. Families often contribute autobiographies or statements expressing their beliefs on various subjects. They may even write their own home-study documents. As adoption becomes more of an interagency venture, the home-study document will serve as the family's passport to the outside world.

Who does the home study? Within an agency, the person who prepares the home study or who leads the group meeting may be a certified social worker, a caseworker, or even another adoptive parent under the supervision of a social worker. Although home studies have usually been carried out under agency auspices, not all states require that a home study be done by an agency. In some states, and for some types of adoptive placements, you may be able to have a home study prepared by a licensed social worker not affiliated with an agency. Check your state adoption unit for specific rules and regulations.

The Traditional Home Study

If your agency will be conducting a home study along the more traditional lines, you can expect to have your first meeting with your caseworker as a couple at the agency. Then, typically, the caseworker will meet separately with you and your spouse at the agency office. One or more additional interviews will follow at your home. If you have older children, the caseworker is likely to interview them together and possibly individually. If you feel that your home study is not moving along (some agencies believe that a home study should stretch out for as much as six months), don't be embarrassed to set up your next meeting. You have a right to show interest and to try to keep things moving.

As part of your home study, you will be asked to submit some basic documents (see Chapters 5 and 6 for a discussion of paperwork) and references. The agency will want to know how your references feel about your potential parenting ability and whether they perceive you as a mature individual. The people you may be asked to use as references may include your employer, your clergyman, your friends, and your neighbors. Each one may have to submit a letter on your behalf, talk by telephone with the social worker, or even come to the agency for an interview. Your references may be cited in your home study by name, and your social worker may quote from the interviews and from letters that were submitted.

Think carefully about the people you will list as your references. Good friends do not necessarily make good references. How do they feel about adoption? How do they feel about your adopting a child? How do they feel about your adopting a particular type of child? Talk with them and explore their feelings and perceptions. Do they think you will make good parents? Why? Do they think you are making a mistake? Don't hesitate to give them some pointers as to what you would like them to emphasize about you, and don't be embarrassed to ask them to read you their letters before they submit them to the agency.

Whom should you choose as references? When the Williamses were applying for their first child to an agency that specialized in intercountry adoptions, they asked one friend who taught nursery school and with whom they liked to talk about raising children. They also asked a friend who had an interracial marriage and could testify to the Williamses' respect for ethnic differences. Their caseworker also insisted on meeting one of their references. They asked the woman who had introduced them ten years before; she was an experienced journalist, a television producer used to talking with people. Three years later, when the Williamses were applying for their second child, they chose a different reference—a neighbor whose son frequently played with their son and who had observed their parenting day in and day out (closer personal friends saw them less frequently).

Doctors—such as your family physician, infertility specialist, psychologist, or psychiatrist—may also be asked to comment on your application to adopt. Be sure to talk with them and explain your reasons for adopting. If you're committed to adoption, you don't want your infertility specialist elaborating on all the other tests that he believes you should pursue. You want him to provide a medical analysis only and to understand fully that adoption is your decision.

If you have had psychological counseling, should you use your therapist as a reference? If you've listed your therapy history under your medical history, then be prepared for the fact that the agency will ask the therapist to submit a report stating why you had the counseling and how he or she evaluates you today. How the agencies react to a psychological report will vary. Sara says:

> We'd had marriage counseling. We used our therapist as one of our three references. I felt that this improved our home study. We always thought that the fact that we'd admitted that we'd had therapy worked to our advantage.

Joan's sense of her agency's response was different:

> We'd put that we'd had psychological counseling on our application. This counseling had centered on our infertility. The social worker was very concerned that we'd felt the need to seek help (most of her previous clients had seemed able to resolve their fertility problems). Our psychologist wrote a very strong letter about how the counseling made us better parents because it showed our ability to reach out for help rather than let problems smolder. Our social worker was still uneasy about the counseling and told us that her supervisor had finally assured her that counseling was acceptable. We felt that we'd opened a can of worms.

Although some U.S. agencies may still warily approach psychological recommendations, some Latin-American agencies request a statement about your mental health.

If you will also be sending your references to an agency abroad, they may very likely have to be notarized, verified, and authenticated (see discussion in Chapter 6). To make the process easier, you may want all your references to come from the same state. But your primary concern should be that your references are able to talk comfortably about you.

What are you likely to be asked during the home-study interviews? Don't be surprised if you must discuss the following:

- Your reasons for adopting a child
- Your strengths and weaknesses
- Your personality: level of patience, attitudes toward life, anxiety levels, sense of humor
- Your marriage—its strengths and weaknesses; how you handle family disagreements
- The causes of a past divorce, your relationship with your ex-spouse, your relationship with your children from a previous marriage
- Your work—its stability and importance
- Your plans for working or for staying home with your children—and if you are planning to continue working, your child-care plans
- Your upbringing
- The kind of parenting you had and how you feel about it
- Your relationships with family, friends, neighbors
- Your extended families' feelings about adoption
- Your past experiences with children
- Your life-style and how a child will fit in
- How you have resolved a fertility problem, if you have one
- How you handled the loss of a child due to miscarriage, stillbirth, or some other cause, if such has occurred, and your feelings about it
- How your children, if you have any, will adjust to a new sibling—how you are preparing them for adoption[2]

If you are single, you will be asked to evaluate what age child you want to consider and what type of child will fit best into your situation. An infant may seem less appealing when you are asked to say how you will provide day care while you work and to consider the constant attention that a young child needs. You can expect your home study to explore the following:

- Your life-style and a child's impact on it
- Your family situation—your support system, your extended network, and the alternatives they can provide in the event of your illness or death

- Your daily plan for the child—how you expect to handle matters from day to day, what arrangements you can make for day care, for after school, for weekends
- Your finances—how you are going to provide for the child over time
- Your work—how flexible it is: Can you take time off from work when the child arrives? When the child is sick?
- How you foresee you and your child handling the special situation of single parenting

Will you enjoy your home study? The worker will tell you to relax and enjoy the experience, but you are involved in a judgmental situation and you will feel intensely who holds the power. Laments one adoptive parent: "When you are going through the home-study process, you are so vulnerable."

What is the final home-study document likely to touch on? If you were able to see your home study, you'd find that it probably outlines the following information:

- The number of times you met the agency
- Who you are—biographical descriptions, which may include a physical description, financial information, description of your personality, employment history, extended family's history, health information, religious affiliation
- Marriage details
- Your motivation for adoption
- The type of child you want to adopt
- If you are childless, your adjustment to childlessness (e.g., how you are dealing with your infertility)
- Your parenting capacity
- Your understanding of, and feelings about, birth parents
- Your home and neighborhood
- Your references (what they said)
- Your preparation for adoption (reading, knowing others, parent-group involvement)
- Your worker's evaluation

The Group Home Study

If the traditional home study has within it the potential for being an isolating experience handled behind closed doors, the group home study has the potential for turning adoption into an open, positive social experience. The group helps people build a network of support that can be called upon both before and after their child enters their home. Since the discussion often focuses on parenting issues, people enter the process with the assumption that there will be a child for them. The business at hand is to decide what kind of child they can parent and to prepare themselves for the task. Over the course of the home study, they, rather than the agency worker, will often decide whether adoption is for them.

Some agencies using group home studies have incorporated components of the TEAM approach (Training and Education in Adoption Methods) advocated by the North American Council on Adoptable Children. According to the *TEAM Parent Preparation Handbook,* "adequate and appropriate adoptive parent preparation, commitment to parenting the child or children on a permanent basis and readily available support services to assist the adoptive families after placement" are the keys to successful placement.[3] The group sessions draw upon the expertise of adoptive parents and community resource people. Using Parent Effectiveness Training, the sessions stress developing individual self-awareness, building commitment, identifying what is involved in parenting a "challenging child," and finding techniques to work with that child.

If you select an agency whose program is modeled on the TEAM method, you are likely to attend a series of meetings:[4]

- Orientation: an overview of special-needs adoption at the agency
- Parenting the Challenging Child: a realistic view of the rewards and challenges of special-needs adoption through panel presentation by experienced adoptive parents

- Transactional Analysis—Preparation for Parenting: a framework for understanding self and others as a base for successful placement
- Transactional Analysis—Building Significant Relationships: special techniques for establishing positive relationships with others including their adopted children
- Accepting Feelings of Self and Others: focuses on the dynamics of acceptance, especially those of accepting a new child into the family
- Values in Parenting: how parents acquire values and pass them on to children
- Support Services for Adoption: identifying the support parents now have and that which they may need to acquire for successful adoption
- Preparing for Adoption—A Wrap-Up: developing empathy for adopted children

Joan and Michael worked with Tressler-Lutheran Service Associates in central Pennsylvania. Meeting at a social worker's house with several other couples, they looked through photo-listing books and marked in the books the children who interested them. At the various sessions, they talked about how children feel when they enter a new home, how it feels to be rejected, how a child already in their home might react to a new sibling, and how they would handle questions about adoption. The couples prepared autobiographies, filled out work sheets about the types of children they wanted to adopt and other sheets about their attitudes and expectations. "It was," says Joan, "a good parenting course. It was interesting." Joan raves about her caseworker: "We felt so comfortable with the social worker. She could almost guess what we were thinking." At the conclusion of the series, they visited a family who had already adopted a child with a profile similar to the one they were hoping to adopt. Says Barbara Tremitiere about the Tressler-Lutheran approach: "We're going to prepare you so that you will take the child and make it work."

At Tressler-Lutheran and other agencies that use the TEAM parent-preparation approach, applicants create most of the documents. Although the staff checks references, visits homes, and writes a brief report of their impressions, Tremitiere emphasizes that the home study is written in large measure by prospective adoptive parents, "presenting themselves to the agency having custody of the children they wish to adopt. We feel this is more realistic than a social worker totally representing a family and writing their life study for them."[5]

Catholic Social Services in Green Bay, Wisconsin, uses the group home study as a "self-education experience." The group members share information about their life histories and the people who shaped their lives; their marital relationships; their childlessness and how it has affected them. The sessions may be tape-recorded so that workers or adoptive parents can review what has been said. The couples role-play situations that help them identify with birth parents, adoptive parents, and adoptees. One couple found themselves confronted with a fifteen-year-old who announced that she was going to go live with her "real" parents, while another couple found themselves playing the birth parents who showed up at the adoptive parents' front door many years later. Says one mother: "The group meetings were a matter of getting you used to accepting an adopted child." This agency does reserve the right to reject applicants after the group sessions. In the final step in the home-study process, the couples write autobiographies and descriptions of the children they can accept. The birth mothers see the autobiographies (the agency worker decides which autobiographies are shown to which birth mothers) and select the parents for their infants.

The home studies done at Tressler-Lutheran and Catholic Social Services are just two examples of the kinds of group home studies that agencies do today. Both agencies have openly called for change in adoption practices and have written up their approaches. Tressler-Lutheran's program has been described in their brochure *There Are Children Waiting* ... (available from the agency, 25 West Springettsbury Avenue, York, Pennsylvania 17403) and in the *TEAM Parent Preparation Handbook,* published by the North American Council on Adoptable Children. This handbook and its companion volume, *Guide to Local TEAM Programs,* set out concrete steps for change and provide a model for helping agencies create more meaningful home studies.

The Home Study as Your Ambassador

All home studies are alike. Or are they? Thomas Morton describes what he learned about home studies:

> As part of a training session, studies of several families were drawn from a state exchange and offered as sample case material. After reviewing the studies, the assembled workers were asked to comment on their understanding of each of the families' strengths, weaknesses, resources, and readiness to adopt a special needs child. One of the families under discussion had been written up by a worker who was present at the session. After the group had completed its discussion of that material, this worker revealed that she'd been the professional involved in that case. She went on to express dismay at the conclusions drawn by the group on the strength of the home-study document. "That's not at all what the husband and wife are like," she said, "and not what I was trying to convey about them."[6]

As this worker learned, what she wanted to say about the family was not what others understood from the home study. That's why many adoption experts urge that families take as active a part as they can in the creation of the home-study document, particularly when it is to be used as a family's ambassador beyond the agency's doors. Writes Pat Shirley of FACE: "Studies seldom say negative things but often give inadequate information, sometimes are written in a superficial or less than readable style. Many childrens' workers are going to read it and it should make your family as real as possible."[7]

Try to read your completed copy. At some agencies, that is now an accepted part of agency practice. Be sure your home study is clearly, cleanly typed with a good overall appearance. It should be dark enough to be successfully photocopied. Any supporting documents, such as value sheets and autobiographies, should also be clearly typed. If your home study is going to be mailed out, you don't want the child's worker to ignore the study because it is unreadable.

Examine your home study for typographical or spelling errors. In one home study for an intercountry adoption, the social worker spelled *Chile* as *chili* and *Colombia* as *Columbia*. Check the chronology of your life (e.g., dates that you attended school, where, what you've done) and other facts carefully. (To ensure accuracy in reporting factual details about your life, you might give your worker a résumé at the beginning of your home study.) If you object to any description of your family, say so. Mary Beth was distressed at the way events in her life were handled. The stillbirth experience that she'd lived through several years earlier was described as "stormy." Her home study dwelled on her childhood and her late father's alcoholism. Her worker reported that she and her husband were motivated to adopt a Korean child "because they were unable to adopt a white child." She approached the social-work supervisor and asked that the home study be revised. Mary Beth rewrote certain sections, correcting factual errors. The agency took out the objectionable language.

There are other things you can do to ensure that your home study presents as full a picture of you as possible. The Sonoma County, California, chapter of OURS (1215 Santa Ana, Santa Rosa, California 95404) has prepared a home-study fact sheet, "What to Do if You Get Stuck." They point out that most agencies will not know your agency and that the child's worker may not trust another worker's home study. So they advise you to do the following:

- Insist that your home-study packet contain multiple copies of photos of you as a family, of your home, and maybe of your activities as a family. It should also contain autobiographies written by you. State your experience with adoptive-parent group meetings and activities.
- Be sure the entire home-study packet is sent every time you apply for a child. Ask that your worker inspect the packet when it is sent. Offer to pay for copying costs or postage. (If you get the costs, you will know whether the entire package has been sent.)
- Include with the package any specific plans for the child's therapy if it will be necessary. Indicate what local resources are available.
- Volunteer to meet with the child's worker in person.

Since the child's agency is not likely to have worked with your agency, ask that your agency include with your home study a brief description of their home-study process and their plan for follow-up should your family be chosen. Recognize also, writes Pat Shirley, that in a special-needs adoption "your chances for a placement may indeed be lessened when your traditional home study is on the table next to a study done by an agency using the group home study concepts."[8]

If you will be sending your home study to a foreign country, keep in mind the value system of that culture. You may have revealed to your worker that you and your husband lived to-gether before marriage—a practice that has become much more commonplace in our society than it may be in another. You may choose to reveal that fact in a home-study interview, but it may be something that should not be written up. One adoption agency found that the discussion of a father's labor-union membership was questioned by a foreign agency since labor unions were illegal in that country. What is regarded as an indicator of stability in one culture can be seen as subversive in another.

You may want your worker to focus on the multiethnic character of your community, if that is so, and how you can take advantage of its resources. Discuss the opportunities your child will have to meet with other people from his birth country and also how he will meet with other adoptees. If you come from a small community, explain how you will go about ensuring that he maintains his cultural and racial identity.

It is up to you, and your agency, to convince a child's adoption worker that you have given a lot of thought and time to the adoption route you are pursuing.

Some Common Problems and Solutions

If all goes well, you will contact an agency and arrange for a home study to be done. But sometimes things don't work out as you think they should. You have rights. You are a consumer of an agency's services whether you pay for them directly by fee or whether they are funded through your tax dollars. The agency and the workers are there to provide you with a service, and you have the right to question those services.[9]

If an agency says that it is unable to do a home study

- Find out why. If you are told that there are long waiting lists for the type of child you seek, consider broadening your range of children.
- Determine whether state law requires them to do a home study, and if so, within what period of time.
- If you find yourself in the position in an intercountry adoption where the local agency will not do a home study unless it receives a request from a foreign agency, and the foreign agency will not accept an application from you unless it sees your home study, see whether the local agency will accept a letter from the foreign agency indicating its willingness to consider placing a child with you upon its receipt of your home study.

- Find out whether you can work with a licensed social worker without agency affiliation.

If you don't get along with your caseworker

- Discuss your problems with other adoptive parents who have previously worked with the agency or worker. They may have suggestions on how to proceed.
- Discuss your problems with your worker.
- Talk with the adoption supervisor.
- Request a new worker. Your home study may take longer, but it may make a difference in the outcome.

If the agency turns down your application for a child

- Find out why.
- Get the decision in writing.
- Appeal the decision within the agency or beyond. Many states have established appeal procedures.
- Don't take the agency's decision as the final answer to your decision to adopt. Some agencies are more flexible than others in approving families.

Considering Intercountry Adoption

Intercountry adoption involves the placement for adoption in the United States of children born abroad. In the 1970s the number of children adopted from abroad averaged about 5,000 annually, with a peak of more than 6,500 adoptions in 1976.[1] For 1980 the Immigration and Naturalization Service reported 5,139 children were admitted for intercountry adoption. For 1981 the number was 4,968, but the numbers since then have been growing. Records at the U.S. Department of State (which issues visas to incoming children) reveal 5,793 children entering in 1982 and 7,350 in 1983. Korean placements seem to be increasing most rapidly, with 2,683 children admitted in 1980, 2,444 in 1981, and 4,545 in 1983—a sizable jump. Intercountry adoption probably accounted for more than 10 percent (and possibly as much as 15 percent) of all nonrelative adoptions in 1983.[2]

This chapter and Chapters 6 and 9 will describe the mechanics involved in intercountry placement. You may decide against it on the grounds that it is too expensive, too complicated, too time-consuming (you may have to spend time abroad), or just too complex for your tastes. Also, intercountry adoption may be fraught with uncertainties: You may decide to try to adopt a child from a country only to have a coup d'état topple the government and the new government have a different attitude toward intercountry placements. A foreign government's regulations may also change, so that the child who is assigned to you at one month old comes to the United States when she is more than one year old.

Although I will often focus on the mechanics of intercountry adoption, keep in mind always why people concerned with children have supported intercountry placements. Father Alceste Piergiovanni Ferranti of the Instituto Chileno de Colonias y Campiamentos in Santiago, Chile, a child-welfare organization that has placed children in the U.S., says that children leave their birth countries because "every child in the world needs a family." For Father Piergiovanni and many others, intercountry adoption is one way to find "families for children, *not* children for families."[3]

There are some very basic matters that will affect your life as a family and your future child's life, and should therefore influence your decision regarding intercountry adoption. Holt International Children's Services has devised a series of questions and comments that you should seriously evaluate as you consider intercountry adoption:

1. What are your ideas about race? What characteristics do you think Asian, Indian, Latin-American, etc., people have? Do you expect your child to have these characteristics? The children become Americanized; therefore try to visualize that cute little baby growing up into a child—a teenager—an adult—a parent. Think about grandchildren.

2. How do you feel about getting lots of public attention, stares, etc.? Possibly your adopted child will get too much attention and other children will tend to feel left out.

3. You will become an interracial family. Do you raise your child to have the same identity as you or your other children? How do you help him develop his own identity? Should his name reflect his national origin? What relationship will the name have to the sense of 'Who am I'? Imagine a child you know and love being sent overseas to be adopted? How would you want him raised? As an Ameri-

can in a foreign country? A native in that country?

4. How can you learn to know what it's like being nonwhite and growing up in a white society if you don't know this from your own experience? You will have to find out how to teach or educate yourself to become sensitive to your child's world.

5. Your family will now be interracial for generations. Adoption of a child of another race or country is not just a question of an appealing little baby. How do you feel about interracial marriage? How does your family feel about interracial marriage? How do you feel when people assume that you are married to an Asian person?[4]

In addition to your qualities and abilities as parents, it is important for you to understand your motivation for this kind of adoption. Do you feel you are doing a good deed for a poor, homeless child, who will perhaps be more grateful to you when he is older than if he were your birth child? This is poor motivation and not very realistic.

If your primary orientation is to help the child become absorbed into your culture at the expense of his own, then transracial adoption is not for you. You must have an attitude of respect for the country and culture of the child.

DO YOU HAVE THE CAPACITY TO IDENTIFY WITH THIS CHILD, to see the world from his point of view and to lovingly supply his physical, mental and spiritual needs? Do you want to learn more about the child's culture and heritage? If you do, then you can consider further the idea of intercountry adoption.

Consider the conversation that Cindy had with a stranger about her three-year-old daughter:

He: What is it?
She: She's a little girl—my daughter.
He: No, I mean, what is it?
She: She's a child.
He: No, where's she from?
She: She's from Korea.
He: You mean your husband's a Chink?
She: No, she's adopted from Korea.
He: Couldn't you just make a baby like normal people?[5]

You'll be asked: What do you know about her parents? What's her real name? How much did it cost? ("I've heard that there's a lot of international baby buying.") Several people are likely to nominate you, in front of your child, for sainthood for rescuing the poor waif. They'll also tell her how lucky she is that you adopted her. Someday, you may have the experience that another parent of a young Korean adoptee had:

> The usual questions continued throughout the dinner (in a restaurant filled with senior citizens)—"Where are the children from?" "Are they related?" "They speak English so well." "Don't you love their eyes?" As we prepared to leave, I took my daughter to the bathroom. She burst into tears—and I assumed that she hit her head on the door. When I asked what happened, she sobbed, "I'm not hurt in my head, I'm hurt in my feelings—why don't people leave us alone?" I said, "Because you are cute children, who happen to look different." She said, "I don't want to look different, I want to look like you, Mommy."[6]

These issues are ones that will confront you as the parent of a child adopted from abroad. Many of the questions will be discussed in later chapters of this book. All of them should be explored by you *before* you adopt a child from another country.

The Risks of Intercountry Adoption

All adoptions have risks. There are the risks associated with the children themselves. Your child may be considered healthy by his or her country's standards, but the child may have an undisclosed illness that becomes apparent only with the diagnostic techniques available in the United States. Many children who have been malnourished or have spent long periods in orphanages catch up. But a child may still manifest some delays. One mother, whose son arrived from Korea at the age of two, reports that seven years later her son suffers from "short-term memory problems" that seem connected to his early poor nutrition. He also tends to hoard food and to be overly concerned about his next meal when the family is away from home (she always packs a snack for him to take with him). She feels that although his fears are not verbalized, her son remembers those hungry times.

Occasionally children die before they are ready to travel to the United States. Or a child may be found to have a medical condition that will not be approved by U.S. Immigration. It also happens occasionally that a child whose referral papers have been sent to an agency in the United States will find an adoptive home (or a relative may reappear) in her native country during the period that the papers are being forwarded and processed.

There are other types of risks—war, change in government, changes in adoption laws, changes in agency policy, illegal dealing and disreputable intermediaries. When the Sandinistas overthrew the Somoza government in Nicaragua, intercountry adoptions stopped. When foreign agencies are swamped with applications, they may temporarily stop their intake. Or U.S. agencies may stop placing from a particular country or agency for a variety of reasons, including long delays.

Finally, there are the risks that come with using a source that you may not know as much about as you should.

How Intercountry Adoption Works

Let's follow four families and see how their childrens' adoptions proceeded.

Agency-to-Agency Placements

Gena and Duane adopted an infant girl from Korea through a local U.S. agency working with a social-welfare agency in Korea. The local agency's worker met with them and conducted a home study. After the local agency approved Gena and Duane as prospective adoptive parents, it forwarded the home study and other documents to its counterpart in Korea. Several months later, Gena and Duane's worker called them into her office and showed them photographs of a five-month-old Korean girl. She also shared with them whatever records, particularly medical information, the Korean agency had provided. Gena and Duane were delighted and accepted the child offered. They filled in some agency papers, including a statement that they would accept financial responsibility for the child, and processed their I-600 with the Immigration and Naturalization Service (see Chapter 6). They then waited while the agency in Korea did its share of processing forms (for example, obtaining her Korean passport). Two months later their worker called to tell them that their daughter would be arriving on a flight later that week, brought by a volunteer escort from Korea.

Dana and Bill adopted an infant boy from the Philippines with the help of a local agency, an agency in another state, and the Philippine government. They applied to the agency in another state because it had an intercountry Philippine adoption program and would take applications from out-of-state people. Bill and Dana arranged for a local agency to do their home study and serve as the "receiving" agency. This local agency agreed to provide postplacement supervision of the child and work with the family toward finalization when the child arrived.

When their home study was completed, the local agency sent it to the out-of-state agency. This agency also approved them as adoptive parents. This agency, working with its counterpart abroad, handled the arrangements in the foreign country: finding an adoptable child, arranging for court procedures, arranging for the child's passport, escorting the child to the United States.

About a year after Bill and Dana submitted their application to the out-of-state agency, their local agency received a child offering. This child offering had been sent to them from the out-of-state agency via the interstate compact officer. All written communication, in fact, between the two U.S. agencies went through the interstate compact officer. Bill and Dana also filed papers with the Immigration and Naturalization Service and waited for their child to be escorted to the United States. Their child was brought to the United States by the agency with the intercountry program. Bill and Dana traveled to an airport near the placing agency, which served as a central arrival point for children coming from abroad.

Facilitated Placements

Linda was a single parent who decided that she wanted to adopt a preschool girl. With the encouragement of a nearby single-parents' group, she contacted an attorney in the United States who worked with an attorney in Chile. Her U.S. attorney advised her about state and federal adoption laws. Through the parents' group, she was referred to several local agencies that would be willing to do a home study for her. When the home study was completed, she brought her materials to the U.S. attorney, who checked them for thoroughness and accuracy and then forwarded them to his associate in Chile.

Several months later, the Chilean attorney, who knew people at orphanages and often had young women approach him directly about relinquishing children for adoption, located her daughter at an orphanage. The Chilean attorney sent a description of the girl to the U.S. attorney, who contacted Linda and showed the referral information to her. She also processed papers through Immigration. Several weeks later, the Chilean attorney notified her that the Chilean paperwork was complete and that she could come to Chile to pick up her daughter. She took a flight later that week and spent a few days in Chile doing some additional paperwork (she had to go to the American Embassy to get her child's visa approval), and then the two of them came to the United States. The U.S. attorney had served as a "facilitator" or "intermediary" in this adoption.

Direct Placements

Mark and Susie wrote directly to the Grupo Nacional de Adopciones of the Instituto Colombiano de Bienestar Familiar (the government adoption program) in Bogotá, Colombia, indicating their desire to adopt a Colombian child and requesting an application. After they had obtained all the required U.S. documents (including a home study, which was done by a local agency), they submitted the package to the Colombian agency. A few weeks later, they heard from the Colombian agency that their application had been accepted. Their names were placed on a waiting list. A year later they were contacted by Bienestar and informed that there was a child available for adoption by them. Again, there was paperwork to do in the United States. Then it was down to Bogotá and on to an orphanage in Cali where their son actually was. There was still some paperwork to do there, but two weeks later they returned with their son to the United States.

In the United States, you may work with a local agency that places children directly from abroad, with a non-local agency that has an intercountry adoption program, or with a facilitator. For some countries, you may apply directly to a source abroad (you will still need to have someone, either a licensed social worker or an agency, do a home study of your family). Your child may be placed through the national department of social services, a national orphanage, a local orphanage, maternity homes, private foundations, or other social-welfare organizations. Depending on the laws of a country, judges, doctors, lawyers, social workers, and other people interested in child welfare may be involved in placing children for intercountry adoption. If you have relatives, friends, business associates, or church contacts in a foreign country, they may be able to help you arrange an independent intercountry adoption.

Because you choose to work with an agency in the United States does not necessarily mean that your U.S. agency will be working with an agency or orphanage in the foreign country of your choice. Some U.S. agencies work with attorneys and other individuals in a foreign country as well as with orphanages and other agencies. International Adoptions, Inc., in Newton, Massachusetts, states in the materials it sends to interested families that it works with "any ethical source, including other licensed overseas adoption programs located in North America, licensed orphanages or agencies in the country of a child's birth, and attorneys or other legal representatives in the country of a child's birth." Be sure the U.S. agencies that you contact tell you exactly whom they work with abroad. You may also find that in some countries, particularly in Latin America, agencies prefer to work directly with families in the U.S. rather than through U.S. intercountry adoption programs. Or you will discover that agencies in other countries, such as Korea, will work only with certain licensed agencies and cannot take an application directly from you.

Working with a U.S. agency that has a relationship with a foreign agency, or applying directly to a national orphanage or well-known private agency abroad, minimizes risks. Observes Betty Laning of the International Concerns Committee for Children: "By using licensed agencies, adoptive parents have some leverage should something go wrong with an adoption program. Parents stand a chance of getting some of their money back if no child is forthcoming. With facilitators or lawyers in a foreign country, there may be no refunds and no way to proceed legally to force a refund." If you are working with a facilitator or with an attorney in a foreign country, proceed cautiously.

A certified social worker in Iowa who counseled people about adoption helped set up a contact in Guatemala. He had met a "good Christian gal," a schoolteacher who knew women who wanted to relinquish infants. According to the original plans, the entire adoption would cost about $2,000 (in addition to the couples' travel expenses to pick up the infants). But as the families' home studies started to be sent to Guatemala, the costs started escalating: The midwifery charges went up, the legal fees went up, the foster-care expenses escalated. Several families did become parents of Guatemalan children, but their total expenses were closer to $9,000. The social worker decided that the schoolteacher was not a reliable source and he stopped making client referrals to her.

Carol decided to work with a woman in the United States who facilitated Mexican adoptions.

> We were assigned a baby in March 1981. We were told that if we wanted this baby we were to send approximately $5,200 to Mexico. We were told that there would be an additional charge of $700 for "baby-sitting" from birth until we picked up the baby. It took a great deal of pressure to get Mexico to say they'd received our money. They said they'd received $4,100 not $5,200. The facilitator kept the rest?
>
> We were led to believe that it would be a matter of weeks until we could bring Karen Jo home. Then it was definitely May. Then June. We heard no more about Karen Jo until September, and then in a roundabout way. Our facilitator called and told us they had the most beautiful baby girl for us. We asked what happened to Karen Jo? We were told that the baby's mother had neglected to sign a paper and she'd disappeared.
>
> We really did want a baby, so we said yes to the second baby at this point. We were told that the baby had been ill and that if we wanted her, we had to send an additional $1600 to pay the hospital bill.

The call to travel to Mexico never came. Carol and her husband subsequently sued the facilitator to try to regain their original outlay of $5,200.

Babette hooked up with another facilitator. She liked the woman's voice on the telephone and felt she was reliable because "she had adopted children from Mexico." Since Babette was told that the lawyer in Mexico placed newborns, "I went out and bought a crib and newborn clothing." There were the usual promises—a baby by Christmas, then in the spring, finally the fall. There was even the day when she was told that their baby was expected to be born momentarily and she sat by the telephone all day. Finally, after months had passed, she and her husband decided to meet this woman who lived in another state. A face-to-face meeting convinced Babette that "this was crazy" and she and her husband returned home and contacted a local agency that placed Korean infants. A year later they welcomed their daughter home.

Carol lost $5,200. Babette spent nine months on an emotional roller coaster. Carol's and Babette's stories, unfortunately, are not unique. Problems sometimes arise for people who pursue independent-placement adoptions here and can plague people who use facilitators for adoptions abroad. The risks may increase if you try to do an adoption yourself abroad, particularly if you use a lawyer or other source *not proved to be reliable to you or others.* All may indeed go smoothly, but there may be problems.

To minimize the chances of an intercountry adoption going sour, examine all sources very carefully. Check with your local adoptive-parent group or a group in the United States whose members have successfully adopted from your desired country. To be blunt, look at references just as you would before hiring someone to work for you. Don't let your heart rule your head.

To help you minimize the risks, here are some questions to keep in mind:

- How long has the source been in operation?
- What type of written materials are there describing the inter-country adoption programs?

- What experiences have other families had in working with this child-placing resource?
- How much money overall is required?
- How much money is required initially?
- How much money is required before you get the child's papers?
- How much money is required before you see the child?
- What written agreements are there?
- If you decide against intercountry adoption, what provisions are there for the return of your money?
- Has it ever been suggested that you can bypass federal or state immigration requirements?
- Has it ever been suggested that if you are unhappy with the child, you can still bring the child into the country and then the facilitator will place the child with another family?
- What type of information is being offered you about the child?
- What has been promised to you about the adoption?
- Has it ever been suggested to you that you put your name on the child's original birth certificate so that there will be no need for an adoption?

Requirements

For an intercountry adoption, you will need to meet the requirements of your state government, the federal government, and the foreign country. Chapter 6, which discusses the special paperwork of an intercountry adoption, explores this at greater length. You may also find that some of the U.S. agencies with intercountry adoption programs may also have special requirements. The most common, of course, is a geographic requirement—that is, an agency will work only within a specific city or state. Other common requirements involve age, marital status, and religion.

The foreign country, or possibly an individual district within the country, usually has laws about guardianship and adoption. These laws may govern such matters as the length of your marriage, your age, or previous divorce. If you are thirty and married for two years, you may be eligible to adopt in one country but not in another. There may be special requirements pertaining to such matters as your religious affiliation or your need to establish a residency abroad. To find out about the laws and procedures for a specific country (if you are not working with a U.S. agency), you can contact the country's consulate in the United States. Remember that agencies within the foreign country may also have their own requirements for prospective adoptive parents.

The ability to travel abroad is not necessarily required of you for an intercountry adoption. Some countries require that you appear before a court or a social-welfare agency before they will place one of their children in your family; others do not. Korean children are usually escorted to the United States. Families adopting from Latin America often must travel abroad. If you are planning to do a direct adoption, it is very advisable for you to travel to see the child.

The Costs of an Intercountry Adoption

Linda and her husband were having trouble getting their home study done. They were anxious to adopt a special-needs child or sibling group of school age and had been waiting for several years for a well-known local agency to do their home study. But the agency wasn't too optimistic about the chances of finding children needing families or when it would be able to study their family. Linda and her husband didn't know about any local parent groups. We spoke about their home-study problems. Had they ever considered an intercountry adoption? They had indeed thought about it, but their minister had told them that intercountry adoptions would be "very expensive." What did they expect to pay in fees to this local agency for a U.S. adoption? Perhaps $3,500 or more, based on their income. I sent them some general information about intercountry adoption and the names of some referral agencies in the country. I'm sharing a letter I received from Linda six months later because it addresses this question as well as the myths that often surround intercountry adoption.

> I have waited so long to write you this special letter. Since I talked to you so much has happened. The day after I talked with you we saw a small article in the newspaper about an intercountry adoption information meeting being held the same week. We decided to attend with CAUTION because our experience with adoption thus far was so negative. We really did not expect much. When the meeting was over I asked John what he thought. He said, "This is the first time in five years anyone has given us any *hope.*"
>
> Last Thursday we received our approval notice from ———. After five years of beginning efforts to be parents (and not including six years of dreaming, planning and saving before 1978) we now *know* that we will be parents. We have requested a sibling group from Korea. Though everyone thinks we've lost our sanity, we have discussed this in depth together and with our caseworker.

A year after Linda and her husband attended that adoption information meeting they became the parents of three Korean children—2 girls and a boy, ages 2, 5½, and 8.

Don't rule out intercountry adoptions because someone has told you that they're very expensive. They are costly when the standard of comparison is with a public adoption agency; the costs may be comparable to certain private agencies' fees. Be aware that intercountry adoption costs are likely to vary from a minimum of $3,500 to upwards of $6,000. Some agencies may charge less when you adopt a sibling group or a special-needs child, but many do not. The cost may be per child. Expenses will also vary depending on whether you must travel to the country and how long you must stay there. Many factors affect costs. A country's distance from the United States, for example, can cause a $500 differential in air fares. (In January 1984, round-trip airfare with a one-week minimum stay from New York to Bogotá on Eastern Airlines was $559; to Lima $700; and to Santiago $1,051.)

The chart shown tries to outline some of the basic costs that you can anticipate with an intercountry adoption. Expenses will differ by country and by program.

INTERCOUNTRY ADOPTION EXPENSES

General Adoption Expenses
- Home-study fee (home study required by Immigration and source of adoption in foreign country and foreign court)
- Medical exams
- Fees for documents (e.g., birth and marriage certificates)
- Photocopying fees
- Immigration and Naturalization Service fees
- Notarization fees required for some documents
- Postage
- Document-translation fees (often required for Latin America)
- Document verification and authentication fees (often required for Latin America)
- Long-distance telephone calls and other communication expenses
- Child's airfare from the foreign country (also possibly escort's)
- Agency fees in the United States or in the foreign country
- Child-care fees in the foreign country (e.g., for foster care)
- Attorney and other court fees in the U.S. or abroad (possibly both pre- and postplacement expenses)

Additional Adoption Expenses If You Travel to a Country
- Round-trip airfare for those who travel
- Lodging expenses
- Meals
- Taxi and other transportation fees (you may have to take another plane if your child is in a distant city)
- Donation to orphanage (if recommended)

The Children

Hee Ra, infant girl, Korean, abandoned at birth on the steps of a police station

Alfredo, infant boy, Colombian, relinquished at birth by his mother at a maternity home

Sharpla, infant boy, Indian, abandoned at birth weighing just three pounds

José and Margarita, brother and sister, ages five and six, living in an orphanage in Costa Rica

Sompit, age three, female, living since infancy in an orphanage in Thailand

These are just a few of the children who have been placed for adoption in the United States. These children have found parents, but there are more like them still waiting to be adopted. Children needing permanent homes (and eligible under U.S. immigration laws) range in age from infancy up to age sixteen. They may be orphaned, abandoned, or have a parent or relatives who cannot care for them because of poverty or other conditions. Some may have lost their families or been separated from their families because of war. Older children waiting for placement may have spent time living on the streets or may have lived all or most of their lives in orphanages. In some countries, agencies may attempt to place infants in foster care, but that is not the general rule. *All* children who come to the United States for adoption must meet federal requirements for the designation "orphan" under federal immigration law (see Chapter 6).

If you are contemplating an intercountry adoption, be sure you try to seek out people who've adopted children from abroad. Attend parent-group meetings, particularly ones where some of the children will be present. If that is not possible, be sure to look at photographs of these children. One parent recalls that "when we were having our home study done in South

Carolina for a Colombian adoption, the caseworker showed us a photo of a child from India. She told us, 'This is the way your child will look.' " Indian children do not look like Colombian children, nor do Chilean children look like Korean children.

In Taiwan, the Philippines, Okinawa, Korea, Thailand, Laos, Kampuchea, and Vietnam, there are children—and adults— who are the offspring, often illegitimate, of American fathers (servicemen or businessmen) and Asian mothers. They are known as Amerasians. Some of their fathers were caucasian; others, black. In their birth countries, Amerasians often face prejudice and restrictions based on their dual heritage and their illegitimate status.

Since the 1950s, some Amerasian children, particularly from Korea, have been placed for adoption in the United States. Their mothers relinquish them for adoption in the hope that they will encounter less prejudice in the U.S. Some of the children are released as infants, but many are relinquished when they are older—perhaps of school age, when the child moves into the outside society and faces increasing prejudice. The birth family and the child may want to maintain contact after the child is adopted. Certain U.S. agencies have specialized in placing Amerasians and in serving their needs. If you are interested in adopting an Amerasian child, see the intercountry adoption directory.

Most likely you've heard about the 1982 federal legislation that makes it easier for Amerasians to immigrate to the United States. The Amerasian Immigration Act (PL 97-359) amends the Immigration and Nationality Act to provide preferential treatment in the admission of certain Amerasians. The law makes it easier for Amerasian children and young adults from Korea, Thailand, Vietnam, Laos, and Kampuchea who were born after December 31, 1950, and before October 22, 1982, to come to the United States. This law is *not an adoption law.* The law provides for sponsorship of Amerasians seeking to come to the United States. The children and young adults coming to the

U.S. will *not* have been relinquished by their birth mothers (children who are coming for adoption are) and will be placed with "sponsors" who promise to support them for a five-year period or until the Amerasian reaches the age of twenty-one, whichever is longer. If you are interested in sponsoring an Amerasian in the United States, the **Pearl S. Buck Foundation** (Green Hills Farm, Perkasie, Pennsylvania 18944) can direct you to the appropriate agencies.

Waiting Children Abroad

Just as there are waiting children and special-needs children in the United States, so, too, are there special-needs children abroad. They are often different from the special-needs children needing placement here. A child may be considered "hard to place" in another country solely because of age—and in some countries or in some circumstances, that may be a four-year-old boy. Young children may be considered hard to place if they are part of a sibling group. Here are some of the children that agencies specializing in intercountry adoption have listed as "waiting."

> *Korea:* A sixteen-month-old girl with tuberculosis of the spine. She was fitted with a back brace and beginning to walk. She would need continuing medical care and possibly orthopedic surgery.
>
> A five-year-old boy whose tiny stature led the agency to test for dwarfism. Since the tests were normal, the agency felt that the child was younger than they had thought.
>
> A sibling group of three girls, ages thirteen, eleven, and eight.
>
> *Brazil:* A two-year-old boy described as aggressive with hyperactive symptoms.
>
> *Colombia:* A six-year-old boy who was developmentally delayed and did not even know how to eat properly when he came into the agency's care.

Consider the overseas waiting-child programs of the Children's Home Society of Minnesota. The children generally available are healthy girls, ages ten to fourteen; healthy boys, ages seven to fourteen; older Amerasian children (younger children are usually of black/Korean heritage); older sibling groups of two; sibling groups of three or more; and handicapped children of any age. The medical conditions that you might find include the following:

- Congenital hip defect
- Heart defect
- Child with missing limb due to accident
- Severe allergies
- Cerebral palsy
- Vision limitations
- Hearing limitations
- Diabetes
- Seizure disorder
- Cleft lip, cleft palate, or cleft lip and palate
- *Severe* malnutrition
- Burns[7]

There is quite a contrast between many of the children "waiting" abroad and the children "waiting" in the United States. However, some of the medical problems are correctable.

Several agencies have programs devoted to the placement of special-needs children. If a special-needs child interests you, and your local agency does not have an active program, contact the Children's Home Society of Minnesota, in St. Paul, which has nationally recognized programs for waiting children and can often work with other agencies around the country. You might also want to check with Adoption Services of WACAP in Port Angeles, Washington; SAME in Bismarck, North Dakota; Welcome House in Doylestown, Pennsylvania; and Holt International Children's Services in Eugene, Oregon.

You will also want to see the photolisting book developed by the **International Concerns Committee for Children** (ICCC) (911 Cypress Drive, Boulder, Colorado; 303-494-8333). U.S. intercountry adoption programs may list with ICCC children they are having trouble placing. Anna Marie Merrill, the editor of the book, also selects from the lists that Holt, WACAP, SAME, and other agencies with intercountry adoption programs circulate to families interested in special-needs adoption. Some of the children featured in this book are already in the United States, having experienced an adoption disruption after their arrival; others are still waiting in their birth countries. Merrill has found that the children featured are typically "bunches of little boys. Most of the girls come in sibling groups." About 150 children appear each year. Families may also list themselves with ICCC (details about waiting families are circulated to the agencies that subscribe to the book). The photolisting book, which comes out six times a year, is available by subscription ($7.50 for the photolisting book; $5.00 additional for a family to register).

Health Problems of Arriving Children

Special-needs children may be identified as having health problems. What about the rest of the children? You've probably heard or read some horror story about people who adopted a seriously ill child. Are those stories grounded in fact?

When Sarah's daughter, Evelyn, came off the plane after her daylong journey from Korea, she was sick, not with a life-threatening illness but with the kinds of maladies that you may find in children coming from abroad. She had ear infections, an upper respiratory infection, scars on her arms from an earlier bout with scabies, a few infected sores, and head lice. She went straight from the airport to the pediatrician. The infections cleared up with a course of antibiotics. Her transformation was quite something—within a week you'd hardly have recognized her.

Evelyn was a healthy child; the problems she brought with her—infections, sores, scabies—are the kinds of small problems that are easily cleared up. Your child may arrive in perfect health. Many do.

But some children do not. Henry is a healthy nine-year-old Korean boy who arrived in the U.S. when he was two. His mother recalls what he was like:

> He was just in bad shape—the size of a nine-month-old baby, but he was two years old. No butt, no waist, nothing. He had rickets and was bowlegged. He looked like our image of an orphan, a little waif. It was a good couple of years before we got his teeth straightened out. We had to have all his teeth pulled.

Wilma's Chilean infant had other problems:

> At eight months he was bloated, had a flat head (having lain most of the time on his back in a crib), and had bowed legs. My doctor did a tuberculosis test, and one test showed elevated levels. He did not have active tuberculosis in his lungs, but the tests showed that he had TB in his body. I took this in stride as my daughter, who'd been adopted from Korea as a five-month-old infant, had been anemic and developed a milk intolerance. So my son was on medicine for the treatment of TB for a year, and at four he's fine now.

These are the types of medical inconveniences you may encounter. Infants may be undernourished and smaller than the average American child. They may weigh less and be developmentally delayed (but the infant who couldn't roll over at nine months may still walk by one year). They may have a low resistance to infection and suffer from anemia. They may have milk intolerances (quite common among Asians and Hispanics). They're not likely to measure up to American "averages" for length, weight, and head circumferences. Older children are likely to have decayed teeth. And they may arrive with few or no medical records.

If you want to adopt a child about whom you can receive an extensive medical and personal history with detailed information about birth parents, then intercountry adoption is probably not for you. Be forewarned that the information you receive is likely to be scanty. Korean infants are often abandoned at birth —left at a hospital or a police station. An older child may have memories but is not dropped off at the orphanage with a long written account of his life. It is quite possible you will receive little information and few medical records. (Medical records may encompass only the child's history with a particular agency or orphanage.)

You may also find that the age estimates given for older children by the agency have little to do with a child's actual chronological age. The agency may have guessed the child's age when he was placed in care. Bone and endocrinological tests performed on children here in the U.S. may reveal that a child is older or younger than the agency and the adopting parent believed. Some children have entered puberty long before anyone expected them to.

Where to Turn for General Information about Intercountry Adoption

Good sources of information about intercountry adoption are people you know who have adopted recently from a foreign country, people who have lived in another country, and people who have family or friends abroad. This is particularly true if you are thinking about an adoption from a country where there are no organized intercountry adoption programs with the United States.

The **Latin America Parents Association (LAPA)** is a parent group whose goal is to help those seeking to adopt children from Latin America. LAPA, a nonprofit, volunteer organization, distributes information about adoption and naturalization requirements to prospective adoptive parents free of charge. It has detailed fact sheets about various Latin-American countries and sources willing to place children with U.S. citizens. LAPA holds cultural, social, and informational meetings during the year, and there is a bimonthly newsletter for all members.

When families travel to pick up their children, they are asked to take down supplies (medical supplies, clothes, toys, formula) provided by LAPA. In 1984 there were chapters in the Washington metropolitan area, Connecticut, Illinois, New Jersey, New York, and Pennsylvania. For information contact LAPA's national headquarters in New York (P.O. Box 72, Seaford, New York 11783; 516-795-7427). Another major parent group is OURS (Organization for United Response), whose headquarters is in the Minneapolis–St. Paul area.

Parent groups are crucial to successful intercountry adoptions since members can offer both support and up-to-date information. You may also find that some agencies have a parent group linked to them.

You can also get information about intercountry adoption from the foreign consulates located in the United States. They can help you locate agencies abroad and can give you information about their countries' laws pertaining to adoption. You may also use the consulate to process your paperwork.

There are some good books about intercountry adoption. OURS produced two compendiums (now out of print) of families' experiences with intercountry adoption: Betty Kramer, ed., *The Unbroken Circle* and *Carry It On*. Parent groups, agencies, and some libraries may have copies, and they're worth reading. Mary Taylor's *A Parent's Guide to Intercountry Adoption*, published by The Open Door Society of Massachusetts, combines both factual information and powerful family stories.

The resource directory at the back of this book lists many of the U.S. agencies that have developed intercountry adoption programs. Contact them for information about their specific programs. Remember that some agencies will have nationwide programs while others will place children only within a particular geographic region. Another invaluable source of information about intercountry adoption is ICCC's *Report on Foreign Adoption*.

5

Paperwork

Paperwork and adoption go hand in hand. Whether you are adopting a child in this country or abroad, you will at some point have to amass documents: birth certificates, financial statements, the birth parents' releases. With intercountry adoption, the paperwork expands since you must meet the requirements of a foreign country, the U.S. government, and your state government. This chapter focuses on basic paperwork. Chapter 6 looks at the special paperwork of an intercountry adoption.

Documents You Can Expect to Need for an Adoption

When a U.S. or foreign agency sends you an application for adoption, or when a foreign country requests information, you will be asked to submit information about yourself. At some point you can expect to show the following:

- Certified copy of your birth certificate.
- Certified copy of your marriage certificate.
- Certified copy of any divorce record.
- Certified copy of the death certificate of any deceased former spouse.
- Medical statement from physician about your health (agency

may provide forms). You may also be asked to submit a statement about your mental health.

- Medical statement about infertility (if applicable).
- Notarized financial statements. (You may be asked to provide bank statements about your various accounts or an accountant's report. You will most likely be asked to send a notarized copy of the first two pages of your most recent federal income-tax return.)
- Verification of your employment, stating salary, position, length of employment, and stability of your position.

You may also be asked to provide the following:

- Certified copy of your children's birth certificates.
- Brief autobiographies, including life experiences.
- Photographs of yourself, your children, your home.

If you are a naturalized citizen, you will be asked to show proof of your naturalization. Do *not* copy naturalization papers —this is illegal. Some states may also require that you be checked for a police record or may send your name to a central registry that lists people who have been accused of child abuse.

As you begin thinking about adoption, you should begin actively working on your documentation. Certified copies of birth, marriage, death, and divorce certificates can take time to obtain since they must be gotten from the states in which these events took place. Since these documents certify past events, they usually do not have to be updated, so you can and should obtain several copies of each document at one time. One family ordered five copies of the relevant documents and were able to use them for two adoptions. The extra money spent may save months in paperwork. (If you are planning an intercountry adoption, find out whether the foreign country must have copies that have been recently certified. Some countries require this; others do not.) You should also try to figure out in advance how many certified copies of each document you are likely to need for any given adoption. (The Immigration and Naturalization Service will accept photocopies of documents if an Immigration officer compares them to the originals and certifies them as duplicates.)

Obtaining Birth and Marriage Records

The chart that follows lists where you can obtain certified copies of birth and marriage records. When writing, be sure to give full identifying information. Call first to find out what the fee is. Be sure to enclose a self-addressed stamped envelope.[1]

BIRTH/MARRIAGE RECORDS

Alabama:
Bureau of Vital Statistics, Department of Public Health,
State Office Building, Room 211, Montgomery, Alabama 36130

Alaska
Bureau of Vital Statistics,
Department of Health and Social Services,
Pouch H-02G, Juneau, Alaska 99811

Arizona
Vital Records Section,
Department of Health Services,
1740 West Adams Street, Phoenix, Arizona 85007

Arkansas
Division of Vital Records, Department of Health,
4815 West Markham Street, Little Rock, Arkansas 72201

California
Vital Statistics Branch,
Department of Health Services, 410 "N" Street,
Sacramento, California 95814

Colorado
Health Policy, Planning and Statistics,
Department of Health, 4210 East 11th Avenue,
Denver, Colorado 80220

Connecticut
Health Statistics Division, Department of Health Services,
79 Elm Street, Hartford, Connecticut 06106

Delaware
Office of Vital Statistics, Division of Public Health,
Department of Health and Social Services,
Jesse S. Cooper Memorial Building,
Federal and Water Streets, Dover, Delaware 19901

District of Columbia
Vital Records Branch, Research and Statistics Division,
Department of Human Services, 615 Pennsylvania Avenue, N.W.,
Washington, D.C. 20004

Florida
Office of Vital Statistics,
Department of Health and Rehabilitative Services,
1217 Pearl Street, P.O. Box 210,
Jacksonville, Florida 32231

Georgia
Vital Records Division, Department of Human Resources,
47 Trinity Avenue S.W., Atlanta, Georgia 30334

Hawaii
Research and Statistics Office, Department of Health,
1250 Punchbowl Street, Honolulu, Hawaii 96813

Idaho
Bureau of Vital Statistics,
Department of Health and Welfare,
450 West State Street, Boise, Idaho 83720

Illinois
Division of Vital Records,
Office of Management Services, Department of Public Health,
535 West Jefferson Street, Springfield, Illinois 62761

Indiana
Vital Records Section, State Board of Health,
1330 West Michigan Street, Indianapolis, Indiana 46202

Iowa
Vital Records and Statistics Division, Department of Health,
Lucas State Office Building, Des Moines, Iowa 50319

Kansas
Department of Health and Environment, Vital Statistics,
Forbes Field, Topeka, Kansas 66620

Kentucky
Division of Vital Statistics,
Cabinet for Human Resources, 275 East Main Street,
Frankfort, Kentucky 40601

Louisiana
Vital Records Registry,
Office of Health Services and Environmental Quality,
Department of Health and Human Resources,
P.O. Box 60630, New Orleans, Louisiana 70160

Maine
Office of Vital Records, Department of Human Services,
State House, Station 11, Augusta, Maine 04333

Maryland
Division of Vital Records, Department of Health and Mental Hygiene,
201 West Preston Street, P.O. Box 13146,
Baltimore, Maryland 21203

Massachusetts
Registry of Vital Records and Statistics, Department of Public Health,
107 John W. McCormack State Office Building,
1 Ashburton Place, Boston, Massachusetts 02108

Michigan
Office of Vital and Health Statistics,
Department of Public Health, 3500 North Logan Street,
P.O. Box 30035, Lansing, Michigan 48909

Minnesota
Department of Health, Section of Vital Statistics,
717 Delaware Street S.E., Minneapolis, Minnesota 55440

Mississippi
Vital Records, Department of Health,
P.O. Box 1700, Jackson, Mississippi 39215-1700

Missouri
Bureau of Vital Records, Division of Health,
Department of Social Services, Broadway State Office Building,
P.O. Box 570, Jefferson City, Missouri 65102

Montana
Records and Statistics Bureau,
Department of Health and Environmental Sciences,
Lockey Street, Helena, Montana 59620

Nebraska
Bureau of Vital Statistics, Department of Health,
301 Centennial Mall South, P.O. Box 95007,
Lincoln, Nebraska 68509

Nevada
Vital Statistics Section,
Division of Health, Department of Human Resources,
505 East King Street, Carson City, Nevada 89710

New Hampshire
Bureau of Vital Records and Health Statistics,
Division of Public Health Services,
Department of Health and Welfare, Health and Welfare Building,
Hazen Drive, Concord, New Hampshire 03301

New Jersey
Bureau of Vital Statistics and Registration,
Administration Division, Department of Health,
John Fitch Plaza, C.N. 360, Trenton, New Jersey 08625

New Mexico
Vital Statistics Bureau,
Health and Environment Department, 604 San Mateo Street,
P.O. Box 968, Santa Fe, New Mexico 87504-0968

New York
Bureau of Health Statistics, Office of Public Health,
Department of Health, 308 Tower Building,
Empire State Plaza, Albany, New York 12237

North Carolina
Vital Records Branch, Division of Health Services,
Department of Human Resources, 225 North McDowell Street,
P.O. Box 2091, Raleigh, North Carolina 27602

North Dakota
Division of Vital Records, Office of Statistical Services,
Department of Health, State Capitol, Bismarck, North Dakota 58505

Ohio

Division of Vital Statistics, Department of Health, Ohio Departments Building,
65 South Front Street, Columbus, Ohio 43215

Oklahoma

Bureau of Vital Statistics,
Vital Records Division, Department of Health,
Northeast 10th Street and Stonewall,
P.O. Box 53551, Oklahoma City, Oklahoma 73152

Oregon

Center for Health Statistics, Health Division,
Department of Human Resources, State Office Building,
1400 S.W. 5th Avenue, P.O. Box 116, Portland, Oregon 97207

Pennsylvania

Division of Vital Records, Department of Health,
Central Building, 101 South Mercer Street,
P.O. Box 1528, New Castle, Pennsylvania 16103

Rhode Island

Division of Vital Statistics, Department of Health,
Cannon Building, 75 Davis Street,
Providence, Rhode Island 02908

South Carolina

Office of Vital Records and Public Health Services,
Department of Health and Environmental Control,
2600 Bull Street, Columbia, South Carolina 29201

South Dakota

Center for Health Statistics, Division of Public Health,
Department of Health, Joe Foss Building,
523 East Capitol Street, Pierre, South Dakota 57501

Tennessee

Division of Vital Records, Department of Public Health,
C3-323 Cordell Hull Building, 436 6th Avenue North,
Nashville, Tennessee 37219

Texas

Bureau of Vital Statistics,
Department of Health, 1100 West 49th Street,
Austin, Texas 78756

Utah
   Bureau of Health Statistics,
   Office of Management Planning, Department of Health,
   150 West North Temple Street, P.O. Box 2500, Salt Lake City, Utah 84110

Vermont
   Vital Records, Department of Health,
   60 Main Street, P.O. Box 70,
   Burlington, Vermont 05402

Virginia
   Bureau of Vital Records and Health Statistics,
   Department of Health, James Madison Building,
   109 Governor Street, Richmond, Virginia 23219

Washington
   Vital Records, Health Services Division,
   Department of Social and Health Services, Airindustrial Park,
   P.O. Box 9709, LB-11, Olympia, Washington 98504

West Virginia
   Division of Vital Statistics, Health Services Section,
   Department of Health, 513 State Office Building 3,
   1800 Washington Street East, Charleston, West Virginia 25305

Wisconsin
   Bureau of Health Statistics, Division of Health,
   Department of Health and Social Services, 1 West Wilson Street,
   P.O. Box 309, Madison, Wisconsin 53701

Wyoming
   Vital Records Services, Division of Health and Medical Services,
   Department of Health and Social Services, Hathaway Building,
   2300 Capitol Avenue, Cheyenne, Wyoming 82002

You may also want to arrange for your physical examination
as soon as possible. Some agencies may insist that the physical-
examination forms be submitted before a home study can
begin, and it may be difficult to see your physician immediately.
As you begin your adoption inquiries, find out about an agency's
medical-exam requirements—particularly about lab tests, such
as the tuberculin test, the blood test for syphilis, and an elec-
trocardiogram. You can often have the physical done and then,

within a few weeks or months, ask your physician to fill in
the form. Be sure to find out how current the examination must
be.

Consents

Before an adoption can be approved by a court of law, certain
consents must be obtained. The child will be asked to consent
to the adoption if he is legally old enough to do so. (This will vary
state by state, but the age of legal consent is typically at least
twelve years.) The consent of the birth parents—both mother
and father—is expected. If the parents are dead or have abandoned the child or lost their custody judicially, then the consent
of the guardian, next of kin, court-appointed "friend," or an
authorized agency will be used. If you are adopting a child
through an agency, the agency will make sure that the necessary surrenders are obtained. The agency will then be authorized to consent to the adoption. If you are adopting a child
independently, you or your attorney must make sure that the
proper consents are obtained. Be sure that if the father is known
(whether or not he is actually married to the birth mother), you
obtain his consent. If you cannot readily locate him, the court
may ask you to show that you made an effort to find him. In
some states that may mean searching for him by placing an
advertisement in a newspaper. States may also have regulations
stating the length of time that must elapse between the child's
birth and the parents' relinquishment. There may also be provisions stating the length of time in which a parental release is
revocable.

Medical Consent Forms

If you are adopting a child independently, before you take
custody of the child, have the birth mother sign a medical
consent form stating that you can legally provide medical treat-

ment for the child. Adoption agencies normally provide you with their consent for treatment.

Finalizing an Adoption

Since a legal adoption is a procedure that establishes a relationship of parent and child between people who are not biologically related, you will have to go to court to finalize an adoption. This may be in your state of residence, your child's place of prior residence, or even the agency's place of (business) operation, depending on state laws. If you are involved in an intercountry adoption, you may be adopting your child abroad.

Some states require a waiting period before you may petition the court to initiate formal adoption proceedings. In other states, you may be able to file your court papers immediately but must still wait a period of time before finalizing the adoption, as is done with independent-placement adoptions in New York State. The process usually begins when you submit to the court a petition for adoption, which is signed by the people seeking to adopt and sets out information about them, the child, and the biological parents. It asks the court to approve the adoption, and may also include your request for an official change of your child's name. Along with the petition, you are usually asked to provide birth certificates, documents concerning guardianships, statements of the consent or termination of rights by the biological parents, the (older) child's statement of consent to the adoption, and the agency's consent to the adoption. The court may require that the consents (of birth parents, agencies, etc.) be submitted with the petition for adoption or at a hearing.

The court usually requires an investigation and the investigator's report before approving an adoption. If a child is placed through an agency, the agency will probably already have done its own postplacement follow-up. If a child has been adopted independently, the court will probably arrange for a study of your home.

The court usually holds a hearing. It may be in a closed courtroom or in the judge's chambers, and you may or may not be present. After the hearing, the court, having approved the adoption, issues an order or decree. The nature of the decree depends on state law. It may be a final decree or an interlocutory decree (a temporary one stipulating that at a later date— perhaps six months or a year—the court will again consider the application). Practices may vary by locality and by state. Which court actually considers your petition will also depend on local statute. It may be the probate court, district court, family court, superior court, or even the county court.

The Richardson family's two adoptions differed procedurally. For one adoption, they submitted a petition to adopt shortly after their son arrived in the United States from Chile. The court issued an interlocutory order of adoption specifying a six-month period during which their home was to be visited by the superintendent of public welfare. At the end of this period, the court could enter a final order of adoption. After the waiting period and the supervisory report, the court issued a final order of adoption. The Richardsons never met the judge; all they did was file the papers.

With their daughter's adoption in another state, there was no interlocutory order of adoption. They had all the visits before approaching the court and were interviewed by the judge on the day that he issued the final order of adoption. The judge, having studied the papers before the hearing, asked them whether they understood that this adoption was final. He approved the adoption, handed out lollipops to the Richardson children, and the family went out for ice cream to celebrate. The children still remember the event, and when they see a man in black robes, they always say that he's a judge.

Should you use an attorney to handle your child's adoption?

Some jurisdictions may permit you to file your own adoption papers, particularly the papers for finalization. Be sure to consult with other adoptive parents who have finalized their children's adoptions, with parent groups, and with your agency. You may find that your agency may even encourage you to do your own paperwork. An OURS chapter in Oregon, for example, has worked closely with the adoption agency PLAN (Plan Loving Adoptions Now) and sends out to Oregonians sample completed forms for filing the papers of children born in Oregon, Korea, Colombia, and India.

Do-it-yourself information often concerns finalizing the adoption of a child born abroad. Among the groups that have do-it-yourself information are FACE in Maryland, OURS in Oregon, and Concerned Persons for Adoption in New Jersey. Take a look also at *Law of Adoption* by Morton I. Leavy and Roy D. Weinberg (Dobbs Ferry, New York: Oceana Publications, 1979), which provides a useful framework for understanding the whole legal process.

Before you consider doing your own adoption, be sure to think it over carefully. Says Blanche Gelber, an experienced adoption attorney in New York City: "No two of my adoptions have been the same, and despite all my experience, the variations on the theme seem unpredictable and endless." Independent adoptions, are particularly complex and often very intricate. Gelber points out that each judge has his or her own beliefs and ways of approaching adoption. One judge may have a pattern of questioning independent adoptions while another may be more favorably disposed.

Consider the experiences of three families in Virginia. The Tellers used the forms that an attorney—whose child had also been adopted from Chile—had obtained from the local court and had successfully used. They essentially filled in the blanks. Their son's adoption went through the local court without a hitch. However, in passing on the "sample" papers to a third family—who also had a Chilean child but lived in another jurisdiction—things went awry. This family's judge was adamant in his insistence that the family provide evidence of having tried to obtain the putative father's consent. So they hired an attorney both in the United States and in Chile and advertised for the putative father.

These three families, living just ten miles apart but in different counties of a state, had different adoption experiences. If you will be following in the steps of someone else, particularly on a road *well trod* and with your agency's support, then adopting without an attorney may be a viable alternative.

In selecting an attorney to handle an adoption, inquire around and do some comparison shopping. For processing the finalization of an intercountry adoption, where all the documents were in order, one family received fee quotations ranging from $250 to $2,000. Be sure to do the following:

- Find an attorney who has some experience with adoption law. The more adoption cases an attorney handles, the more familiar the attorney should be with the forms, the courts, and the local clerks.
- Ask parent groups or the local bar association for recommendations.
- If you have worked with an adoption agency, check with them, but be aware that the agency lawyer is not necessarily the best suited to handle your case. The agency attorney may have an arrangement to handle adoptions for a set fee. You may find an equally competent attorney who charges less. The agency attorney, because he also handles all agency legal matters, may be very busy and finalizing adoptions may be a low priority on his agenda.
- Inquire about not only an attorney's fees but also how long it will take for him to get to the paperwork. Courts may be backed up, but if your attorney's case load is too heavy, there may be delays because he or she simply does not have time to work on your case.

- Inquire about hidden fees. One attorney, when asked to break down his fees, said that he charged $200 to file a child's naturalization papers. (See Chapter 6 about doing this yourself.)
- Check into an attorney's reputation. Some adoption attorneys may not be well regarded by the court because of the poor quality of their paperwork or their questionable legal practices.

The Sealed Record

With the issuance of the final order of adoption, the adoption proceeding is completed and the case is closed. The legal practice has been to keep the adoption records confidential. In the past they have been available in most states for inspection by court order only. In most states the child's original birth certificate and the other documents collected for the adoption petition are placed in sealed court files. (Agency records are not necessarily sealed, but many agencies do not release the information.) Access to this basic information can thus be very limited, even to adult adoptees.

An adult adoptee born in Kansas, however, might quite easily learn about his past since Kansas law states that "such sealed documents may be opened by the state registrar only upon demand of the adopted person if of legal age or by an order of court."[2] He could receive his original birth certificate if he requested it from the Bureau of Registration and Health Statistics. In Michigan and some other states, adoptees can now receive "nonidentifying" information about their birth parents. They can request identifying information (name of child before placement, parents' names, most recent address of birth parents), but this information will not be released until Michigan receives statements of consent from the birth parents. The state also maintains a central adoption registry—a file of birth parents' consents or denials to release information to adult adoptees. In still other states no registries exist and no information is disclosed. Under federal law, a foreign-born adoptee can obtain the records that were filed with the Immigration and Naturalization Service.

Chapters 10 and 12 discuss at length the importance of getting information about a child. Keep in mind that any information you turn over to the court may indeed be sealed and no longer accessible. If you are concerned about sharing with your child information about his background, be sure to keep a copy of whatever information you have received, and push your agency or contact to share information with you.

Obtaining a New Birth Certificate

It is customary, upon the adoption of a child, for the state to issue a new birth certificate or an amended birth certificate giving the new name of the adopted child. The certificate will usually give your child's name, will list you as parents, and may give the child's birthplace and other details. The new birth certificate will not reveal any information about the child's birth parents, nor does it usually state that the child is adopted.

Your attorney may handle this routinely as part of the adoption process. If you are not using an attorney, check with your state office of vital records. It is always a good idea to order more than one certified copy of the new birth certificate as your child may need the birth certificate when entering school, when obtaining a driver's license, and when marrying. (For details about birth certificates for children adopted abroad, see Chapter 6.)

6

The Special Paperwork
of an Intercountry Adoption

The magnitude of paperwork increases with an intercountry adoption. Even if you will be working with an agency, you must be well informed, well organized, determined, and willing to assemble what in advance may seem like an awesome array of personal documents. It can be done and has been done by thousands of people. The paperwork is extensive because you are meeting the requirements of a foreign country, our federal government, and your state system.

Meeting the Immigration Requirements of the Federal Government

Everyone bringing a child into the United States for the purposes of adoption must file an I-600 petition—a "Petition to Classify Orphan as an Immediate Relative." This petition is filed with the Immigration and Naturalization Service (INS) which has offices throughout the United States (see page 107). When you file the I-600 with INS, you will need to submit a variety of supporting documents and pay a filing fee by check or money order. The I-600 form (see Figure 1, page 100) also states that you must meet certain federal requirements:

- The term *orphan* under the immigration laws means an alien child who is under the age of sixteen years at the time the visa petition in his behalf is filed and both of whose parents have died or disappeared or abandoned or deserted the child, or the child has become separated or lost from both parents. If the child has one parent, that parent must be incapable of providing for the child's care and must have in writing irrevocably released the child for emigration and "adoption."
- To enter the United States, the orphan either must have been adopted abroad or must be coming to the U.S. for *adoption* by a U.S. citizen and spouse jointly or by an unmarried U.S. citizen at least twenty-five years of age.

In sum, the child must be under sixteen years of age; both parents must have died or disappeared, or, if there is one known parent, that parent will have had to release the orphan irrevocably. If there are two known parents, then the child does not qualify as an orphan under the I-600.

The I-600 also states that you must meet state preadoption requirements, and that if the child has not been adopted abroad, you must certify that he will be adopted in the United States.

There is no way around filing an I-600. Children brought in for medical procedures are brought in on different visas. If you try to bring a child into the country on a temporary visitor's visa, you are asking for trouble.

Processing through the Immigration and Naturalization Service

Long before your child arrives in the United States—even before a particular child may be assigned to you—the paperwork for adoption begins. As outlined in the previous chapter, you should begin gathering your documents in advance so that

UNITED STATES DEPARTMENT OF JUSTICE

Immigration and Naturalization Service

Form approved
OMB No. 43—R0992

PETITION TO
CLASSIFY ORPHAN
AS AN IMMEDIATE
RELATIVE

(Section 101(b)(1)(F) of
the Immigration and
Nationality Act, as
amended.)

Date Filed

Fee Stamp

File No.

TO THE SECRETARY OF STATE:

The petition was filed by:

☐ Married Petitioner   ☐ unmarried Petitioner

The petition is approved for orphan:

☐ adopted abroad   ☐ coming to U.S. for adoption.
                         Preadoption requirements have been met.

Remarks:

DATE
OF
ACTION

DD.

DISTRICT

(PETITIONER IS NOT TO WRITE ABOVE THIS LINE)

Petition is hereby made to classify the orphan named herein as an immediate relative.

BLOCK I.—INFORMATION ABOUT PETITIONER

1. My name is (Last) (First) (Middle)	2. Other names used; (including maiden name if married woman)

3. I reside in the United States at (C/O, if appropriate)   (Apt. No.)   (Number and street)   (Town or city)   (State)   (ZIP Code)

4. Address abroad (if any)   (Number and street)   (Town or city)   (Province)   (Country)

5. I was born: (Month)   (Day)   (Year)   In: (Town or city)   (State or Province)   (Country)   6. My phone number is

7.

I am a citizen of the United States   ☐ through birth in the U.S.   ☐ through parents   ☐ through naturalization   ☐ through marriage

(1) If acquired through naturalization, give name under which naturalized, number of naturalization certificate, and date and place of naturalization: _____

(2) If acquired through parentage or marriage, have you obtained a certificate of citizenship in your own name based on such acquisition? _____

   (a)   If so, give number of certificate and date and place of issuance:

   (b)   If not, submit evidence of citizenship in accordance with Instruction 2.a.(2).

Have you or any person through whom you claim citizenship ever lost United States citizenship? _____
If so, attach detailed explanation on separate sheet.

8a. My marital status is   ☐ Married   ☐ Widowed   ☐ Divorced   ☐ Single

b. I   ☐ Have   ☐ Have not been previously married.

c. If you have been previously married, state number of times _____

9. If you are now married, give the following information

   a. Date and place of present marriage

b. Name of present spouse (include maiden name of wife)	c. Date of birth of spouse (Month) (Day) (Year)
d. Place of birth of spouse (City) (State) (Country)	e. Number of prior marriages of spouse.

f. My spouse resides   ☐ with me   ☐ Apart from me at address (Apt. No.)   (No. and street)   (City) (State)   (Country)

(over)

Received	Trans. In	Ret'd-Trans. Out	Completed

FORM I-600
(Rev. 11–20–79)N

Figure 1

Block II.—Information pertaining to orphan beneficiary

10. Name at birth   (First)   (Middle)   (Last)

11. Name at present   (First)   (Middle)   (Last)   12. Sex

13. Any other names by which orphan is or was known   14. Date of birth   (City)   (State or Province)   (Country)

15. The beneficiary is an eligible orphan because: (Check one) ☐ He has no parents ☐ He has only one parent who is the sole or surviving parent.

16. If the orphan has only one parent, answer the following:
State what has become of other parent _____
Is the remaining parent capable of providing for the orphan's support? ☐ Yes ☐ No
Has the remaining parent, in writing, irrevocable released the orphan for emigration and adoption? ☐ Yes ☐ No

17. The orphan ☐ has ☐ has not been lawfully adopted abroad by ☐ petitioner and spouse jointly ☐ unmarried petitioner. If adopted abroad, did ☐ petitioner and spouse ☐ unmarried petitioner personally see and observe the orphan prior to or during the adoption proceedings? ☐ Yes ☐ No
Date and place of adoption:

18. If the orphan has not been lawfully adopted abroad by the petitioner and spouse jointly or by the unmarried petitioner, or if adopted abroad, the orphan has not been seen and observed personally by the petitioner and spouse or by the unmarried petitioner prior to or during the adoption proceedings, give the following: Do petitioner and spouse jointly or does the unmarried petitioner intend to adopt the orphan in the United States? ☐ Yes ☐ No.   Have the preadoption requirements, if any, of the orphan's proposed state of residence been met? ☐ Yes ☐ No.

19. To petitioner's knowledge, does the orphan have any physical or mental affliction? ☐ Yes ☐ No. If so, name the affliction:

20. Has petitioner or spouse or unmarried petitioner ever petitioned for the adoption of any other child? ☐ Yes ☐ No. If so, give the name of each child at birth and the date and place of birth.
_____
Is petitioner or spouse or unmarried petitioner, in the process of petitioning for the adoption of any other child? ☐ Yes ☐ No. If so, give the name of each child at birth and the date and place of birth:

21. Is the orphan the ward of a foreign country or a political subdivision therof? ☐ Yes ☐ No

22. Name of child welfare agency, if any, assisting in this case:

23. Name and address of attorney abroad, if any, representing petitioner in this case:

24. Address in the United States   (Number)   (Street)   (City)   (State)   (Zip Code)
where orphan will reside

25. Present address   (Apartment)   (Number)   (Street)   (City)   (State or Province)   (Country)
of orphan

If orphan is residing in an institution, give full name of institution

If orphan is not residing in an institution, give full name of person with whom orphan is residing

Give any additional information necessary to locate orphan such as name of district, section, zone or locality in which orphan resides

26. Location of American Consulate   (City in Foreign Country)   (Foreign Country)
where application for visa will
be made

AFFIDAVIT OF PETITIONER	CERTIFICATION OF MARRIED PETITIONER'S SPOUSE
I swear (affirm) that all the statements I have made in this petition are true and correct to the best of my knowledge and that I will care for the beneficiary of this petition properly if the beneficiary is admitted to the United States.	I certify that my spouse and I will care for the beneficiary of this petition properly if the beneficiary is admitted to the United States.
_____ (Signature of Petitioner)	Dated at _____ This _____ day of _____ 19____
Subscribed and sworn to (affirmed) before me this _____ day	_____ (Signature of Petitioner's spouse)
_____ 19 ____ , at _____	Signature of Person Preparing Form, if Other Than Petitioner.
_____ (SEAL)	I declare that this document was prepared by me at the request of the Petitioner and is based on all information of which I have any knowledge.
My commission expires _____	Signature:
_____ (Signature of Officer administering oath)	Address: Date:
_____ (Title)	

U.S. GOVERNMENT PRINTING OFFICE   o70—10—88188p-1

your application can proceed. Accompanying the I-600 will be the documents that describe you and your child.

The I-600 requires that you submit the following for yourself:

- Proof of U.S. citizenship
- Proof of marriage (or proof of divorce)
- Home study favorably recommending adoption
- Fingerprints (Form FD-258)

You can have your fingerprints taken at your local police station or at an INS office. INS personnel often recommend that you use their own service because fingerprints provided by local police are often smudged and illegible. Remember that a fingerprint check can take up to forty days and that a smudged fingerprint may need to be redone, causing additional delays.

You will also be asked to offer proof of your financial ability to support a child. This may include your last year's income-tax forms, statements about your bank deposits, and a statement from your employer. Some immigration offices require that you submit the Affidavit of Support (Form I-134).

You may also file an "Application for Advance Processing of Orphan Petition" (I-600A) with INS before you have identified a specific child—that is, you present all your documents, the I-600A, and a nonrefundable filing fee. Thus INS can run a fingerprint check on you and look at your documents. You can even file the I-600A before your home study is completed. (The home study must be submitted to INS within one year of the filing date of your application.) When you obtain your child's documents, you file an I-600, and the I-600 is processed. You do not need to resubmit with the I-600 the material that was presented to INS for the I-600A. Nor do you need to pay an additional fee unless your application is more than a year old. Advance processing can shorten your wait. Nothing is more frustrating than to have all your documents ready, know that your child is ready to emigrate, but fail to have fingerprint approval.

For an I-600 application, you will also be showing your child's documents to INS for approval. If your child's documents are in a foreign language, you must provide a translation. For the child that you are planning to adopt, you must show the following:

- Proof of age of orphan (e.g., birth certificate)
- Certified copy of the adoption decree, together with certified translation if the orphan has been legally adopted abroad
- Evidence that the sole or surviving parent is incapable of providing for the orphan's care and has in writing irrevocably released the orphan for emigration and adoption, if the orphan has one parent
- Evidence that the orphan has been unconditionally abandoned to an orphanage, if the orphan has been placed in an orphanage by his parent or parents
- Evidence that the preadoption requirements, if any, of the state of the orphan's proposed residence have been met, if the child will be adopted in the U.S.

If you are adopting more than one child, you will need to file a separate I-600 for each child.

Once INS has approved the I-600 application, they can notify the embassy in the country where the child is located that he or she has permission to enter the U.S. Regulations have now been changed so that you can also submit the completed I-600 to the U.S. Embassy in your child's birth country. If you file the I-600 in the U.S., the local INS office will cable the visa-petition approval to the embassy. Ask for confirmation from INS. If you are not going to be traveling to pick up your child, you will want to follow up with the agencies to be sure the visa approval was received. After your child has had a medical exam, the U.S. Embassy can issue a visa permitting the child to enter the United States on a permanent basis.

The wait for your child after you file the I-600 will vary, depending on the type of foreign adoption you are doing. With an agency adoption, such as an adoption from Korea, you can expect to file the I-600 as soon as you receive the child's documents and then possibly wait a month or more before the agency completes the paperwork in Korea. If you will be adopting your child abroad, the submission of the I-600 may come at the end of your wait, when your child is already with you, and you and your child may enter the U.S. shortly afterward.

Meeting State Preadoption Requirements

To meet preadoption requirements, some states may demand that you submit certain documents to them before they will approve the child's entry. Virginia, for example, requires that a family show the state's Interstate Placement Unit their home study, social and background information about the child and birth parents, documentation describing the child's legal status, a statement of financial responsibility for the child by the adoptive parents, and a statement of how the adoptive parents learned of the child's availability for adoption. In Wisconsin, if a family is granted guardianship of a child abroad, they must post a $1,000 bond as part of the preadoption requirements. Not all states have preadoption requirements, but be sure to inquire with your state's department of social services and the state's interstate compact administrator what requirements you must meet and what procedures you must follow.

If your child will be entering the United States with a final adoption decree, you do not need to meet preadoption requirements.

Notarization, Verification, Authentication

If you are adopting from Latin America, you are likely to be told that all your documents must be "notarized, verified, and authenticated at the consulate." Your home study, for example, will bear the seal of a notary public, who attests that the signatures on your documents are valid. The county clerk or the secretary of state for the state in which the notary resides will verify that the notary public's seal and signature are valid. (Birth and marriage certificates are certified copies, so they do not usually require this step.) Your notarized and verified documents, with translations if required, then go to the consulate. The consul of the country to which you are applying to adopt will attest to the authenticity of the documents and letters by his seal and signature. Some countries may require that everything you submit (your references, your birth certificates, your home study, your doctor's report) be notarized, verified, and authenticated. Costs can mount to several hundred dollars. Be sure you call ahead to the consulate in advance to ask about hours and costs (cash payment may be expected) and to make an appointment if necessary. Be prepared to leave the documents and have them returned to you by mail.

Translations

Your documents may have to be translated into a foreign language. Your child's documents will have to be translated into English. If you are working with an agency, they may have the translations done. If you are asked to arrange this yourself, be sure to use a competent, experienced translator, preferably someone working in his or her native language. Your translator will need to provide you with a statement of competence bearing an official raised seal. The statement might read: "I, ———, hereby certify that the above is a complete and accurate translation of the original and that I am competent in both English and ——— to render such a translation."

For the I-600, a "summary translation in English" is acceptable. Since the documents contain information about your child, you will want to get a full translation for your own information.

Getting Help

As you do the paperwork for an intercountry adoption, it's useful to talk to people who have recently completed the process. They can give you tips about whom to see at INS, what process to follow, and how long things will take. Local parent groups have often written up the local INS or foreign-consulate procedures.

Legwork

As the volume of paperwork grows with intercountry adoption, so, too, does the time it takes to process the papers. If you live near the offices of the Immigration and Naturalization Service, or indeed within any reasonable distance, it often pays to do your paperwork in person. Be sure to call ahead to find out opening and closing hours, lunch hours, and the days when the people you need to see will be on vacation or out of the office. Most families carry as many of their documents as possible by hand. They may spend one day at their state's secretary of state's office getting documents verified (if that is required by the foreign country), another at the foreign embassy getting the papers authenticated, and still another filing papers with INS. One family found that the only time they mailed in their documents—for their son's naturalization—they received a notice from their local INS office four months later stating that the letter had just been opened and their application assigned a file number. If you must mail your documents to your state government, for example, send them certified, return receipt requested. If there is a specific person who will be handling your documents (such as the interstate placement officer), you may want to follow up your letter with a telephone call a week later. Be sure also to send a self-addressed stamped envelope for the documents' return.

Getting in Touch with the Immigration and Naturalization Service

The offices listed below can give you information about immigration. Addresses marked with an asterisk are the INS district offices.

ADDRESSES FOR IMMIGRATION INFORMATION

Alabama
See Georgia or North Carolina.

Alaska
Federal Building, U.S. Courthouse, 701 "C" Street, Room D-229, Lock Box 16, Anchorage 99513*

Arizona
Federal Building, 230 North First Avenue, Phoenix 85025*

Arkansas
See Louisiana.

California
300 North Los Angeles Street, Los Angeles 90012*;
880 Front Street, San Diego 92188*;
Appraisers Building, 630 Sansome Street, San Francisco 94111*

Colorado
1787 Federal Office Building, 1961 Stout Street, Denver 80202*

Connecticut
900 Asylum Avenue, Hartford 06105*

Delaware
See Pennsylvania.

District of Columbia
25 "E" Street N.W., Washington 20538*

Florida
   Post Office Building, 311 West Monroe Street,
   P.O. Box 4608, Jacksonville 32201;
   155 South Miami Avenue, Miami 33130*;
   500 Zack Street, Tampa 33602

Georgia
   Richard B. Russell Federal Office Building,
   75 Spring Street S.W., Atlanta 30303*

Hawaii
   595 Ala Moana Boulevard, P.O. Box 461, Honolulu 96809*

Idaho
   See Montana.

Illinois
   Dirksen Federal Office Building, 219 South Dearborn Street,
   Chicago 60604*

Indiana
   104 Federal Building, 507 State Street, Hammond 46320

Iowa
   See Nebraska.

Kansas
   See Missouri.

Kentucky
   Room 601, U.S. Courthouse Building, West 6th and Broadway,
   Louisville 40202

Louisiana
   Postal Service Building, 701 Loyola Avenue,
   New Orleans 70113*

Maine
   76 Pearl Street, Portland 04112*

Maryland
   E.A. Garmatz Federal Building, 101 West Lombard Street,
   Baltimore 21201*

Massachusetts
John Fitzgerald Kennedy Federal Building,
Government Center, Boston 02203*

Michigan
Federal Building, 333 Mt. Elliott Street,
Detroit 48207*

Minnesota
927 Main Post Office Building, 180 East Kellogg Boulevard,
St. Paul 55101*

Mississippi
See Louisiana.

Missouri
324 East Eleventh Street, Kansas City 64106*;
200 North Tucker Boulevard, St. Louis 63101

Montana
Federal Building, 301 South Park, Room 512, Helena 59626*

Nebraska
Federal Office Building, 106 South 15th Street, Omaha 68102*

Nevada
Federal Building, U.S. Courthouse,
300 Las Vegas Boulevard, South, Las Vegas 89101;
350 South Center Street, Reno 89502

New Hampshire
See Massachusetts.

New Jersey
Federal Building, 970 Broad Street, Newark 07102*

New Mexico
See Texas.

New York
U.S. Post Office and Courthouse, 445 Broadway, Albany 12207;
68 Court Street, Buffalo 14202*;
26 Federal Plaza, New York 10007*

North Carolina
1111 Hawthorne Lane, Charlotte 28205

North Dakota
See Minnesota.

Ohio
U.S. Post Office and Courthouse, 5th and Walnut Street,
P.O. Box 537, Cincinnati 45201;
Anthony J. Celebrezze Federal Building, 1240 East 9th Street, Cleveland 44199*

Oklahoma
Federal Building and U.S. Courthouse,
200 N.W. 4th Street, Room 423, Oklahoma City 43102

Oregon
Federal Office Building, 511 N.W. Broadway, Portland 97209*

Pennsylvania
U.S. Courthouse, Independence Mall West,
601 Market Street, Philadelphia 19106*;
Federal Building, 1000 Liberty Avenue, Pittsburgh 15222

Rhode Island
Federal Building, U.S. Post Office, Exchange Terrace, Providence 02903

South Carolina
See Georgia or North Carolina.

South Dakota
See Minnesota.

Tennessee
Federal Building, 167 North Main Street, Memphis 38103

Texas
Federal Building, 1100 Commerce Street, Dallas 75242*;
343 U.S. Courthouse, El Paso 79984*;
2102 Teege Road, Harlingen 78550*;
2627 Caroline Street, Houston 77004*;
U.S. Federal Building, 727 East Durango, San Antonio 78206*

Utah
230 West 400 South Street, Salt Lake City 84138

Vermont

Federal Building, St. Albans 05478*

Virginia

Norfolk Federal Building, 200 Granby Mall, Norfolk 23510;
See also District of Columbia.

Washington

815 Airport Way, South, Seattle 98134*;
691 U.S. Courthouse Building, Spokane 99201

West Virginia
See Pennsylvania.

Wisconsin

Federal Building, 517 East Wisconsin Avenue, Milwaukee 53202

Wyoming
See Colorado.

Passports

If you will be traveling to pick up your child, you will need a valid passport. You can apply for a passport at a U.S. government passport office, at federal or state courts, or at some U.S. post offices. With the application, you must present your birth certificate (naturalized citizens must present their naturalization certificates), recent identical signed photographs of a specified size, and a fee. If you are applying for a passport for the first time, you must apply in person. You will also be asked to prove your identity. If you've had a passport within the past eight years but it has expired, you may use it to apply for a new passport.

Since passports are now valid for ten years, you should apply for your passport as soon as you can. Some Latin-American agencies will ask for your passport number on their applications, and the foreign consulate may ask to see your passport when you present your documents. Even if you do not plan on traveling abroad, you should have a valid passport so you can travel if you need to.

Your child will also need a passport issued by his birth country to travel to the United States. If you are adopting through an intercountry program, your agency will most likely make these arrangements. If you are adopting independently, you may have to make these arrangements when you go abroad.

Paperwork Abroad

As part of the intercountry adoption process, you will be submitting basic documents, including your home study, to a foreign source. This usually precedes the assignment of a particular child. If you are working with a U.S. agency, they may handle all communications abroad. If you are adopting independently, you may be doing all your own paperwork. If you are working independently with a foreign agency or attorney, you may be asked to send a "power of attorney" permitting them to act on your behalf.

You will need to meet the adoption requirements of your particular source (foreign agencies have requirements) and also of the foreign country. A country or an agency may have requirements pertaining to age, length of marriage, religion, residency, divorce, or marriage. *If you do not meet the foreign country's or foreign agency's requirements, you cannot adopt even if you satisfy all your state and federal requirements.*

To find out about the laws and procedures in a specific country, you can contact that country's consulate in the U.S. or parent groups whose members have adopted in that country. The U.S. consulate in the foreign country may also be able to help you.

If you will be traveling to pick up your child, you may have to appear before foreign authorities and do some paperwork at that time abroad. You can also expect to visit the American Embassy to obtain your child's visa. You may be asked to do such things as submit affidavits to a department of welfare or documents to the court, obtain statements from a physician about your child's health, or file an application for your child's passport. Your agency or attorney abroad may do this, or you may have to do it yourself.

Miriam describes what she and her husband did when they traveled to Bogotá and Neiva, Colombia, to adopt their daughter through the Instituto Colombiano de Bienestar Familiar. She says that after they arrived in Bogotá,

> we checked in with the consulate general of the U.S. and made sure that we understood the embassy procedure for Juanita's visa approval. A list of documents and other necessary steps was provided to us.
>
> Since we were hand-carrying most of our documents required by Bienestar, our next step after the embassy visit was to have each document verified and stamped at the Ministry of Foreign Relations. This office verifies that the Colombian Consulate in San Francisco who stamped our documents is legitimate.
>
> The lawyer at Bienestar handled all of the legal aspects of Juanita's adoption: preparation of adoption papers, representing us before the judge, and arranging for Juanita's passport.
>
> The adoption interview with the judge in Neiva went unobserved by Juanita. She was asleep in my arms the whole time. We promised to care for her in all the ways we care for our son.
>
> After the adoption, the time had come to leave Neiva (Juanita's Colombian passport in hand) and travel to Bogotá to arrange for her visa. It took four days to arrange for her visa. We then flew home.

Keeping Track

You will want to devise a method to keep track of all the documentation you need to accumulate (see Figure 2, for example). Be sure to keep copies of all correspondence and all documents.

Remember that you are preparing at least three sets of documents: one for the agency or person who is placing your child; one for the Immigration and Naturalization Service; and one for yourself (a duplicate set that you can use if necessary).

Figure 2 Checklist of Documents

	Request					
	Sent	Rec'd	U.S. Agency	Foreign Agency	INS	State (Preadopt)
Application: 1. 2. 3. 4.						
Documents **Birth Certificates** No. Needed Husband Wife						
Marriage Certificate No. needed						
Divorce Record						
Death Certificate						
Medical Reports Husband Wife						
Bank References Savings Checking						
Employer's Reference Husband Wife						
Income Tax Form 1040						
Home Study Date started: Date completed:						
References 1. 2. 3.						
Form I-600A			✕	✕		
Fingerprint Cards (2 for each of you)			✕	✕		
Form I-600			✕	✕		
Passports Husband Wife			✕	✕		✕
Your Future Child's Documents Proof of Age Parental or Agency Release Medical Report Background Information: Others:	✕	✕	✕	✕		✕

Alien Registration

When your child immigrates to the United States, he or she enters as an alien, not as an American citizen. You will receive from INS an alien registration card. This card should be carefully safeguarded along with other important papers. Until your child's naturalization, whenever you move, you must notify INS of the change of address. (In the past, aliens were required to register with INS every year. That procedure has been discontinued.)

Readoption

If you legally adopted your child abroad, the adoption is valid. Still, most adoption authorities recommend as an additional safeguard that you readopt your child in the United States under the laws of your state. This will also give you readily available evidence of the validity of your child's adoption. Some states may not permit readoption, so check locally to see if this can be done.

If your child left his or her country of birth under a guardianship, not a final adoption, then you *must* adopt in the U.S.

Naturalization

If you adopted your child abroad, you can apply for his or her naturalization immediately. Otherwise, as soon as your child has been legally adopted, you can apply to INS for naturalization. (The requirement that a child reside in the U.S. for two years before applying for naturalization has been discontinued.)

You will submit to INS an "Application to File Petition for Naturalization in Behalf of Child" (Form N-402). The application must be accompanied by special photographs taken within thirty days of the filing of the petition.

At a later date, you will be called for a hearing before an Immigration officer. Bring your child's birth certificate, a certified copy of the adoption decree (if your child was adopted abroad, be sure you have the adoption decree translated and that you have your translator's statement of competence), your various documents (birth, marriage, divorce certificates), the alien registration card, and the filing fee *in cash*. Even if INS fails to tell you to bring your documents, do so.

Only one parent need file the naturalization petition. If there is a family emergency or illness, only the parent who filed the petition must attend the hearing and naturalization.

Be prepared for a wait. You may be called by your local INS office immediately, but in some areas of the country the wait has been known to take up to two years.

Sometime after your meeting with the Immigration official, you will be summoned to the "swearing in" naturalization ceremony. It can be quite lengthy. It is for all new citizens, not just adoptees, and takes place in a courtroom. No cameras are permitted in the courtroom. The amount of fanfare surrounding the ceremony will vary by locale (in some areas of the country, the local Daughters of the American Revolution distribute souvenir American flags at the ceremony's conclusion). Sometime after the naturalization, INS will send you a naturalization certificate for your child.

Must a young child be present? It is the parent, rather than the young child, who takes the oath of allegiance on behalf of the child. Most parents want their young children present, but it is apparently not mandatory.

Obtaining a Birth Certificate for a Child Adopted Abroad

If you have adopted a child abroad, some states will permit you to apply for a state birth certificate without readoption;

others will insist upon readoption. Some states will issue a birth certificate for foreign-born adoptees upon receipt of proof of naturalization in the United States; others permit parents to submit a copy of the child's translated birth certificate and a translated copy of the child's final adoption decree. Check with your state's Vital Records Office (see Chapter 5). The policy of issuing birth certificates to foreign-born adoptees has been changing in recent years, so that even if you previously inquired and were told that your state does not issue a certificate, it is wise to keep calling periodically.

Some states will issue a foreign-born child a birth certificate that is the same as the birth certificate issued to all people born in the state. Other states issue a "certificate of foreign birth."

The Immigration and Naturalization Service will issue a "Certification of Birth Data" (Form G-641) to foreign-born children under twenty-one years old who have been admitted to the United States for permanent residence. INS can provide this certificate before naturalization. If you want INS to list your child's new name (if the name has been changed), INS will do this "where documentary evidence is presented to show the child's name has been legally changed."

Follow-up Contact with the Agency Abroad

Once your child's adoption has been completed, there's a strong desire to "get on with living" and put the past behind you. That feeling may extend to failing to keep in contact with the people who helped in your child's birth country. You may not be legally required to keep in touch with the agency or court, but intercountry-adoption advocates urge you to do so. Send cards on your child's birthday or at holidays. You may also want to send packages of clothing, small donations of money, and, of course, photographs that show your child's development. The judges and social workers in foreign countries who are involved in intercountry adoption are concerned about the welfare of those children who have left. Send letters not only the first year but for the next five or ten years so that others can see that your child is loved and cherished. It's good for you, good for your child, and good for intercountry relations. A judge or an agency that never hears about the outcome of intercountry adoptions might just decide to stop approving placements to the United States.

Searching for a Baby Independently

Pat and Gary contemplated adoption for several months before attending an adoption-orientation class run by a local parent group. When the discussion got around to independent-placement adoption, another couple mentioned that they were running advertisements for a newborn in several newspapers around the state. The two couples chatted about possibly pooling their resources. Nothing more was said. Pat went home and started compiling a list of newspapers in which she might run such a personal advertisement. A month later the other couple called her. They'd had two responses to their ads and both birth mothers had already given birth. Were Pat and Gary interested in talking with the birth mother of a week-old boy? They were, and a week later, after contacting an attorney, they picked up their new son.

Not all nonrelative independent (nonagency) placements happen like this, but some do. Most independent placements, in fact, involve a stepparent adopting the child of a spouse, or a relative adopting, for example, a niece or nephew. But private infant adoptions, or "direct adoptions," as nonfamilial independent placements are often called, can have an element of drama about them. An independent adoption counselor describes one such case:

Last month I got a call from a woman about adoption. When I called
back, I was told that she was in the hospital for minor surgery. Two
weeks later I learned that while she was in the hospital, another
woman came in, gave birth to a baby boy, and said that she wanted
to give the baby up for adoption. Her doctor apparently mentioned
to her that there was another patient on the floor who was interested
in adopting a child. The woman came in for minor surgery, and she
left [as] the prospective adoptive parent of a young boy.

While there are no national statistics showing the number of
infant nonrelative independent placements as compared to the
number of infant agency adoptions, there are some tantalizing
suggestions. In 1982 Nevada reported about 200 agency adoptions and about 50 independent nonrelative adoptions, while
Idaho reported 176 agency adoptions and 128 independent
nonrelative adoptions.[1] According to Grace Lichtenstein, who
described some independent adoptions in *New York* magazine
in 1981, Spence-Chapin Services to Families and Children and
Louise Wise Services, two well-known New York agencies, reported 55 Caucasian adoptions for 1980; while a well-known
New York adoption attorney, whose case load was primarily
infants, handled over 100.[2]

Bonnie Gradstein, Marc Gradstein, and Dr. Robert H. Glass,
who conducted a study of private adoption in California and
reported their findings in the journal *Fertility and Sterility*,
found that of the couples known to have successfully adopted,
over 90 percent had adopted privately.[3] These couples had
received counseling about private adoption and then were able
to pursue it. The couples surveyed did not encounter a long
wait—the majority had a baby in their home within four months
of the time they actively began trying to adopt: Twelve children arrived within a month of their parents' initiating the
search, and all but two of the 105 infants were placed in adoptive homes within a year of their parents' beginning attempts
at adoption.

Perhaps the best way to understand independent placement

is to contrast it with the traditional agency infant adoption practice, as the following chart shows.

AGENCY ADOPTION COMPARED TO INDEPENDENT ADOPTION

Agency Adoption	Independent Adoption
Birthparents surrender child to agency, which later places child with adoptive parents.	Birth parents consent to place child directly with the adoptive parents.
The adoption agency serves as the intermediary.	Various intermediaries—attorneys, physicians, teachers—may be used to help facilitate the placement.
Birth parents usually don't know the identity of adoptive parents and may not have any biographical information about them. Agency maintains anonymity.	Birth parents may know the identity of the adoptive parents and may have biographical information about them. Varying degrees of anonymity maintained.
Birth parents usually will not have had any contact with the adoptive parents. The agency serves as the intermediary.	Birth parents often have been in contact with the adoptive parents—either by telephone or in person.
Birth parents usually have released the child for adoption before the child is placed in adoptive home. If release has not been obtained, placement is called "legal-risk adoption."	Birth parents usually surrender child for adoption after the child is residing in the adoptive home. Birth parents may have right to remove child from home.
Infant may be placed in foster care until all the releases have been signed and all waiting periods have passed.	Infant usually placed in adoptive home after discharge from the hospital.
Agency social worker usually selects the parents for a specific child.	Birth parent often selects the adoptive parents for her child.
Adoptive parents have sought out an agency, filed an application, been approved, and waited for the agency to assign a child to them.	Adoptive parents often are actively involved in searching for an infant to adopt.

The Legality of Independent Adoption

Independent placement is legal in most states, although the laws governing it will vary. Some states impose few or no restrictions on independent placements. Others say that a child must be placed for adoption directly by the birth parent with an adoptive parent; intermediaries are forbidden.

Your state department of social services can tell you exactly what is legal in your state. (The directory at the back of this book provides a brief summary.) In 1984, independent placements were not permitted by state law in Connecticut, Delaware, Massachusetts, Michigan, Minnesota, and North Dakota. If you are considering an independent placement across state lines, you will need to learn what is legal in both states and how the interstate compact will be involved. Some adoptive-parent groups may offer guidance. Many groups cannot assist since their memberships may not include parents who have done independent adoptions. Be prepared to encounter hostility since many people are not familiar with how independent placement legally works and may be uncomfortable with it. The **Adoptive Parents Committee** (210 Fifth Avenue, New York, New York 10010) is one parent group that has advocated independent adoption. Many of its members have successfully adopted independently and the group has written pamphlets and held workshops that stress independent placement as a legal, viable adoption alternative.

No doubt as you ponder independent placement you'll be warned about "gray market" adoptions, "black market" adoptions, and "baby brokering." These are terms that people have coined to identify nonagency adoptions. What do these terms imply? A gray market, as the dictionary defines it, is a market using irregular channels of trade or undercover methods not actually or explicitly illicit and chiefly in scarce materials at excessive prices. The implication is that nonagency adoptions are gray-market in that they use irregular—that is, nonagency—channels. A black-market adoption, technically speaking, involves an illicit market in which goods are sold in violation of price controls or other restrictions. Huge amounts of money are reportedly passed along in trade for babies. Using an intermediary, when one is forbidden by state law, would also be a black-market adoption. Baby brokering also suggests schemes and trading in babies.

As adoption practices continue to evolve, it becomes hard to use these terms meaningfully. What about an agency that charges a high fee or advertises on park benches for birth parents? Agency adoption, like independent adoption, can also involve "brokering" if one recognizes that the agency can "act as an agent for others in negotiating contracts for a fee." Independent-placement adoption is just what it says: a nonagency placement that results in an adoption whose circumstances adhere to the rules of the state. Some practices can smell fishy and be illegal whether they are handled by individuals or agencies.

Deciding for Independent Adoption

Carrie was seventeen, unmarried, and living at home with her parents in a rural town. Just a few months before, she had given birth to a child. She was now struggling to raise that child while still attending high school. She had thought that she was using birth control, but now found that she was pregnant again. First she delayed telling anyone, because she was embarrassed. Then she decided that, for her, abortion was out of the question. So when she was six months pregnant, she told her minister's wife of her situation. She wanted to release the child for adoption, but was adamant in her refusal to approach the local agency; she did not feel comfortable talking about her situation with strangers, particularly when she felt that they might question how she could become pregnant twice in less than a year.

Said the minister's wife: "She was not what we think of as a trampy kind of kid. She was a good student. She was extremely reticent to talk to anyone who would ask her questions. She had a fear of interrogation by adults, a fear of sexual questions, a fear that she would have to tell her story to many people. She just wanted one person who would be her advocate, whom she could tell what she wanted and when." The minister's wife became her advocate and her intermediary.

Meanwhile, Earl and Alice, a couple who wanted to adopt, had approached a local agency and placed their name on a waiting list for a home study. Through mutual friends, the minister's wife heard that they had been making inquiries about adoption and had been thinking about the possibilities of an independent adoption, so she contacted them on Carrie's behalf. After Carrie's son was born, Earl and Alice became his parents.

Ron and Dorothy chose an independent-placement adoption because they wanted to adopt a newborn and were able to take their daughter home directly from the hospital. Still other couples end up adopting independently because they happen to hear of a pregnant woman willing to place her child for adoption. Like Earl and Alice, they take the chance that comes up.

Birth parents may decide to place their children for adoption independently because they want more control over the situation. They may feel it is important to select the adoptive parents, to talk with them, and even to meet with them. Financial needs may also play a role in birth mothers' seeking out independent placement. Many agencies cannot pay medical bills or other expenses, although they may direct a woman to public assistance and other forms of help. Many states, however, will permit adoptive parents to pay for reasonable expenses in an independent placement. A birth mother may also be reluctant to approach an agency for counseling, fearing that the social worker will be passing judgment on her. She may fear too much probing. Or she may have gone for an interview at an agency and been turned off.

Adoptive parents may seek out an independent placement because there are long waiting lists with local agencies or too many agency restrictions (age, fertility history, length of marriage, and religion are common barriers). Or there may just be a lack of agencies in their area. Some adopters may feel strongly that they want to have more information about their child and the birth parents than local agencies traditionally provide. They want to ask questions about the birth parents' family history, medical history, intellectual capacity, and other pieces of a person's life story. Despite what you may hear, most people who adopt independently are not forced to do so because of their rejection by an agency but rather choose to because they believe it is most suitable for them.

If you want to have direct contact with a birth mother, it is quite possible in an independent adoption. In fact, some states have laws mandating direct contact between birth parents and adoptive parents. For a more complete sense of open adoption's potential in independent placement, see *To Love and Let Go* by Suzanne Arms (New York: Knopf, 1983), which chronicles several families' experiences, including such opportunities as being present at the child's birth.[4] Arms's book is particularly strong in portraying birth mothers and their wants and needs.

Getting Prepared

If independent placement interests you, your first step will be to find out what is permitted. Here are some basic questions to ask the state social service department:

- Must you meet directly with the birth parents?
- Can you use an intermediary if you don't wish to meet with the birth parents directly?

- What type of parental releases and/or consents must you obtain?
- What are the waiting periods required for the releases?
- What are the rights of the putative father? (Once you identify a particular child, be sure to ask who the putative father is, where he is now, and whether he's agreed to the adoption plan.)
- Does the state require that adoptive parents and birth parents be of the same religion?
- Can religious restrictions be waived?
- Does the state require a home study before placement?
- Does the state have a residency requirement?
- What expenses related to the adoption can you legally pay for?

If you are adopting in another state, you will need to contact that state's department of social service to find out what is legal there. You must also consider the standards of the interstate compact before you carry a child across state lines for the purposes of adoptive placement.

Meanwhile, you still have more questions to ask and answer for yourself:

- Do you want to have contact with the birth parents?
- What do you mean by "contact"? Face-to-face? Letters? Photographs? Telephone calls?
- Do you want to use an intermediary?
- How much anonymity do you want?
- What questions do you want to ask the birth parents?
- What medical risks are you willing to assume?
- Will you accept a child born with a birth defect?
- What is the state of your savings?
- Can you afford to pay the legitimate pregnancy-related expenses?
- Can you afford the expenses of a cesarean section if it occurs?
- Are you willing to travel to pick up your child?

- Are you willing to live for several months in another state if that is necessary?
- Are you willing to bring the birth mother to your state to give birth to her child?
- If you bring a birth mother to your state, what facilities and costs are involved in providing shelter and maintenance for her?
- Whom will you turn to for legal advice?
- Whom will you turn to for both obstetric and pediatric medical advice?
- How much risk and uncertainty are you willing to live with?

This last point should be carefully weighed. People often hear of a woman in her third month of pregnancy who is thinking about surrendering her child for adoption. You will have to wait out her pregnancy realizing that she may change her mind either before or after the child is born. It is also possible that the woman will miscarry or her child will be stillborn or have other medical problems. There is a financial risk, too. You may have paid for medical bills, counseling, or other legally permissible bills, but you won't necessarily get your money back if the adoption fails to go through. Sometimes you can ask, but the chances of getting it back are mighty slim. Moreover, after the child is placed in your home, depending on your state's law, the birth parents may still have the right to change their minds for a specified period of time. If the birth parents have received proper counseling and their decision was made without duress, this is unlikely to happen. But it can. Can you live with that uncertainty? With a traditional agency adoption, the risks are lessened because you will not have learned about a child until the child was freed for adoption.

Mike and Eve's situation illustrates how involved an independent placement can become. Someone from another state told them about a baby who would be born soon. Checking with a local attorney in the state where the birth mother resided and with attorneys in his home state who advised him on the general legality of the situation, Mike learned that he and his wife would have to be residents of the state where the birth mother lived in order to successfully adopt. They would have to set up an apartment and live there. This state's preadoption requirements involved a home study before the child could enter their home. Their costs would include an attorney's fees, medical expenses, and living costs in two states. Mike would continue working and commute by air on weekends to his new home.

They decided to take the chance. They did their preadoption paperwork and had their home study done. Eve sat in their new home waiting for the baby to be born. Then things got even more complicated. The birth mother, a young teenager, gave birth under an assumed name, left the baby with a friend, and ran away. She was frightened. At that point, says Eve, "we were getting ourselves psychologically prepared to pack up and cut our losses." The birth mother returned, however, and had additional counseling. She eventually surrendered the baby. Several months after Mike and Eve had traveled to the new state, they returned home with their new son. Would they do it again? Yes, and no. "We wouldn't be separated for almost four months. For our second child, we'd probably not go out of state like that." But, continues Eve, "for William, we were willing to do almost anything."

Seeking Legal Advice

As you pursue an independent-placement adoption, you will need to consult with an attorney. To find the right one, check with adoptive parents and organized parent groups for recommendations for attorneys who have handled independent adoptions. Local and state bar associations often make referrals.

Ask your attorney what role he expects to play in the independent placement process. Following are some questions to ask:

- Will he interview the birth parents on your behalf?
- Will he arrange for counseling?
- Will the attorney take charge of the medical arrangements?
- Will he represent you in court?
- Who will represent the birth parents in court? (Some courts do not permit one lawyer to represent both you and the birth parents, since there may be a conflict of interest.)
- How many independent adoptions and agency adoptions has the attorney handled?
- How many interstate adoptions has he handled?
- What are his fees? (Compare his fees with those of other adoption attorneys.)
- What do his fees include? Are you billed for services rendered or is there a set fee for every adoption?
- If you want to, can you participate actively in the process and reduce the lawyer's time and fees? What would you do?
- Should you have a written agreement with the attorney, before the child arrives, as to what services he will provide?
- Do you feel comfortable with the lawyer who is about to share the intimate procedure of obtaining your child? Do you trust him?

Be sure that you check the lawyer's reputation among his colleagues and other adoptive parents. Has the court ever questioned the independent adoptions he's handled? You can also check with your state attorney general's office. If you have any doubts at any point, get other legal opinions.

Spreading the Word

In her Christmas cards, Fay wrote: "We're trying desperately to adopt and if you hear of anything, let me know." Shortly after Christmas, she got a call from a physician for whom she had once worked who had moved out of state. One of his patients had just given birth to a baby boy. Were they still interested in adopting? She was, and she traveled across the country to pick up her son. Five months later, Fay got a call from her obstetrician, who told her he knew of a baby. Not right now, Fay said, but thanks and keep me in mind for the future. And two years after those cards went out, Fay's sister's obstetrician called from another state to ask whether they were still interested in an independent adoption.

Spreading the word—telling others that you are interested in adopting a child and are willing to adopt independently—is a wise first step—and possibly the only step you will have to take in pursuing an independent placement. If you want to adopt, you must talk about it. That means telling your parents, your aunts and uncles, your cousins, your neighbors, your friends, and whomever else you can think of. "I called everybody I knew," recalled Roberta, whose daughter arrived several months after her inquiries began. "I promised myself that I'd make one telephone call a day. At parties I'd walk up to people, complete strangers sometimes, and say, 'Hello, my name is Roberta Rolfe and my husband and I want to adopt a baby. Do you know of anyone who wants to put up a baby for adoption?' " (She'd hand them her business card with the handwritten message "Hoping to Adopt.") When Roberta accompanied her husband on a business trip to Louisiana, she picked up the telephone and called the local department of social services to inquire about adoption. "It was an obsession. There was nothing more important than this," says Roberta. "I was monomaniacal."

Was Roberta crazy? No. The more people she told, the greater the likelihood of turning up someone who knew someone. Beyond family, friends, neighbors, colleagues at work, reach out to other people within your community. Go through your address book, your parents' address books, your sister's address book. Are there some old college chums who might help? Adoption counselors particularly recommend that you contact nurse-midwives, physicians, social workers, and other health professionals; clergymen; teachers and high-school principals; and even beauticians. These people often come into contact with pregnant women. Establish as extensive a network as you can; indeed if state laws and finances permit, explore the possibility of contacting people in another state.

How should you go about letting people know? Some people use the telephone; others, like Fay, send out letters; while still others try to talk to people in person. Encourage the people you contact to talk with others about your desire to adopt.

Keep track of all your contacts. Get a notebook and record details about everyone you approached and exactly what they were told and what they told you. Follow up on as many leads as possible—and be prepared to retrace your steps at a later point.

There are also more formal ways to alert others to your needs. Bonnie Gradstein has advised her clients to do a mass mailing of letters to some 500 obstetricians, pediatricians, and family practitioners whose names have been taken from phone books and medical directories (including the membership directory of the American College of Obstetricians and Gynecologists).[5] Other counselors have suggested contacting abortion clinics, right-to-life groups, planned-parenthood centers, and free health clinics.[6] Reni L. Witt and Jeannine Masterson Michael's book for pregnant teenagers, *Mom, I'm Pregnant* (New York: Stein and Day, 1982), is also a useful resource for people seeking to adopt since it has an extensive state-by-state directory of where to go for help, including hot lines and service agencies.

Some people have tried sending out detailed autobiographies along with their letters.[7] The autobiography should contain much of the basic information that would be found in a home study and should be written in an open, appealing manner. It can describe your desire to become parents, your education, jobs, home, community, and outside interests. The autobiography should include a phone number where you can be reached —collect! You might also give the names of other contacts (for example, your attorney). To round out your profile, enclose good color photographs of yourself, your home, and your other children.

Be sure that your autobiography conveys your personality. Do you like to swim? Do you play tennis? Do you enjoy movies? Do you have a pet? Do you come from an extended family that gets together frequently? What is important to you in raising a child? How long have you been trying to have a child? How has your desire to parent a child affected you? The autobiography should make a person want to reach out and help you. Your autobiography may well be passed on to a birth mother. You want her to feel that she can envision her child's future with you.

Placing advertisements in newspapers is another technique that adoptive parents have begun to utilize. Just as agencies are finding that featuring a waiting child can bring a response when trying to find a home for a special-needs child, prospective adoptive parents have found that placing an advertisement in the personal section of the classifieds alerts birth parents to their desire to parent a child. The ads convey their concerns:

> ADOPTION, NOT ABORTION: Let us adopt your baby. We are a young, happily married couple who wish to adopt a white infant into our home. If you can help us, our gratitude goes to you. Expenses paid.
> ADOPT—Childless couple will be wonderful parents and give terrific life to newborn. Answer our prayers.
> ADOPT—Happily married couple will provide love, finest education, country home for baby, confidential, expenses paid.

The couple that places the advertisement often takes out an unlisted telephone number specifically for adoption inquiries. Typically, they have talked with their attorney in advance to discuss the legal requirements. They receive responses either directly from the birth mother or from an intermediary of her choice. They may talk several times and may then refer her to their attorney, if state law permits, to make the arrangements.

Don't be surprised if your ad is not the only one appearing

in a particular newspaper. You may want to make your ad as personal as possible. Try to put yourself in the place of the birth parent who will be reading the newspaper. Don't pinch pennies when writing these ads—they speak for you.

Be aware also that you may need to run your ad for several months in several newspapers. You may receive many calls and talk with many people who never follow up.

The advertisement method has been successfully used by people. In fact, people are often astounded at the speed with which things may happen. John and Rhoda placed their ad in a newspaper in the Midwest. The first day their ad ran, a parent who had just recently learned of her thirteen-year-old daughter's pregnancy was reading the personals column of the local newspaper to pass time while the girl was in labor. She spotted the ad and approached her daughter after the delivery. "It's amazing how disconnected some people are until they see the ads," says an adoption attorney. The family felt very positive about the independent placement, and within the month John and Rhoda had become parents.

Be sure you find out whether it is legal to place an ad for an adoption in a state. Check with the state department of social services, a knowledgeable adoption attorney, and parent groups. You may also have to search around for a newspaper willing to take your ad.

The Cost of an Independent Adoption

You've probably been told that independent-placement adoptions are very expensive and you've probably been quoted figures—$10,000, $15,000, and even $25,000 are among the amounts that I've heard bandied around by people who knew very little about adoption. People who had successfully completed independent adoptions gave me different figures. The costs might be as low as $3,000, no more than a couple might pay to a private agency that had a sliding fee scale.

It's difficult to come up with an exact or typical dollar figure, because costs vary tremendously case by case. If the birth mother is living at home and has health-insurance coverage under her parents' policy, the expenses of the adoption are going to be much less than if the birth mother has no health insurance and delivers the child by cesarean section. If the birth mother travels to your state to give birth and resides there before delivery for a month or more, the costs will be higher. The difference to you can be as much as $5,000.

A cardinal rule for assessing costs in an independent placement ought to be that all expenses be reasonably documented —there should be receipts for all expenditures. Sometimes a preadoption agreement clarifies the financial expectations of all parties.

If an intermediary has been involved, he or she should not receive a fee for bringing you together. Attorneys should be paid for the professional legal services they perform. Physicians should be paid for the professional medical services they render. Social workers or clergy should be compensated for any professional counseling services they perform. *You should not be paying any "finder's fee."*

WARNING: You should not be paying for the birth mother's college tuition, the down payment for her house (or her parents' house), a vacation in Europe, or "designer" maternity clothes. You may be asked, *but these expenses are not considered "reasonable expenses."* When you finalize the adoption in court, you may be asked to submit a sworn accounting of all payments made, or your actual receipts, and the judge may look very carefully at all expenses incurred.

Your expenses for an independent adoption are likely to include:[8]

- Birth mother's hospital and doctor bills
- Birth mother's lab fees, vitamins, tests, and drug bills
- Infant's hospital-nursery and pediatric bills

- Infant's drug bills
- Counseling for the birth parents
- Your attorney's fees
- Birth parents' attorneys' fees

Additional expenses that can sometimes come up are:

- Birth mother's lodging and maintenance expenses for one or several months
- Birth mother's or birth father's travel expenses (for the surrender of the child)
- Long-distance telephone calls
- Putative father's pregnancy-related expenses
- Postage for mailing out your résumé
- Advertising expenses in several newspapers for several months
- Installation of a separate phone for your adoption search

Things to Watch Out For

If you decide to pursue an independent-placement adoption, you should proceed cautiously at all times. Be especially alert in the following areas:

Parental consent: Don't pressure anyone into releasing a child for adoption. Be sure that the parent has made the decision without duress. Be sure that you obtain the father's release. If there is no father's release, you may be asked to locate him.

Attorney expertise: Be sure that your attorney is experienced in adoption law, particularly for independent adoption and for the county where you will be adopting your child.

Pressure from intermediaries: Don't let anyone tell you that this is a "once-in-a-lifetime situation."

Costs: Examine these carefully. Are you being asked to put down money to place your name on an intermediary's waiting list? Are you being asked to advance large sums prior to placement? Are you being asked to pay for everything in cash? If you are being asked to put money into escrow, what is it for? Are you receiving an itemized bill for expenses?

Health: Arrange to have the infant assessed by your pediatrician or by another physician of your choice. Get as extensive medical records as you can about the birth parents and the child. Don't hesitate to ask questions.

Counseling: Be sure that the birth parents have adequate counseling and, again, that their decision is not made under pressure from you or anyone else.

Remember, in an independent-placement adoption, you are relying on yourself, rather than on an adoption agency, to ensure that your child's placement proceeds legally and successfully.

8

Searching for a Waiting Child in the United States

If you are interested in adopting a waiting child or a special-needs child and your agency says it does not have any children available, what can you do? The last chapter showed how people looking for infants can go outside the agency system to try to locate a child. Families seeking to adopt older children need not go outside the agency system, but they may also have to search—using local, state, and national programs that have been created to serve waiting children.

Today there are local, state, regional, and national adoption exchanges that can act as "matching services," registering children, and sometimes families, to make links. Many of these adoption exchanges have created photographic listing books that describe available children. These books, resembling the multiple-listing books that real-estate brokers use, provide capsule portraits of children.

Exchanges also use other recruitment devices, such as weekly newspaper columns or regular television newscasts featuring waiting children. In New York City, the Human Resources Administration sponsors a twice-yearly Adoption Exchange Conference. Social workers from various local agencies show slides of individual children available for adoption. Prospective adoptive parents have ballots that include a photograph of each child presented, some basic information, and the name of the agency that is overseeing the child in foster care. As the social worker presents the child to the group pictorially, the people in the audience look at their ballots and check off the children who interest them. After the presentation, the prospective adoptive parents go to the agency's information table and register their interest in a particular child. (At the agency's information table, more photos of other waiting children in the agency's care are invariably displayed.) Families interested in a child will be contacted by the agencies.

The Massachusetts Adoption Resource Exchange (MARE) has experimented with adoption parties where social workers, prospective adoptive parents, experienced adoptive parents, and waiting children get together in informal settings. A trip to the zoo, for example, featured a picnic lunch, a tour of the zoo, and a chance for interested people to mingle, share information, and become more familiar with adoption. At one event, eight children were also linked with new families. Although the children come to the event, there is no pressure for families to accept a child. Events such as this, however, give children the chance to meet adults—and offer you the chance to find that special child.

State Adoption Exchanges

Many states operate some form of adoption exchange where agencies—both public and private—can list waiting children and, in some instances, waiting families (see the directory at the back of this book for a state-by-state list). If an agency has a child needing to be placed in an adoptive home, and the agency does not have a suitable family available, it can register that child with the exchange. Some states even mandate by law that agencies *must* register their children with a state adoption exchange if they fail to find an adoptive home within a specified period of time. The exchanges do not have children in their custody;

rather, they take referrals and try to facilitate placements. The exchanges provide their services free of charge.

The Massachusetts Adoption Resource Exchange, which celebrated its twenty-sixth anniversary in 1983, is typical of a full-service exchange. Its programs include adoption information, referral (trying to match a referred child to one of their registered waiting families), photolisting (the *MARE Manual*), recruitment (the *Boston Sunday Globe* column "Sunday's Child" and WBZ's television program "Wednesday's Child"), exchange meetings, and adoption parties. At any given time, some 200 children and some 400 families are listed with MARE. In 1982, for example, MARE responded to 3,453 inquiries and was responsible for creating 117 matches (77 boys; 40 girls). All the children matched had either physical, emotional, or intellectual special needs. The average age of all children registered with the exchange was nine years old, while the average age of minority children was six and a half years old.

In 1982 the photolisting book, the *MARE Manual*, accounted for some 30 percent of the matches. The photolisting provides a profile of each child through a detailed biography and a photograph (see Fig. 3). Updated monthly and usually containing the write-ups of almost all the registered children, the manual is circulated to adoption agencies, community centers, public libraries, and parent groups—places where interested people might turn for information. If a person sees a child featured in the *MARE Manual,* he or she can contact the MARE office and be put directly in touch with the child's social worker if that child is still available. If a child is "placed" or "on hold," then the telephone number of the worker is not given out.

As a person seeking a special-needs child, you should touch base with one or more exchanges. If waiting families are permitted to register with your exchange, then do so yourself or ask your worker to register you. Try to list yourself also with other states' exchanges, particularly those nearby. Consult as many photolisting books as possible (see directory at back of this

Walter, who previously appeared on pgs. 139
& 140, is an attractive 12 year old boy of
Black parentage. He is of small build with
a medium brown complexion, large dark brown
eyes, and dark brown hair.

Walter has an appealing smile and is very friendly
and outgoing. If one were to describe Walter
in one word, it would be "energetic". He is
very sociable and loves to please. He especially
enjoys showing off his skills with sports and
academics. His hobbies are watching television,
reading and sports of all kinds, he also likes
to pose for pictures and is a natural model.

At a very early age, Walter suffered major
losses and rejection; "As well as being affected
by lead paint poisoning which has left him
moderately retarded". He functions intellectually
and emotionally like an eight year old child.
He attends a special class which includes speech
therapy in a public school. He gets along very
well with his teachers and peers and is very
much at ease with strangers.

Walter has no behavioral problems, and despite his past physical and emotional traumas,
he is now felt to be in good health.

Walter has been in the same foster home for the past seven years. It has been a positive
experience for him since the family has provided him with much love, care and attention.

The agency is looking for a small family for him
and would prefer a two parent Black home able
and willing to devote their time and love. Walter
will need a lengthy period of visiting before
moving into his new home.

Walter is a loving and lovable child with much
potential and should be able to live independantly
as an adult.

He is legally free for adoption.

545. (update of pgs. 139 & 140) (841) 4/82 MA

Figure 3 Sample Photolisting from *MARE Manual*

book), not once but at frequent intervals. Find out whether your local parent group, or a local agency, has the photolisting books of other states' exchanges. Some parent groups or agencies, particularly those with an interest in placing special-needs children, subscribe to out-of-state listing services. You may not want to look at every exchange's books, but it's recommended that you look at the books of neighboring states, or states that have a large number of children in foster care. New York State, for example, has mandated that all children freed for adoption and not placed in adoptive homes within a period of time be photolisted. Its book, *New York State's Waiting Children,* typically lists several hundred children and is updated every two weeks. Over the course of a year, it will spotlight several thousand children. Remember, however, that the children listed in these books will be those for whom an agency has not been successful in finding a home locally. Don't expect to see infants, toddlers, or elementary-school-age white children.

Using a photolisting book, even for out-of-state children, can result in a successful adoption. Carol and Bob Wilson had been consulting their state photolisting book and those of several other states for several months. They saw the photos of their children—a brother and sister with several developmental and physical handicaps (including congenital cataracts that severely limited the childrens' sight)—in the photolisting book of the Texas Adoption Resource Exchange. It took seven months and many interstate telephone calls, and they had to contend with the childrens' social worker's belief that it would be best to place the children in-state. But, says Carol, "persistence paid off." The caseworker confided to her afterward that the biggest selling point—what broke down her resistance to an interstate placement—were the letters Carol sent expressing the family's sincere wish to adopt the children. All the other families under consideration had provided only factual information. "Our file was more personal," Carol says, "and that's what made the difference." That and the willingness to use a photolisting book —and to follow through.

Regional Exchanges

Regional exchanges take referrals of children from several states and circulate information about adoption. Very often the children listed with the regional exchanges have special problems that have made these children's placement more difficult. Agencies contact a regional exchange to seek a wider exposure for such children and to recruit families. Like the state adoption exchanges, regional exchanges usually register children, often register families, and may distribute a regional photolisting book. They run recruitment programs and provide technical information to social-service agencies.

You may want to touch base with your nearest regional exchange or other regional exchanges around the country. A list of them follows.

AASK (Aid to Adoption of Special Kids)
3530 Grand Avenue
Oakland, California 94610 (415)451-1748
(Serves primarily Arizona, California, Hawaii, and Nevada, but takes registrations from all states.)

Adoption Center of Delaware Valley
1218 Chestnut Street
Philadelphia, Pennsylvania 19107 (215)925-0200
(Serves Delaware, the District of Columbia, Maryland, New Jersey, Pennsylvania, Virginia, and West Virginia.)

Exchange of Mid-America
Kansas Children's Service League
P.O. Box 517
Wichita, Kansas 67201 (316)942-4261
(Serves Missouri, Iowa, Kansas, and Nebraska.)

Maine-Vermont Exchange
Maine Department of Human Services
Bureau of Social Services
221 State Street
Augusta, Maine 04333 (207)289-2971
(Serves Maine, Vermont, and New Hampshire.)

Minority Exchange Component of Region IX
Nevada State Welfare Department
700 Belrose Street
Las Vegas, Nevada 89158 (702)648-8550
(Serves Arizona, California, Hawaii, and Nevada.)

Northwest Adoption Exchange
909 N.E. 43rd Street
Seattle, Washington 98105 (206)632-1480
(Serves Alaska, Idaho, Oregon, Utah, and Washington.)

Rocky Mountain Adoption Exchange
3705 East Colfax, Suite 105
Denver, Colorado 80206 (303)333-0845
(Serves Colorado, New Mexico, North Dakota, South Dakota,
Utah, and Wyoming.)

SEEUS (Southeastern Exchange of the United States)
P.O. Box 11181
Columbia, South Carolina 29211 (803)799-1234
(Serves Alabama, Florida, Georgia, Kentucky, Mississippi,
North Carolina, South Carolina, and Tennessee.)

Southwest Regional Adoption Exchange
227 North 23rd Street
Oklahoma City, Oklahoma 73103 (405)525-2451
(Serves Arkansas, Louisiana, New Mexico, Oklahoma, and Texas.)

Three Rivers Adoption Council
239 Fourth Avenue
Pittsburgh, Pennsylvania 15222 (412)471-8722
(Serves Pennsylvania and West Virginia.)[1]

National Adoption Exchanges

June, a seven-year-old black girl with Down's syndrome, was
living in Georgia and available for adoption. She was registered
with the state exchange; featured in the state photolisting book,
Be My Parent; shown on an Atlanta television show; and named
child of the month in a local newspaper. All this was done to try
to find an adoptive family for her. Finally her social worker
registered her with *The CAP Book,* a national photolisting service in Rochester, New York.

Bertha, a single black woman in her fifties, was searching for a child to adopt in upstate New York. She looked through *The CAP Book* and saw June's photograph. She called her social worker; her social worker called June's social worker; Bertha's home study went to Georgia; June's biographical information came to New York. June and Bertha's search was over; a new adoptive family had been formed.

The CAP Book registers children from throughout the United States who need wider exposure. Workers must be willing to place the children across state lines. This photolisting book contains 500 children and has biweekly updates. Both adoption social workers and families can contact the staff of *The CAP Book*, who serve as a clearinghouse and direct people to the appropriate agency and caseworker. All the children featured in *The CAP Book* are hard to place. Check your local adoptive-parent group or specialized agency for the book. For further information, you can also contact The CAP Book, Inc., 700 Exchange Street, Rochester, New York 14608 (716-232-5110). An annual subscription to *The CAP Book* costs $50. For a look at the type of children featured in the book, you can consult the *National Enquirer,* which spotlights one youngster a week.

In 1982 the **National Adoption Exchange** (1218 Chestnut Street, Philadelphia, Pennsylvania 19107; 215-925-0200) got under way. According to director Marlene Piasecki, the exchange has been designed as a resource for any child for whom national recruitment would be helpful in locating a permanent family. A child may be listed simultaneously with a state exchange and with the National Adoption Exchange. (An agency might list a teenager with the National Adoption Exchange at the same time it lists the youth with the state's adoption exchange, anticipating that it might not be successful finding a potential adoptive family within the state.) Families with completed home studies can register themselves directly with the exchange. This is important, says Piasecki, because "many families don't know that they can take the initiative."

The National Adoption Exchange is using a computer to facilitate matches. The computer, by handling basic biographical data, expedites the paperwork involved in trying to match families with children, leaving the staff more time to look at other, less quantifiable data. The National Adoption Exchange's staff will notify you, the child's agency, and your agency of any potential matches. Piasecki hopes that the exchange can serve about a thousand children and several thousand families annually. In addition, the exchange publishes a photolisting book (updated monthly and available by subscription) and a quarterly newsletter.

Although the National Adoption Exchange is an exciting addition to the adoption scene, Piasecki is quick to point out that it is not for everyone seeking to adopt. "You have to be clear as to what a special-needs child is," she says. "We get registration forms from families for whom there are no children waiting." Before contacting the exchange, be sure to look at several state or regional adoption-exchange books so that you will know what types of children are awaiting placement. If you are looking for a younger, healthy, white child, there is little the National Adoption Exchange can do for you, although it will keep your application on file. As a national organization, however, they'll be glad to answer questions and refer you to other resources.

Some Specialized Referral Programs

In addition to state, regional, and national exchanges, there are some specialized exchanges and programs with which you may be able to link up:

National Down's Syndrome Adoption Exchange
  c/o Janet Marchese
  158 Longview Avenue
  White Plains, New York 10605 (914)428-1236
    A voluntary adoption exchange providing services to birth parents, adoptive parents and agencies. Accepts listings from agencies of children needing

placement. Families seeking to adopt children can also list themselves. Can also help birth parents seeking to place a Down's syndrome infant with an agency or independently.

Native American Adoption Resource Exchange

c/o Council of Three Rivers American Indian Center
200 Charles Street
Dorseyville, Pennsylvania 15238 (412)782-4457
   Serves dependent Indian children by providing recruitment and referral of adoptive Native American families. Families can apply for registration with the exchange if one or both parents are American Indian. You will be expected to provide documented evidence of Indian ancestry (for example, your enrollment number, census number, certificate of degree of Indian blood, or a letter from your tribe on tribal stationery). Be sure your home study also mentions the name of your tribe and your cultural life-style.

Spina Bifida Adoption Referral Program

c/o Judy Grafstrom
1955 Florida Drive
Xenia, Ohio 45385 (513)372-2040
   Provides liaison services to birth parents, adoptive parents, and agencies. Accepts listings from agencies of children needing placement. Families seeking to adopt children can also list themselves.

Transracial Adoption

In the 1960s, black children were placed for adoption in white homes. That policy came under increasing attack in the 1970s, and today many agencies will not place black or other minority children in white homes. Yet as you look through the exchange books, you'll discover that many of the children waiting for homes are members of minority groups. If you are a white person seeking to adopt a waiting child, can you—should you—offer your family as a resource for a waiting minority child? Barbara Tremitiere, the parent of ten adopted black children, as well as the director of adoptions at Tressler-Lutheran Service Associates, describes her agency's policies: "Tressler-Lutheran Service Associates has a policy of *not* placing young, easy to place Black children across racial lines, and of only placing harder to place Black children across racial lines if they have no other possibilities and if the adoptive family knows full well what such adoptions entail and are willing to make life style and/or location changes."[2]

Tremitiere's agency asks families to write out an integration report before they adopt transracially. The report focuses on the family's life-style, their place of residence, and their plan for providing their children with adult black role models. Says Tremitiere: "Adopting across racial lines requires of us as parents that we also move into life styles that may differ from what we are in now in order to allow our children to grow up in an atmosphere that will enable them to feel a part of the world they will be entering as American Black adults."[3]

The Indian Child Welfare Act was passed by Congress in 1978 to protect the rights of Native American families and tribes. It requires that the extended family of an Indian child be given first priority for adoption, followed by a member of the child's tribe, and then a member of another tribe. An agency that seeks to place a Native American child in a non–Native American home may in fact be violating federal law.

Transracial placements still occur, but if you inquire, be prepared to encounter many hurdles and questions. Consider whether your family is the appropriate resource for the particular child you hope to parent. Evaluate carefully how you will meet your child's special needs. If you feel strongly, then you should persevere. Says the white mother of a black girl: "To me, a choice for a permanent parent is by far preferable for a child to a long wait in foster care. I believe there's more damage that can be done in the wait than in the issue of race."

The Frustrations of Working with Exchanges and Photolistings

We first started looking at the Books (with an eye toward a two to three member sibling group around ten years of age) during the time we attended Parent Preparation Classes. By the time we received the letter from the agency certifying us as "perfect" prospective adoptive parents we already had selected a sibling group here we wanted to adopt. Several nervous weeks later we were told that unexpectedly relatives had come into the picture and those children were no longer up for adoption. But, "please try again."

We did. This time we chose two boys from another state's book we thought would fit into our home. It was several days later when we discovered that, unknown to the agency in our state, the boys were already in the process of being adopted. So, "please try again."

A week or so later one of the social workers from the agency called to say that she had just received a new book, *Exchange of Mid-America,* and that there were three siblings she felt were definitely suitable. We asked that she call about them rather than write, thus cutting down on the suspenseful waiting time. Within an hour she called back with the information that just the week before the children had appeared on "Wednesday's Child" in another state. They too were already on their way through the adoption process.

Shortly thereafter we chose two children from another state. The news from their social worker, please try again.

Several days later our social worker told us that another state had gotten information on us through the *Exchange of Mid-America* book and had sent a computer match-up of two brothers they believed would be suitable for us. These children were in no way anything like the sort of children my husband and I felt that we could deal with. The social worker came back to us with that information and then urged us to "please try again."[4]

When Alice wrote about her experience, she had been trying to adopt for a year. Shortly after that, she and her husband gave up. They were not a young couple (they were in their late forties and her husband had grown children from a previous marriage) and they had not been trying to adopt young children. But they got tired of trying and decided to get on with other things in their life.

Alice's litany of woe is unfortunately not that unusual. Many people hoping to parent waiting children report that their search is unending despite the fact that they've seen children listed for adoption. Parent-group newsletters are full of stories in which people report that when they inquire about a specific child, they are told that the child is on "hold." Yet these people report that months later they still see the child's photo in an exchange book. They have found, too, that social workers may be reluctant to place a child out of the county or out of the state —despite the fact that no adoptive family has yet been found locally. There is also the sense that social workers are "collecting" home studies, poring through as many as sixty before beginning to make a decision. Alice even found, when she inquired about one child in another state, that the social worker had listed the child for adoption only because the state mandated it; the worker had no plans for placement and was surprised—and not very interested—when Alice contacted her. Be aware also that only a small percentage of the children legally free for adoption may be listed with an exchange or photolisted. In states where listing is mandated by law, the number will be higher than where listing is voluntary.

Exchange books and television appeals that heighten a child's visibility are clearly important tools in placement and recruitment. But, as people seeking to adopt will tell you, they're hard on families. Reporting on the impact of a local Connecticut television program, "Thursday's Child," the Connecticut Adoption Resource Exchange noted that for three black brothers, ages six, five, and three, it received forty-six calls; and for an eighteen-month-old girl of mixed parentage with developmental delays, it got thirty-two calls. In both cases one of the responding families became the adoptive parents.[5] The television program worked, but if you, as a family, had set your heart on one particular child, you were likely to be disappointed. These types of recruitment programs are good for children, but they are often very hard for "waiting families."

Some Tips on Searching for that Waiting Child
- Be sure you understand who is a waiting child or a special-needs child. You may be searching for a child who is not likely to appear in the exchanges.

- Consider how flexible you are. See how much you can broaden your scope.
- Be sure you are listed with all local exchanges and informal exchanges available for your area.
- List yourself with the state exchange if possible.
- List yourself with the regional exchange if possible.
- When your home study is complete, you may want to contact the National Adoption Exchange.
- Be sure your home study is as complete as possible.
- Check your state photolisting book (and others that you decide to consult) frequently and try to respond to *as many* as possible. Don't feel shy about requesting information on more than one child listed in the book. Let your agency know promptly about your interests.
- If you see a child who interests you in a photolisting book, either you or your worker should call, rather than write, to get some initial information about the child. If you're still interested, follow up immediately by sending out your home study.
- Don't wait to hear about one child before inquiring about another.
- Note the date when you talk with your worker, and follow up —your worker can get busy. Keep track also of when you contacted the child's agency and be prepared to follow up.
- Keep track of which children you inquired about, when you made the inquiry, whom you talked with, and what was done. Follow up.
- When you are rejected for a particular child, ask why.
- Don't set your heart on one particular child that you've seen featured. Chances are you will be successful in adopting a child like the one that attracted your attention, rather than that particular child.
- If you are having trouble adopting a child who appeared in a photolisting book or a listing service, let the exchange or listing service know that you are having problems. They can often help expedite the process.

Be persistent. Just as people seeking to adopt independently must work hard to spread the word, so will you probably need to. You know there are children who need you. It may just take some time to make the connection.

9

Searching Independently for a Child Abroad

Jocelyn and Dave were in their late thirties when they decided they wanted to adopt an infant. Several people they knew
had adopted infants from abroad, so they decided to look into
an intercountry adoption. First they talked to people who had
adopted children from Colombia. "We talked to a couple who
had adopted a newborn through La Casa de la Madre y El
Niño," Jocelyn says. "They showed us movies of their experience in Colombia, including pictures of their daughter when
she was three days old. It helped me to feel that intercountry
adoption was a viable way to adopt." With this couple's help,
they wrote to La Casa requesting an application.

Jocelyn also went to the meetings of her local adoptive-parent group, some of whose members had successfully adopted
internationally. She talked to people who had lived abroad
about the possibilities of intercountry adoption. "Our daughter
actually came from an orphanage in Ecuador," Jocelyn reports,
and goes on to explain:

> I told a woman I worked with about my interest in adoption. She had
> lived in Ecuador and had friends there. She wrote them. My col-
> league got a letter from her friends sending me an application and
> saying that I should send the completed application to them. So I
> did. I was lucky. It turned out that her friend knew the director of
> a private orphanage there.

Her friend continued to help, calling the people she knew in Ecuador and checking for her. One day the agency called them up and said, "Congratulations, you have a newborn baby boy." Since she had already advance-processed through INS, she and her husband were able to fly to Ecuador.

In Guayaquil she and her husband stayed with these friends of friends. "It was just unbelievable," she says. "Total strangers took us into their lives. They had gotten a crib for us and they took us over to the orphanage." The agency had arranged for a lawyer to handle the legal matters, so they went to the family court and received custody of the baby. But there was still more paperwork to do. Her husband went home to file papers related to their state's preadoption requirements. She stayed on with her son and the family while the paperwork was processed. "I was all by myself. I didn't know how to care for a baby. I didn't speak any Spanish, so we tried communicating in French. I finally asked for a shortwave radio so that I could hear English." When her son was four weeks old, the paperwork was completed and the two of them came to the United States.

If you were to inquire about intercountry adoptions from Ecuador in 1984, you'd probably be told that families and agencies—both in the United States and abroad—have found that the time span between the assignment of a child and the completion of the paperwork can now be as long as a year or two. So parent groups recommend other countries.

But Jocelyn and Dave's experience with an intercountry, parent-initiated adoption is similar to that of people who adopt independently from Colombia, Honduras, and other countries, bypassing U.S. intercountry adoption programs. Lauren and Bob's Chilean adoption came about through a personal connection. Their son had joined their family through an agency that placed Korean infants, and they expected to contact the agency to process a second application. Lauren's mother, however, tutored children, and one of the children she tutored was Chilean. The child's mother became friendly with Lauren and learned she was thinking about another child. Was she interested in a

Chilean adoption? Lauren said yes. Six months later this friend called Lauren and told her to contact an attorney in Chile. That phone call led to the placement of her son, Ted.

Why do people choose a direct intercountry adoption over a U.S. agency's intercountry adoption program? Some people do so because they want a child of a particular nationality and there is no agency placing those children. Others have family or friends who make a connection for them. Still others feel that they want to do the adoption themselves—and that includes finding their own child abroad. Others feel strongly that in a country like Colombia, where there is a well-established social-service system and a well-trod path involving intercountry adoption, there is no need to pay a U.S. agency an "overseas handling fee." Since families may have to do most of the paper-work—that is, the verification, authentication, and notarization—why not do everything? Finally, there are some organizations abroad, such as La Casa de la Madre y El Niño in Bogotá, Colombia, that have not established intercountry adoption programs with U.S. agencies and prefer to work directly with the adopting couple.

Deciding to Pursue a Direct Intercountry Adoption

A direct overseas adoption is not for everyone who is thinking about an intercountry adoption. You should ask yourself:

- Is it important to have someone help you through the adoption process step by step?
- How much of the legwork are you willing to do yourself? There may be a parent group familiar with your prospective "source," but you will not be working with an established program in the United States.
- How much uncertainty can you live with? With any intercountry adoption, things may not go as you would like. With a direct adoption, delays or snafus may arise.

- What is the state of your finances? If there are unanticipated expenses, can you absorb them? With an agency's intercountry adoption program, there are fees that you can anticipate. (If you must travel to a foreign country—whether under an agency intercountry adoption program or for a direct adoption—there may be additional expenses.)
- How do you feel about traveling abroad?
- How do you feel about spending time in another country, perhaps as much as two or three months?
- How do you feel about spending time abroad alone, without your spouse and possibly without contact with another English-speaking person?
- How self-reliant are you?
- What foreign languages do you speak? You may have to deal with attorneys, bureaucrats, and other officials in a foreign country. How do you plan to communicate with them?
- What "risks" are you prepared to assume?

Some of the above questions apply to any intercountry adoption, whether independent or through a U.S. agency program. With a direct adoption, however, more of the burden of bringing the adoption to fruition lies with you.

One mother describes some of the uncertainties that went along with her child's direct overseas adoption:

> You know your baby will need a passport; how do you get a passport? Have you ever had the frustrating experience of making a long distance call to find out information you desperately need only to hear someone answer the phone who speaks only Spanish? Even when you find someone who speaks English you often realize the question you asked and the answer you received just don't go together. You write so many letters that are never answered and you often receive conflicting information from the letters you do receive answers for. When you've done a private adoption you become aware of how much an agency does that the waiting clients never are aware of.[1]

Getting Prepared

If you think that direct intercountry adoption appeals to you, it's wise to do some basic homework. You will need to contact your state's department of social services and its interstate-compact officer. You will also want to contact the embassy in the United States of the country that interests you. You'll need to ask:

- Is intercountry adoption permitted from the country?
- Is direct intercountry adoption permitted in the country?
- How frequently have people adopted from the country (many children a year, a handful a year, a handful every few years)?
- Who are the children available for intercountry adoption?
- What are the country's requirements regarding the adopter's age, marital status, length of marriage, divorce, and residency? (If you've been married one year and the country's adoption law states that you must be married five years, then clearly you don't qualify.)
- What are your state's laws concerning adoption? Are independent placements permitted? Are there preadoption requirements that must be met?
- What are the requirements of the Immigration and Naturalization Service? Be sure you understand the requirements of INS.

If you are thinking about a Latin-American adoption, Hector Faundez Ledezma's *Adoption Laws in Latin American Countries* covers the laws of Argentina, Bolivia, Brazil, Chile, Colombia, Costa Rica, Ecuador, Mexico, Panama, Paraguay, Peru, and Venezuela (available from the International Social Service/American Branch, 20 West 40 Street, New York, New York 10018). International Adoptions, Inc., in Massachusetts has compiled some fact sheets, including "Direct or Parent-

Initiated Adoptions," which families have used successfully. The Latin America Parents Association also has fact sheets for various countries and agencies; they outline who to contact and what documents you will need. There is even a fact sheet on traveling to Colombia, listing places to stay, taxi drivers, and other useful information. You may also want to take a look at *Gamines* by Jean Nelson-Erichsen and Heino R. Erichsen, and *How to Adopt from Asia, Europe and the South Pacific* by Jean Nelson-Erichsen, Heino R. Erichsen, and Gay R. Hallberg. Both books offer helpful descriptions of the steps of parent-initiated adoptions.

Making Contacts Abroad

Direct or parent-initiated intercountry adoptions occur in many countries. But how are you going to go about making contacts abroad? You can do the following:

- Check with adoptive-parent groups.
- Contact the foreign country's embassy in the United States. The Consulate General of India in New York, for example, sent me a description of the legal requirements as well as the names of some agencies to contact in the United States and in India. Clearly I was not the first person—nor will I be the last—to inquire. In fact, in one day's telephoning, I found that I'd gathered quite a bit of information from embassies.
- Contact the U.S. consul abroad. The embassy may send you information about various organizations. Some embassies will send you a list of accredited lawyers in the country who do adoptions.
- Write the national agency concerned for the welfare of children in a particular country. (The embassy here can give you that information, and so might your public library.) The foreign agency may send you information and an application, or they may send you a list of other organizations to write to.

- Get in touch with family, friends, and friends of friends abroad. They may refer you to an organization. They may refer you to an attorney or other person who works in adoptions. They may know someone themselves.

The list that follows notes a few Latin-American countries and some agencies abroad that you can contact. All have worked with American families interested in intercountry adoptions. The list is not all-inclusive; rather, it singles out a few overseas contacts that U.S. families have used successfully in the past.

CHILE
Casa Nacional del Niño
Unidad Adopción
Antonio Varas #360
Santiago, Chile
> This is the national orphanage of Chile. The children placed are usually over two years old.

COLOMBIA
> Colombian agencies take applications directly from prospective adoptive parents. Keep in mind that many of the U.S. agencies that specialize in intercountry adoption (see the directory at the back of this book) have developed active programs with the agencies listed below. OURS has a helpful booklet, *Colombian Adoption Information Package*.

Grupo Nacional de Adopciones
Instituto Colombiano de Bienestar Familiar (Bienestar)
Apartado Aéreo No. 18116
Bogotá D.E., Colombia
> The National Group for Adoption Coordination was formed in 1981 to cooperate with private and public foreign institutions responsible for adoption programs in their respective countries and to cooperate with international organizations in matters relating to adoption. Bienestar is the national organization that oversees the nation's adoption program.
> If you are interested in adopting through Bienestar, you should send a letter to the National Group for Adoption explaining your motives for adoption, your age, and the age and sex of the child that you wish to adopt. (If you have no preference, say so.) You will receive an application. You will submit a home study and other documents with the application. Although Bienestar places children of all ages, the wait for infants can extend up to two years; people

seeking children over the age of four are likely to have a much shorter wait.

Your application is sent to Bienestar. The National Group decides which branch of Bienestar to send your papers on to.

There are some general age criteria:

- For newborns to three years, parents should be twenty-five to thirty-five years old.
- For three- to seven-year-olds, parents may be thirty-five to forty-five years old.
- For children older than seven years, parents may be forty-five to a maximum of fifty-five years old.

You can also contact these nongovernmental organizations:

La Casita de Nicolas
Carrera 47 No. 56–47
Apartado Aéreo 3800
Medellin, Colombia

Centro de Adopción Chiquitines
Calle 23 No. 33A–67
Apartado Aéreo 4558
Cali, Colombia

Centro de Rehabilitacion y Adopción del Niño
Calle 27 No. 27–21
Bogotá D.E., Colombia

Fundación para la Adopción de la Niñez Abandonada (FANA)
Calle 71A No. 5-67
Apartado Aéreo 051023
Bogotá, Colombia

Fundación Los Pisingos
Carrera 1a No. 68-79
Apartado Aéreo 50090
Bogotá D.E., Colombia

La Casa de la Madre y el Niño
Calle 48 No. 28–30
Apartado Aéreo
Bogotá, Colombia

This is a private orphanage that places children, including newborns. They work with couples, not singles. Write them to request an application.

COSTA RICA
Patrono Nacional de la Infancia
Apartado 5000
San José, Costa Rica

This is the national agency that oversees the placement of children. They usually place children over the age of four for adoption abroad. Younger children who are handicapped or part of a sibling group may also be placed abroad. (One family adopted three siblings—ages one and a half, three, and four and a half.)

GUATEMALA
Programa de Adopciones
Dirección de Bienestar Infantil y Familiar
9a Avenida, 7-01 Zona 11
Guatemala
This is the national program. Write them to request an application. They can also send you information about other programs in the country.[2]

No doubt you've heard about direct adoptions from other Latin-American countries—El Salvador, Peru, Brazil perhaps. Adoptions are possible directly from the Philippines and Thailand by applying to their departments of social welfare. Families who have applied directly have sometimes waited over two years. Families adopting from Thailand have had shorter waits when they used an intercountry adoption program such as Holt International Children's Services. For some countries, you may learn through parent groups about attorneys or social workers abroad who place children in the U.S. Adoptions from Honduras, for example, are often done with the help of attorneys. Be aware that all Korean adoptions take place through licensed U.S. agencies. You cannot adopt directly.

Writing a Letter of Inquiry

Most likely you will be sending out some letters to learn more about intercountry adoption and to request applications. If at all possible, as a courtesy, write in the language of the person to whom you are addressing the letter; your contact may not have access to a translator. Make your letter warm and friendly, not businesslike. You are writing to people. Let them know who you are. The impression you create in your introductory letter is critical. This is a time when you can permit your feelings to come through. Says one adoptive parent, who spent time working at a Colombian orphanage: "The letters that the women in the orphanage read to me were flowery ones, with statements like 'We wanted a baby all our lives and just found out that we will have to adopt' or 'We have a house and we are anxious to paint the nursery.' The women would say, 'Oh! we want to help them!' "

So what do you say? Describe yourself, your occupation, and your interest in children. Say how long you have wanted to adopt. Mention the status of your home study and ask for more information about their program. If you know people with foreign-born adopted children and they have been influential in your decision-making, say so. If you know people who have worked with the agency, let them know. You might want to include a photograph of yourself, your family, and your house.

Should you state a child preference? Many agencies are truly offended if you say that you want a child who is "as light as possible" or who looks like you. If you feel that this is something you must emphasize, consider again why you are pursuing an intercountry adoption. If you want only a boy or only a girl, be prepared to explain why. You can sketch out some parameters, but be flexible. If you are writing to an attorney, or another individual, be sure your letter does say that you are seeking a "legal, ethical adoption."

One couple sent out the following letter to several agencies:

> My wife and I are writing to you for further information and guidance about the process of adopting a child in ———. We are not able to conceive children and are therefore very eager to learn about opportunities for adoption. We are especially excited about the prospect of perhaps being able to adopt a child who needs a home.
>
> My wife and I are young professionals [the letter then gave information about them]. We have been married for ten years. The child who came to us would be received with love and care and every

opportunity for a good education and a successful future. We would like to adopt a boy or girl, as young as possible, although we are willing to consider children up to the age of four.

Our own marriage has always been firmly rooted in the values of family life that shaped us as children. We have always wanted children very much to complete ourselves as individuals and as a married couple. Even before discovering that we could not have children biologically, we had always planned that at least one of our children would be adopted. The medical therapy that we have undergone for infertility has been a long and frustrating process; however, it has convinced us all the more strongly that we want to raise children, and that we have the love, maturity and the commitment to each other to be fine parents.

This couple sent out several letters of inquiry since they were unsure of their plans and felt that some agencies might reply that they were not taking applications currently. They heard from most of the agencies. One response told them what an impact their letter had made: "I must first say that I appreciated your letter very much since usually the letters we receive in such cases are very dry and concerned only with the technical details and devoid of all human feelings for future parents and child."

Should you contact more than one agency? For initial letters of inquiry, you can. Policies may have changed or intake may be temporarily closed. At the beginning you are gathering information. Singles, particularly, may find that they have to search around for the appropriate place to apply.

What about filing more than one application? Some parent groups believe it is unethical to do so. One social worker specializing in intercountry-adoption home studies feels differently: "I recommend more than one application because I have seen long delays. I tell people that if they are up to all the paperwork, they can apply to more than one agency. I tell them that at a later point they should send a donation to the other orphanage." (Don't, however, send any donation to an orphanage prior to the adoption. Your donation might be construed as a bribe.)

You'll have to make the decision about what's appropriate. If you do apply to more than one agency, *be sure to notify the other agency immediately when you are offered a child.*

Any letters you send should be accompanied by return postage. You can use international reply coupons, which are available at your local post office.

Working Out the Details

Once you receive a reply to your inquiries and the direct-adoption process gets under way, there are still more things that you are going to have to work out:

- What legal steps must you take to realize the placement of a child?
- Who will be doing your legal work abroad?
- Exactly what paperwork will you be required to do?
- What are the expected costs? Try to get a breakdown of probable expenses—lawyers' fees, court costs, foster care, orphanage or agency donation, medical care.
- What expenses, if any, must be paid "up front"? (This is particularly relevant if you will be working with an attorney.)
- When are fees to be paid?
- What references can the person provide (if he or she is not known to you)? Has this person ever helped with a U.S. inter-country adoption before?
- How long is the whole process likely to take?

Be sure you make clear to your contact overseas exactly what documents you will need in order to bring your child legally into the United States. Your contact may know the requirements for a legal adoption in his country; you may have to tell him what is required for U.S. Immigration. You will also want to get a listing of *all* services and *all* fees *in writing*.

There may be a significant time lapse between when you first approach people about intercountry adoption and when you finally become a parent. During that time you will want to keep in touch. Do so by writing letters about your continuing interest and plans for the future. It's alright to remind them that you're eagerly waiting.

Getting Information About Your Child

The day will finally come when you will receive a telephone call or a photo and a description of a child. Don't hesitate to ask for more information. If you are concerned about medical information, ask for it. If you are adopting a child who's been abandoned, the agency may not be able to give you much in the way of background information, but they can give you a full report about the child's current health. If your child is being placed by an attorney, social worker, or other helping professional, this person may well have met one of the birth parents or another relative. Ask for information.

If you have been sent a medical report, show it to your pediatrician (see chapter 10). If your pediatrician has questions, don't hesitate to refer them to your foreign source. If possible, get someone in the foreign country to take a look at the child. Recalls one mother whose child was in an orphanage in Colombia: "We knew someone who knew a physician in Bogotá. We arranged to have our baby checked. The doctor found that our son had a fungus infection—thrush. He was severely underweight. The doctor arranged to have him treated." Not every child will be ill, but if there is a problem, it's best for your child if the condition can be detected as soon as possible.

If you need to locate a foreign attorney or doctor, you can get in touch with the U.S. consul in the country, or you can check with parent groups or with the agency abroad that you are using. The International Association for Medical Assistance to Travelers (IAMAT) (736 Centre Street, Lewiston, New York 14092) also publishes a directory listing medical centers around the world. The center abroad can give you a list of approved doctors—internists and other specialists. IAMAT physicians will provide a medical report if you need it, make referrals for you, and report to your own physician.

Traveling Abroad

If you do a direct intercountry adoption, you probably can expect to travel abroad—to finalize the adoption, to work out the guardianship, or to bring your child home. Everybody's travel experience is different, but here are some general guidelines to keep in mind:

- Contact a parent group before you go to learn about places to stay, things to take with you, local transportation, and the like.
- Contact the foreign embassy or foreign tourist office for information about the country.
- Try to learn a little of the language. Don't feel hesitant to use a dictionary and point to words. People appreciate your making the attempt to communicate even if it isn't perfect.
- Bring donations to the orphanages—clothing, medical supplies, formula. Your local parent group can probably give you supplies to carry with you.
- If advisable, give a financial donation.
- Don't complain.

Be prepared to feel homesick, confused, and lonely. You're likely to be very excited, but you also may feel terribly unsettled. It may not feel like a vacation. When you're staying in a hotel or other accommodation, there's nothing romantic about having to boil baby bottles in a hotpot rather than in a fancy sterilizer. Says one parent who traveled to Medellin, Colombia: "Staying in a country club [which is where families adopting through one agency were housed], the American couples were operating in a social vacuum without supports. No family, no friends." Whatever your situation, she says, "you must under-

stand that you are a *guest* in another country and understand
their ways of doing things. They are giving you a precious gift."

A precious gift—that is what your child adopted from abroad
is. A gift from one country and one culture to another. Your
travel to your child's country is the beginning of your learning
about his land. Respect the people and their culture. Dress and
act appropriately for *their* culture, not *yours*. From now on,
your child's country is yours.

10

Preparing for Your Child

The wait—all adoptive parents have to go through it, whether for a few days, a few weeks, a few months, or years. Waiting is a critical part of adoption: Children wait for homes; parents wait for children. When you've done all that paperwork, when you've done all the preliminaries that you need to do to make your adoption happen, you may still have some waiting to do.

Keep busy. If you're working, keep working. If you plan to take time off for parenting, wait until your child is ready to enter your home; don't quit your job, or start your leave, in anticipation of your new status. Do other things that you'd planned; don't defer a vacation or other project "because the agency's call might come." Let your life continue.

Get involved in your adoptive-parent group. Others have been through the waiting and they may help. You, too, can offer support to someone else. Betsy Guinn, an adoption worker with Holt International Children's Services, Inc., and herself a parent who waited for a Korean child, says: "With my luck, I'd call a friend or relative who did not understand. When I told them I was going crazy, they would probably respond with 'Are you sure you want to do this?' Or, 'How can you handle a child if you're already crazy?' You don't need to hear these things the day you are going crazy, so call up your new friend who has adopted. They won't have any answers, but they can say they understand; you don't wait forever; your child *will* come home."[1]

The waiting period should be the time when you sit down and read about child care and adoption. Think about the future. How do you see yourself as a parent? What do you think your life will be like once your child arrives? What roles will your spouse, other children, family, and friends play in the upcoming adoption? How will your relationships with them change? What do you expect of your new child? "Waiting parents," says Claudia Jewett, "are wise to discuss openly their dreams and fears and plans for their coming child."[2]

Consider those early days and weeks after your child arrives. If you are working, will you be taking time off? If so, how much? Do you want help at the beginning from a spouse, parent, or friend? What kinds of support will you require? When?

This chapter outlines some of the things that you will want to get done in preparation for your role as an adoptive parent. You may want to change your insurance policies and wills, take a leave of absence from work, arrange for a pediatrician and possibly a dentist in advance. If you are adopting an infant, you may want to set up your child's room and do some shopping. If you are adopting an older child, you may want to do some fix-up yourself and leave some things to do with your child. Time is likely to be in short supply once your child arrives.

Leaves of Absence

Carole Fezar wanted to take an unpaid maternity leave to spend time with her infant daughter—a common request among working mothers. But unlike most mothers, Carole had to file a grievance with her union to get that opportunity.

For Carole had adopted her daughter. A federal arbitrator in November 1983 ruled that she was entitled to her leave. Said he:

> It is apparent that the term *maternity* does not singularly embrace conception and childbearing but rather that it encompasses the duties and responsibilities of motherhood. The very fact that maternity leave can cover a period of time up to one year in duration serves to establish the fact that it sets a major portion of the time for child-rearing. It must follow then that the adoption of an infant child requires the same care, the same responsibility as would be with an infant born to a natural mother.[3]

Yet maternity leaves and adoption leaves are clearly treated differently by employers. The parent group FACE turned up some basic facts about leaves in a survey they conducted.[4] FACE found that 95 percent of the employers surveyed had a policy allowing biological maternity leave, while only 39 percent had an adoption leave. Three-fourths of the employers provided paid maternity leaves, while less than a quarter offered paid adoption leaves. The rationale for offering paid leave for maternity and unpaid leave for adoption rested on the premise that pregnancy created a physical disability, while adoption did not. Most employers had health-insurance programs covering pregnancy expenses; only two employers provided adoption benefits. There were even differing job guarantees, with 86 percent of the employers guaranteeing job reinstatement following pregnancy leave but only 63 percent after adoption leave.

If you are a working mother waiting to adopt a child, you will want to explore your employer's leave policies. You will need to find out the following:

- Does your company grant adoption leave?
- Is your company's adoption leave a formal policy or has it been granted informally, on a person-by-person basis?
- What are the specific provisions of the adoption leave?

- How does the adoption leave differ from the company's maternity leave?
- How many weeks of adoption leave are you entitled to?
- Are you entitled to paid weeks of adoption leave? If so, how many?
- How far in advance must you request an adoption leave?
- Are you guaranteed your job—or a similar job—when you return?
- How are your health insurance, disability, and other plans in which you participate affected while you are on leave?
- Is there a restriction on the number or frequency of your adoption leaves?
- If you are adopting an older child, can you take an adoption leave?

If your company does not offer an adoption leave, Marcie Schorr Hirsch, author of *Managing Your Maternity Leave* (Boston: Houghton Mifflin, 1983), recommends that you start by asking your boss to support your request for a leave, and that you then talk with your company's department of human resources. Says she: "People get maternity leave because it makes sense for the company because they are a valued employee." You can also contact Catalyst (14 East 60th Street, New York, N.Y. 10022), which has been looking at corporate policies on maternity and parental leaves of absence to develop guidelines for corporations. You might also ask your labor union to back your request, as Carole Fezar did.

Advocates of equal rights on the job have called for paternity leave also. You may want to ask about one, particularly if you are a single father, but don't be surprised if you are rebuffed.

You'll need to decide when to inform your employer about your adoption plans and your interest in taking a leave. When you discuss your plans, you may find that your employer has some difficulty dealing with the timing of an adoption leave. Employers and benefit managers are used to having people tell them, "My baby is due on March fifth and I want to leave work two weeks before that." Employers usually can deal with medical complications that suddenly force a woman to leave work earlier than she had planned. It's much more difficult to grasp the reality of adoption: that people don't know when the blessed event will take place; that families will not have much notice; that working parents can't give much notice. Your employer may be stymied by such statements as "We don't know when the agency will contact us" or "My daughter's coming from Korea in two to four months and I want to leave when I'm told that she's on the flight." You may also have difficulty getting people to understand that you won't have time for a while to come back to the office to take care of things unexpectedly left hanging. You'll need to explain to them that you're going to be swamped at home for a while. You may not be exhausted from the birth of your child, but that's only a small part of new parenthood. Adjusting to a new child—whether by birth or adoption—will require your full attention.

Health Insurance

Before your child enters your home, you should be sure that you have proper medical coverage. Some agencies may require a statement about the exact coverage that you have. If you are adopting a child with special needs, be sure you understand the details of any health coverage or subsidy that the child will receive. In all cases you want to be sure that your child will be covered upon *arriving* in your home, not upon finalization.

Check with your health-insurance company to find out about your plan's coverage for dependents. Some plans cover foster children; others do not. One may state that it covers *"legally adopted"* children, while another begins "coverage for an adopted child on the day you begin legal proceedings for the adoption of the child." Find out what you must do to get your child covered under your policy. Be sure to explain that the child is not adopted at the time he enters your home but that you are fully responsible for the child's well-being. If your health insurance will not cover your child upon arrival in your home, you will need to take out additional coverage through your insurance company, or else contact other insurance carriers to arrange for separate coverage for your child. (An insurance broker or your agency or adoptive-parent group may be able to help you find a company.) Try to find a policy that covers preexisting conditions, both diagnosed and undiagnosed, and be sure to get a letter verifying your coverage.

If you have individual coverage under a group plan (sometimes spouses are covered individually by their employers), be sure to convert to *family* health-insurance coverage. This is particularly important if you are a single parent, because you will need a family policy in order to cover your child. Check also to see whether there is a waiting period before coverage begins.

Wills

If you don't have a will, you'll want to write one to be sure that from the time your child arrives in your home, he or she is provided for. Your will gives you a chance to name the executor of your estate as well as the guardian of your child and your child's property. In naming guardians, you will need to explore with them their feelings about adoption and about raising an adopted child. Just as seriously as you prepared for adoption, you will want to talk at length with the people who might end up raising your child.

You'll need to look closely at your will to be sure that it protects your child. Wills and trusts often include terms like *issue, heirs of the body, born to, next of kin,* and *descendants,* which are not always legally understood to include adopted as well as biological children. To protect your child, you should insert a clause stating that all biological and adopted children are to be considered equally as heirs and beneficiaries. One family's wills state that "whenever the terms *child, children,* or *descendants* are used or are relevant under this will and in the disposition of my estate, adopted children shall be considered and treated in all respects the same as natural children." Such a clause protects your adopted child, but not necessarily during the period before you've been to court to obtain the final order of adoption. Many attorneys recommend that to protect your children fully, you should state their names (both the names under which they are currently known and any other names they have had in the past). Be sure that you update your will whenever you add a child to your family.

You may want to ask relatives, such as grandparents, who may be making bequests in their wills to your "descendants" or "issue," to insert similar clauses to ensure that all your children inherit equally.

Life Insurance

Life-insurance policies may also use terms such as *descendants* or *issue* or *heirs of the body,* so be sure to name your children. It is also recommended that you advise your insurance company in writing (keeping a copy) that you have adopted children and request confirmation that the policy applies to them.

Some adoptive parents have also taken out life-insurance policies for their children. "When our son was an infant," Laura said, "we took out a ten-thousand-dollar life-insurance policy. We had adopted our child from abroad and had used up our savings. We felt that if something were to happen to our child, we would not otherwise have the financial resources to undertake a second adoption. We felt funny taking out the policy, but we did it."

Finances

All states have now developed some adoption subsidies (sometimes referred to as "adoption assistance"). Subsidies are based on the special needs of children and help hard-to-place children find families. The subsidy provides the financial base for a family so that the adoption of a special-needs child will not result in expenses beyond the reach of many adoptive parents. Thus the expenses involved in raising a special-needs child are no longer a deterrent to the child's placement. There may be monthly cash stipends for a child or payments for specific medical, surgical, psychiatric, or other costs. Subsidies vary state by state: Some states have restricted programs; others, more inclusive programs. Subsidies can come from federal or state money. Subsidies deriving from federal funds can be taken to another state, and some states will permit all subsidies to travel with the child. A subsidy may be paid for a period of time or until a child reaches maturity. One-time expenses, such as legal fees, may also be subsidized.

Contact your department of social services to learn about your state's subsidy program. If you are considering adopting an out-of-state child, check with the social-services department of the state where your potential child resides. You can also ask your agency or parent group for help.

Once your child enters your home, you should be able to declare him or her as a dependent on your federal income-tax return. You may also be able to deduct medical and dental expenses; special care for handicapped persons; contributions; and qualified adoption expenses. If you have adopted a "child with special needs" (defined by the IRS as a "child with respect to whom adoption assistance payments are made under Section 473 of the Social Security Act") and you itemize your deductions, you may deduct up to $1,500 for "qualified adoption expenses." You may also be able to take a credit for child care if you and your spouse worked or looked for work. The IRS has several booklets describing these allowances in greater detail: *Exemptions, Medical and Dental Expenses; Child and Disabled Dependent Care;* and *Tax Information for Handicapped and Disabled Individuals* (available free from the Forms Distribution Center for each state). Contact the IRS, an accountant, or another qualified person for help.

Some states also permit income-tax deductions for adoption expenses. The state of California, for example, permits people to deduct that portion of child-adoption expenses which exceeds 3 percent of their adjusted gross income up to $500 for a separate return and $1,000 for a joint return. (People adopting hard-to-place children are not subject to the 3-percent base.) These expenses include any medical and hospital costs of the birth mother and any child-welfare agency, legal, and other fees relating to the adoption. Check with your state's department of revenue to learn whether your state permits any deductions.

In recent years the corporate world has also begun to recognize the strains placed on a family's budget when they adopt a child. Some companies now provide adoption benefits. Hewitt Associates, an independent consulting firm, reported in an influential study that some companies "provide adoption benefits primarily as an equity consideration. Adoptive parents are not covered by pregnancy benefits but may incur considerable expenses through adoption, often greater than if they had the child naturally."[5] Hewitt found that companies either reimbursed employees for specific expenses, set dollar allowances, or paid for medical expenses. Benefits ranged from $75 to more than $2,200. At Time Inc., for example, employees are reimbursed for legitimate expenses (up to $2,100) incurred as a direct result of the adoption, including legal fees, agency fees, pregnancy expenses of the mother, temporary-foster-care charges, medical exams, and foreign adoption fees.

Getting Medical Advice and Arranging for Medical Care

You'll want to line up a pediatrician before your child arrives. If you are considering a child with special needs or a child who will be coming from abroad, you may consult a pediatrician before you apply for a specific child or at the time you receive a child referral. Says Peggy Soule, executive director of *The CAP Book:* "Be sure to let your physician tell you the *facts* about specific diseases or handicaps. The doctor should tell you what to expect but should not put his own value judgment on whether or not you should adopt. That is your decision. Too often because the doctor would not adopt a child with the specific handicap you are considering, she will advise the family not to do it."

Ask others—particularly parents whose children may have the same needs as your prospective child—for recommendations. When selecting a pediatrician, take the time to have a sit-down discussion about your child. (Some pediatricians will talk with families on the telephone, but many will not.) A meeting at a doctor's office means that you will have to pay him for his time, but it's well worth it. In your consultation, you may want to ask:

- Does he see other adopted patients in his practice?
- Has he treated other children from Asia or Latin America? Your pediatrician should be able to accept, for example, that a child adopted from abroad might not have reached the developmental milestones or the weight and height that American children of the same age have.
- How does he feel about adoption? One family learned their pediatrician's opinion about adoption when he examined their newborn and discovered that the child had a heart murmur. He recommended that the family not keep the child.
- How many patients in his practice have been in foster care?
- What is his policy about Medicaid? Some doctors refuse to accept Medicaid payments, so if you receive a subsidy for your child and if it involves Medicaid, be sure your physician will accept it.

- How does he feel about not receiving complete medical records? There may be a lot that is unknown about children who have been in foster care in the U.S. and about children born abroad. Adoptive parents report that U.S. pediatricians are often very uncomfortable working with children who do not have complete medical histories.

Raise issues that concern you. You may want to discuss child care, child-rearing, or even your plans for feeding. One Jewish couple, for example, interviewed a pediatrician and mentioned that their infant son coming from Latin America would not have been circumcised. The couple asked whether this could be done in the United States. The pediatrician told them that circumcision was no longer medically advised. Even if the parents wanted the child circumcised, he would not advocate the procedure for a two-month-old child. This couple consulted a pediatric urologist, who told them, "It is probably going to be more difficult for your son to be uncircumcised in a Jewish home than it is for the child to have this procedure done later than is customary." Based on this second opinion and their own preference, the couple decided against using that pediatrician.

Linda had told her pediatrician about the uncertainty of her child's arrival from Korea and the possibility that her daughter might arrive on a Saturday. Would the doctor see her? Sure, he said. But when she called him on Friday night to tell him that her daughter would be coming the next day, she found out different. Linda recalls:

The agency called us that night to say that Martha, who had been flown into another city, had developed a rash on the flight but no fever. The agency felt that she should be seen when she arrived in our city. I called my pediatrician and told him that we wanted him to see her. The pediatrician refused, saying that he did not have office hours and that he didn't trust an agency's opinion about whether a child should be seen. This agency had brought thousands of Korean children to the U.S. and had called us long-distance to urge us to make medical arrangements. Here was a pediatrician doubting their word. We switched pediatricians.

If you are adopting a child from abroad, you will want to be sure that your pediatrician does a few basic tests when the child arrives. If you are working with a U.S. agency that has an inter-country adoption program, they will probably tell you what tests they require. You will want to have your pediatrician do the following:

- Stool culture to check for ova and parasites.
- Complete blood count.
- Blood test for syphilis.
- Test for tuberculosis. (Be aware that in some countries children are vaccinated at birth against tuberculosis—the BCG vaccine—and may test positively.)
- Hepatitis B surface antigen test. (Strongly recommended for children born in Eastern Asia, including Korea, Taiwan, Vietnam, and the Philippines. Even if your child is born elsewhere, consider having him tested.)

Getting a full medical evaluation is important. Hepatitis B, for example, is hyperendemic in Eastern Asia. Dr. Mark Kane, medical epidemiologist at the Centers for Disease Control in Atlanta, Georgia, says that approximately 10 to 15 percent of the population born in Korea will be Hepatitis B carriers. A child may become a carrier at birth from an infected mother. The child may *not* have symptoms but *can* transmit the disease to family members. The carrier child can also be at risk of future liver disease.

Many U.S. agencies have prepared fact sheets about the health and care of the children they are placing. Holly van Gulden Wicker and Judy Walker Haavig's *Today's Child—The Health Care Needs of IMH Infants* (available from Today's Child Publications, 4558 29th Avenue South, Minneapolis, Minnesota 55406) focuses on Indian children. LAPA has also produced a fact sheet, "Medical Considerations of Latin American Adoption."

If you are adopting a child who is not an infant, you will probably want to take your child to a dentist shortly after arrival. Indeed, since older foreign-born children often have extensive tooth decay, you may want to talk with a dentist in advance.

Getting Background Information About Your Child

The amount of information you receive about a child may vary. Mary Ann Jones, in a 1976 study of the sealed-adoption controversy for the Child Welfare League,[6] reported that agencies usually shared the following information about birth parents with adoptive parents:

- Age
- Race
- Ethnic group
- Religion
- Education
- Occupation
- Personality, temperament
- Medical history
- Psychiatric history
- Intellectual capacity
- Circumstances of birth (if illegitimate)

She found, however, that 99 percent of the agencies did not release the names of birth parents, and 92 percent did not release the birth parents' place of residence. Agencies were also less likely to give adoptive parents information about the existence of siblings and did not always explain why the birth parent relinquished the child for adoption (if the birth parent was imprisoned, only 50 percent of the agencies told the adoptive parents). If the circumstances of a child's birth involved rape or incest, only 45 percent of the agencies provided this information to adoptive parents, and only 16 percent of the agencies felt that the parents should tell the child. Although agencies recommended that parents provide their children with non-identifying, descriptive information, Jones found that "except for medical history" the information relayed by agencies to adoptive parents "is not usually given in writing." She also found that agencies usually do not recommend that information about the problems of the biological parents be shared.

Families involved in independent adoptions have the opportunity to obtain much more information, since they are more likely to have contact with the birth parents. Yet they often shy away from asking questions, fearing that they are rocking the boat.

Whether you are adopting through an agency, a birth parent, or an intermediary, try to get *as much information* as you can about your child. Ask for basic demographic information—age, religion, education, occupation, reasons for relinquishment. You might also consider these questions that Jayne Askin, author of *Search*, compiled for adult adoptees to use when they contacted an agency:

• What were my birth parents' first names?
• Were they both living at the time of my adoption?
• Were my birth parents married to each other?
• Was either of them married to someone else?
• Were my birth grandparents alive at the time of my birth? What was their attitude? Did they participate in the relinquishment/adoption proceedings?
• What was the color of my birth parents' eyes? Hair? And so on?[7]

Try to get as much medical information as possible about the birth parents and their families. Push your worker or intermediary for any personal descriptions (e.g., "She enjoys singing"). There are also the little details in a birth parent's life that you might want to inquire about. When did the mother get her first menstrual period? Does she bite her nails? When did she cut her first tooth? When did she first talk? If you had a child by birth, you might ask your parents some of these questions about yourself as you tried to think about what family traits your child has inherited. So—ask your child's birth parents for him. If you're wondering how your child may look when he grows up, then requesting photographs—or even meeting—can offer clues.

If possible, get the information in writing. Don't trust your memory. Take detailed notes during any interview or telephone conversation, and be sure to save your notes.

If you are adopting a child from abroad, you may find the names of birth parents or other relatives on your child's documents. Be sure to keep copies of all documents for your child. Although INS requires only a summary translation for the I-600, get a full translation for your child's sake. Keep any attorneys' letters, health reports, even medical bills that you may have been sent. These are the scraps of information that adult adoptees say they cherish.

If you are adopting a U.S. special-needs or older child, your agency may provide a current medical report, school reports, and psychological and social evaluations. Be prepared, however, for the fact that a child's condition may have been misdiagnosed—hence the labels attached to the child may not accurately reflect his situation. Paula describes what she learned when she took her son, identified as a slow learner and a behavior problem, for a full medical checkup:

> He had a 60 percent hearing loss because of a fibrous tumor in one ear that had gone undetected in his fourteen foster homes. He was

an underachiever because he couldn't hear. He's actually quite bright and taught himself to lip-read, which is why the tumor went undetected for so long.

You may also find that a worker has glossed over a problem or not disclosed full information, feeling that it could jeopardize the child's placement. Claudia Jewett, in *Adopting the Older Child*, writes:

> One of our daughters came to us from a foster home that was being suddenly closed because it had been determined that the children there had been exposed to sexual abuse. Hesitant to share this information, our daughter's worker deliberately omitted mentioning the abuse to our agency or to us. This information would have made no difference in our willingness to adopt our child, but it would have saved us valuable time and lessened our concern at her seemingly unreasonable terror of men and of bedtime.[8]

For an older child, Jewett suggests that prospective adoptive parents ask:

- Why is this child not living with his biological parents?
- What has the child been told about his first family? What was his last contact with them?
- How old was the child when he came into care? Where has he lived? If he has lived in more than one other family, what were the reasons he moved?
- How is the child's physical and emotional health? What is his history—shots, allergies, dental care?
- How well does the child's worker know him? How long has she been assigned to him?
- How does this child feel about himself? How does he respond to other people?
- How does this child handle failure, anger, anxiety, fears, happiness, success, pain, disappointment, sadness, affection, discipline, daily routines?
- Does he understand about adoption? About foster care?
- Why did they pick this child for you?[9]

Preparing for an Infant

When Susie learned that she was pregnant, she began eight months of planning and reading about infants before her baby arrived. Closer to her due date, she and her husband took a class in prepared childbirth. Although the class focused on the childbirth experience, the last session included a film about an infant's first three months. The instructor gave her a checklist of things to pack for the hospital and things to have at home for the new baby. Susie also took a class at the hospital to prepare herself for breast-feeding. After her daughter was born, she was kept busy in the hospital with a series of classes: the feeding of infants; general child care (e.g., how to diaper a baby, how to bathe a baby); infant development. When she took her daughter home on the fourth day, she felt shaky but informed about her new role.

Prospective adoptive parents often find themselves less well informed. Although they may have read a few books about child care, they have usually not received community support. Fran had read some books about child care but lacked much experience. She enrolled in an infant-care course at her local American Red Cross, but withdrew the first day when she found that everyone else was eight months pregnant. "Too awkward," she recalls. So, she says, "when I traveled to Chile to pick up my baby, I knew very little about babies. I'll never forget my first diapering of her—alone on an airplane, not too sure which end went where. Nor did I know how much formula she should take, how frequently to feed her, and how to burp her."

Amanda has another story that she likes to tell about her adoption experience: "I didn't know what a bunting or a layette was. When we were expecting Jonah, we bought newborn-size clothing. Since he was seven weeks old when we brought him home, he outgrew it all in a week."

Agencies and parent groups have begun to realize that prospective parents need to be better informed. Terry Allor, a public-health nurse in Michigan, has developed "Expectant Adoptive Parent" classes, which she has offered since 1982. The classes, in four three-hour sessions, cover basic child care (clothing, diapering, bathing, buying baby furniture, babyproofing a house), infant development, adjustment to parenting and adoptive parenthood. Allor, an expert on infant care who teaches at the University of Michigan, developed the classes because she found that "when we adopted our son, there was much that we didn't know, including the adoption-related issues."

Obstetrical nurse Virginia Brackett of Illinois, also an adoptive parent, felt that people were concerned about such issues as bonding and attachment and that "going to a prenatal class was not appropriate." Her class features a discussion of questions that concern adopters: "Will we find it difficult talking about adoption?" "Will we receive support from family and friends?" "How will we handle insensitive questions about adoption?" Allor and Brackett teach the courses with their husbands since they feel that adoption involves both partners equally.

The classes offered by Family and Children's Services of Chattanooga feature a session with a foster mother. Recognizing that adoptive parents do not have children placed in their homes at birth, this agency devotes time to a discussion of a baby's first weeks of life. The agency also has plenty of handouts —brochures about diapering, baby-sitters, formulas. Says social worker Carolyn Baton: "We try to make things as easy as possible."

You may find that you have to enroll in an American Red Cross class or a hospital-related class to get any infant-care preparation. If you have friends with infants, spend some time with them. Volunteer to baby-sit for a day or evening so you can get some "hands-on experience."

If you are adopting a young infant, you might want to explore the possibility of breast-feeding, which some adoptive mothers

have successfully done. Breast-feeding an adopted infant usually will not satisfy all of the infant's nutritional needs, but it
offers the chance to enrich the mother/child relationship
through this special physical relationship.[10] Although women
can stimulate the breast to produce some milk, most have to
supplement their milk by using Lact-Aid. This is a presterilized
bag, hung from the breast or bra, which holds milk and feeds
the infant through a flexible tube. When the infant sucks at the
breast, he receives his nourishment from the Lact-Aid bag. If
you are interested in breast-feeding, contact the **La Leche
League International** (9616 Minneapolis Avenue, Franklin
Park, Illinois 60131). La Leche has pamphlets about breast-
feeding an adopted infant and can put you in touch with a local
leader who will work with you toward your goal.

Preparing for a Child from Abroad

As you prepare for your foreign-born child, "know your child
by his culture," says Cheryl Markson, director of FCVN, a
Colorado agency that places Korean children. Find out about
the child-care practices in his culture, and try to use them to
ease him into your home. If you know people from his birth
country, ask them what they found strange when they first
came to the United States. Talk about differences in cultural
patterns between the two countries. Ask about family relationships and how they differ. Ask other adoptive parents about
their experiences. If your child has been used to physical closeness with adults, even sleeping with them at night, then he is
likely to be petrified of sleeping alone in a bed or crib. Korean
infants and toddlers are usually carried on their mothers' backs;
if your child has been with a foster mother, carrying him in a
backpack may provide a soothing and familiar manner of loco-
motion.

If your child has been in an institution, then you need to learn
about orphanage life. He may not have received much individ-

ual attention. His days there may also have been so tightly regulated that he is not adept at making decisions, knowing how to use free time, or playing independently with toys. FCVN, for example, has prepared orphanage-information sheets on different orphanages in Korea.

Your child may be fearful. If your infant has been in a foster home where no man was present, he may be scared of men. Even if he's been around men, the differences in appearance from what he's used to, including full beard, may frighten him. The physical size of adults, which may be radically different from those in his previous environment, may be upsetting. He may be scared of pets, particularly dogs, since in some cultures they are used as guards or run wild in the streets. And, of course, he will have to cope with dietary changes. You can help him by having familiar foods on hand. It's worth keeping in mind that many children from Asia and Latin America will have a lactose intolerance or sensitivity, and that infants from these areas may need soy-based formulas. This is something you should discuss with your pediatrician.

If you are adopting an older child (toddler and up), learn some basic words and phrases in your child's language so you can communicate with her in both her language and yours. You may also want to line up an interpreter who can help explain things in the early weeks. One parent whose Korean-born daughters have served as translators for other adoptees says that they were able to "answer children's questions, relay parents' questions and messages, and help clear up misconceptions. One child, for instance, wanted the two boys 'visiting' her new home to go to their own house and was surprised to learn that they were her brothers."

Be sure, however, that you let your translator know exactly what you want communicated. Says Markson: "You don't want your translator to tell your child that 'you must behave or they'll send you back.' And you do want your translator to tell your child that 'it's okay to cry.' You must *educate* your interpreter."

Ask your agency and people in your parent group for help. Some agencies and parent groups offer workshops that focus on preparing. Other parents may be able to share tips with you about specific child-rearing customs that will ease your child's transition.

If you will be adopting an Asian child, you will want to read Frances M. Koh's *Oriental Children in American Homes: How Do they Adjust?* (Minneapolis: East-West Press, 1981). The book is a study of Oriental culture, particularly Korean, as it relates to cross-cultural adoption. Koh examines the physical and emotional adjustments that the children undergo; the social structure of Asian countries; and the contrasting methods of American and Asian discipline, education, and family dynamics. Writes Koh of her task:

I decided to cover some of the most basic and important areas directly related to the experiences of adoptive families, in which the American parent and the Confucian child are most different in their cultural orientations. For instance, what kind of adjustments must the child make in his eating and sleeping habits? These are relatively simple areas of adjustments; more complex adjustments must be made in the psychological, social and linguistic areas. The older the child, the greater the challenge. How can parents help the child overcome his trauma of separation or cope with the stress which results from change of culture? How does the child who had never been kissed or hugged respond to his American parents' kissing or hugging? How does the child who had learned only Confucian relationships of inequality adjust to American relationships of equality? How does the child who had been oriented to dependency from his infancy adjust to American orientation of independence? Do the parents find the American way of discipline effective with the child? What aspects of the child's basic personality did the parents find most difficult to cope with in terms of their own? What kind of errors did the child most frequently make in learning to read or speak English, and why? How was the child's general performance in school, as well as his motivation to learn? How did the parents and teachers handle name-calling the child encountered in school or in the street? These are some of the questions I have attempted to answer.

A comparable book for children adopted from Latin and South America has yet to be written. Jean Nelson-Erichsen's and Heino R. Erichsen's *Gamines: How to Adopt from Latin America* gives the best introduction thus far. Adoptive parents have also reported that personal accounts of adoption experiences helped them prepare. Check your library for Jan de Hartog's *The Children,* which provides practical information based on his adoption of two older Korean girls.

Preparing for an Older Child

As you prepare for the arrival of your child, particularly an older child, you've got to try to put yourself in his place. It is important that you keep in mind the environment he came from and the environment he will be entering. Think about the impact that moving has had on you and on other families you know. How might a child react to change? What can you do to ease the transition?

"Parents have to be prepared to deal with the child who should not be happy to come to your house," says Jack Frank, a family therapist associated with Tressler-Lutheran Service Associates who has done extensive counseling of youngsters. "They're glad that these people have said that they'll be their parents, but they're not glad to be adopted."[11] For kids who have not known permanence, adoption is just another move. In fact, since adoption is described as a "forever family," a youngster may feel that he is permanently trapped. Says Frank: "You need to be in touch with what your kid's expectations are."

How are children helped to make the move? As part of the adoption-preparation process, your child may have created a "life book," which tells the story of his life through pictures, drawings, and other materials. His social worker will have used this to help him talk about his life. Childrens' life books, writes Claudia Jewett, may "include pictures and comments about foods that they love and hate; people that they love and hate;

things that make them feel good and bad; some of the things that they are afraid of." The book will "express feelings, so that the child is less concerned about what his new parents will think of the things he considers unacceptable about himself, less fearful that his new parents wouldn't want him if they knew what he was like inside."[12]

What are some of the steps you will want to take as you get ready for your child?

Read Some Parenting and Child-Development Books.

If you've had a home study utilizing the TEAM approach, then you've already begun to focus on parenting issues. If not, now's the time.

Claudia Jewett's book *Adopting the Older Child* (Boston: The Harvard Common Press, 1978) is a basic primer for adoptive parents. Based on case studies, it's a balanced, insightful book that will help direct your thinking. Her other book, *Helping Children Cope with Separation and Loss* (Boston: The Harvard Common Press, 1982), and a pamphlet that she's written, *A Parent's Guide to Adopting An Older Child* (available from the Open Door Society of Massachusetts), are also informative reading.

Evelyn Felker has written a sensitive book, *Raising Other People's Kids* (Grand Rapids, Michigan: William B. Erdman, 1981).

I'd also look at the *TEAM Parent Preparation Handbook* (available from NACAC).

Thomas Gordon's *P.E.T.—Parent Effectiveness Training* (New York: New American Library, 1975) is a book that many families recommend.

Katherine Nelson's *On Adoption's Frontier: A Study of Families Who Adopted a Child with Special Needs* (New York: Child Welfare League, 1984) examines the experiences of 177 families and the types of services they needed. The book is designed to help adoption professionals and families understand the problems they will face.

Adopting Children with Special Needs: A Sequel, edited by Linda Dunn (available from NACAC) is a collection of stories of different families.

Be sure you also do some reading about child development. You want to understand a child's behavior at the age of your future child—how he thinks, acts, feels—and the common developmental landmarks. Some of your child's behavior may be typical of his age group rather than a response to his move to your home.

Line Up Postplacement Support.

Building a family is hard work. You and your child may need help initially—and over the long term. Programs such as TEAM emphasize the importance of preparation and support. To whom will your family turn—your social worker? a parent group? a family therapist?

Talk with families who have adopted older children. Explore the services in your community. Barbara Tremitiere insists that "you can't drop these kids in cold."

Larry, a parent whose four-year-old son almost started a fire in their house, describes how he and his wife floundered. "We planted our own seeds of failure," he recalls, "because we didn't understand what was going on. We'd been told that our son had a deprived background. What we found was that the things we accept as part of our everyday life (how to eat at a table, how to interact with others, how to take a bath), he hadn't been taught." Larry and his wife were embarrassed to talk to their social worker about their problems—"I was scared that people would think I was a rotten father." The relationship deteriorated: "It was like drowning in molasses. You couldn't move fast enough to get out. There was no one to throw a rope."

Two and a half years after their son was placed with them,

Larry and his wife relinquished their adopted son. That was in 1974. Looking back, Larry says: "Now Jamie would be no problem. In foster care [which they've done since 1974] we've had thirteen different children. We've had children who've been physically and sexually abused, children who've been physically and emotionally handicapped. We've learned a great deal about how children work and how children think. We adopted one of our foster children, a girl with spina bifida. Today I spend a good deal of time talking and sharing with others."

At Family Resources, Inc., an agency in Ossining, New York, that focuses on hard-to-place children, therapy is seen as an integral part of the adoption process. "It is expected and accepted by staff and families," says director Bernard McNamara:

> We introduce the idea right at recruitment and incorporate it within our parent training as well. Our philosophy is 'not if there are problems,' but 'when there are problems' here are ways to handle them. Therapy needs to be an automatic part of the adoption process and placement, not just a response to difficulties later on. It's a tool for the family to help with adjustment and reduce the stress that any new placement naturally brings, even with children with no obvious problems. It's a reassurance for a 'good start' that avoids or tempers future issues. At Family Resources, therapy is started within hours or days of placement with a new family.[13]

Observe other children.

If you have never parented an older child, observe children about the age of your expected child to familiarize yourself with their interests and behavior.

If possible, visit with your child before the move.

When an agency places an older U.S. child, the prospective parents and the child may meet, perhaps a few times or over an extended period of time, before the child moves. First visits might revolve around outings to a park, zoo or other neutral surrounding. You may visit with the child at his foster home. Children may also spend time in your home, including week-end sleepovers. There is no prescribed way or specific length of time that visiting will take place before the child is placed in your home. The circumstances vary with the individual child.

Prepare a book of photographs featuring your family, your home, and your neighborhood.

All children appreciate photographs to look at, but this is particularly important if your child will be coming from abroad or if you will be unable to visit. Sending photos and letters before your child enters your home gives him an introduction to you and helps to familiarize him with his new surroundings. He can thumb through them as much as he wants, just as you are probably looking at his photograph and spinning dreams based on it. If several weeks or months will elapse before he arrives, you will want to continue the contact, just as your agency is probably sending you updates. If you are adopting a toddler or young child, ask your agency if you can send a toy or other item that he can bring with him as a transitional object.

Think about how your household operates.

If this will be your first child—or your first older child—consider your household and the rules that you will want observed. When is bedtime? What about homework? What about television? What household chores will he be asked to perform? Keep in mind that your child's understanding of tasks may be different from yours. You'll need to give clear messages about your expectations. When you tell a child to "clean your room," you may mean that you expect him to pick up the trash from the floor and make his bed. In your child's previous home, that may have meant to wash down the walls.

*Visit the school your child will attend
and talk with the staff.*

Since school will play an important role in your child's life, you should begin working with the school before his arrival. Does the school offer special services that you can tap? You might want to get a copy of *The Special Student,* a pamphlet published by the Illinois Council on Adoptable Children (5 Park Road Court, Lombard, Illinois 60148). It's intended to acquaint educators with issues that have concerned the parents of older adoptive and foster children.

Adopting older children is very complex, and I've just sketched out a few of the many issues. Barbara Tremitiere believes that successful adoptions occur when parents are realistically prepared. Do your homework.

Renaming the Named Child

All parents of adopted children, particularly if their children are past infancy, are confronted with this question: Can you change a child's name? Observed one parent:

When my son arrived from India at age 3½, he was wearing what was probably his first pair of shoes—used, too small, and with no socks they were rubbing his toes raw. But he would not give them up. Only through much hand waving could I convince him that the removal of his shoes was temporary, and only then did he part with them in order to take a bath. They had to be returned to his feet immediately following—over the sleepers with the built-in feet— and then into bed with him. How little and simple were his possessions! The other item he was attached to was the bag (you know, the one on the airplane for emergency use) he was carrying with two pennies in it. His shoes, the bag and pennies, and, yes, his name, were his only possessions—his security. And I wanted to change his name. The shoes he gave up for brand new ones. The bag was eventually set down and lost in the shuffle. But the name? Something he had for 3½ years? How would I? How could I take that?[14]

Unless you are adopting a very young infant, your child will have a name by which he has been identified and which he recognizes. But you, as a parent, may feel strongly the need to give him a name that you—rather than a birth parent, a social worker, or someone else—chose. Should you?

Dr. Vera Fahlberg, who has written extensively about children and attachment, told the editor of the newsletter *Adopted Child* that parents should not change children's names unless they have a very good reason.[15] Dr. Fahlberg believes it is as important for younger children as for older children to keep their given names: "Children know their first name by the time they are one year old and may recognize and respond to it before that time." She points out that a child may find it difficult to understand why a first name is changed and may even decide, by a kind of magical thinking, that the one name is "bad" and the other one "good." Says Fahlberg: "Adopted children have enough issues to deal with without having to understand what it means to have their names changed."

You may want to consider renaming a child if there is already a child in the family with that name. Parents of foreign-born children often change a child's name when it is difficult to say or spell. They may retain the child's original name as a middle name. Rachel and David changed the name of their Colombian infant from Jesus to Joshua, because, says Rachel, "We are Jewish and he would have had difficulty being accepted in a Jewish community today with that name."

Not everyone is as adamant as Fahlberg on the inadvisability of name changing. You may have waited for the day when you could confer a name upon your child. You may feel that it helps build attachments. Your family may have a naming tradition. You will need to weigh your needs with your child's.

You will probably want to call your child by your last name from the day that he is placed in your house. You may have to battle with your child's school, however, to recognize this name change before the adoption is finalized. Says Fahlberg: "Most families carry the same last name. It's one of the ways families describe who are family members and who are not." Gloria Peterson in the pamphlet *The Special Student* brings the point home most graphically: "One of our children was not riding the school bus for weeks. I was at work when our son arrived home on foot and was unaware of the situation. When it was discovered, the answer was that his bus pass was in his old name and he simply refused to show it to anyone and so he walked."[16]

Even here, however, there are two sides. Jack Frank points out that youngsters who have bounced around from one situation to another have one thing that traveled with them—their names. Their reaction to adoption may be " 'and now you even have to give up your last name.' "[17] Joyce Kaser and R. Kent Boesdorfer agonized about what to call the six-year-old boy they were adopting from Colombia. They write:

> We found that we wanted to keep Jorge's Colombian name for the identity he had associated with that name and as a link with his heritage. We were resistant to changing the name of a 6-year-old whom we hadn't yet met, but we were fearful of causing Jorge concern if we did not give him a new family name. Finally we were reluctant to demand that our son have one spouse's last name and not that of the other.[18]

Their son was named Christopher Jorge Cruz Kaser Boesdorfer, although "when we met in Colombia, our son declared himself to be Jorge Cruz."

Preparing Family and Friends

You may want to give your family and friends Pat Holmes's *Supporting an Adoption* (available from the author, 11502 41st

Avenue Court N.W., Gig Harbor, Washington 98335). The booklet gives a quick run-through of the adoption process and postplacement.

Think carefully about revealing to others the background information that you have about your child—this is information for you and your child. (For a full discussion, see Chapter 12.)

If you have older children, no doubt you began preparing them at the time of the home study. If you are adopting an infant, you'll need to help them understand what infants are like. A young child will have to be prepared to share his parents and toys.

If you are adopting an older child, make your children aware that the new sibling may seem less than overjoyed at joining their family. Indicate that there are likely to be rocky times ahead and that the new child's behavior may be different from what they expect. They should realize that the child may hoard, may hit, or may act like he doesn't like them. Says Markson: "Prepare the siblings for the worst, just as if you were bringing home a new baby and wanted to educate your child in advance." There are also some children's novels that focus on the foster-care experience and the feelings of children moving to a new home. These books are listed in the directory at the back. Your children might want to read one of them before their new sibling arrives.

11

Adjustments

What's it like to become a parent through adoption? In our society, with its current emphasis on the early bonding of mothers and infants—via birthing rooms, soft music, nonviolent births, etc.—adoptive parents are often reluctant to discuss what they felt when their families were formed. They will acknowledge that the process is different, but how it differs and how they worked at forming a family are often very private topics. People who have adopted older children may be more open about acknowledging that they didn't feel instant love and that the bonds between parents and child will have to grow over time. Families with newly adopted infants or toddlers are usually less open about telling others how they felt in those early weeks or months. As new parents, you may be left in the dark as to exactly how other adoptive families got through this transition period.

The outsider is often left to believe that "instant love" and "rapport" magically occurred. Parent-group newsletters are replete with stories such as the following:

> We had yearned for this baby through nearly two years of infertility testing and treatment and another 17 months on a waiting list, and now that we have her, we know that the many months of frustration really were worth it.

This baby who's been ours for under two weeks is totally a part of us. Her looks, her expressions and gestures, her feel, her baby smell are all very dear to us."[1]

Parent newsletters have begun, however, to feature accounts of the adjustment process suggesting that things do not always go so well:

I was ready to pack our bags and leave. That was my first reaction to the baby we had traveled so far to adopt. Here we were in Santiago, Chile, tired, anxious, no sleep in two days, and faced with a screaming, sweaty, red-in-the-face, quite unpleasant, almost 7-month-old little boy. The only thing that prevented me from leaving was having to face friends and relatives upon our return home.

The weeks before our trip were filled with excitement. There was furniture to buy, wallpaper to hang, curtains to sew. I made tons of stuffed animals, interviewed doctors and bit my nails. I also spent many hours drooling over the pictures.

Throughout this time people continually asked, "Aren't you nervous?" My answer was, "Well, a little," but in truth, I felt pretty calm. I only fell apart when we were introduced to our son—a tired, screaming, ugly baby.

I was unprepared for negative feelings towards the baby we longed for. I had spent two years reading wonderful stories in adoption newsletters about parents meeting their children for the first time. Perhaps some of these stories did describe negative encounters, but I must have selectively ignored them. Nobody wrote about wanting to leave the kid behind, or wanting to throw up!

Needless to say, my trip to Santiago was not very enjoyable. I saw no sights, unfortunately for our son bought no souvenirs, got no sleep and easily lost five to seven pounds in four days. The plane trip home, though uneventful for the baby, was a very anxious time for me. I was only able to relax when we landed in Miami.[2]

Dorothy W. Smith and Laurie Nehls Sherwen, in their book *Mothers and their Adopted Children—the Bonding Process*, challenge us to look at bonding—the factors that lead to it and the factors that lead to its opposite, distancing—and its role in adoptive families. The authors write that "a great deal of literature on adoption makes light of the difficulties while somewhat sentimentally stressing the joys of instant parenthood. Our data suggest that the advantages of adoption for children and parents are very great, but that the path to achieving a close family tie with some children may be steep and rocky."[3]

Smith and Sherwen break the bonding process down into three stages: (1) prior to entry (preadoption), (2) entry into the family (adoption), and (3) after entry (after adoption). In the first stage of maternal bonding, a woman prepares for motherhood. She begins to take on the role of mother, fantasizing about her child-to-be, solving problems through fantasy, and manipulating her environment. She develops a support group and carries out nesting behavior such as preparing the infant's room and clothes. The authors question how much maternal fantasy actually occurs before an adoption since parents may have very little notice before the child arrives. If they are involved in an independent adoption, they may be reluctant to dream at all, fearing that the placement may fall through. Smith and Sherwen also note that "because those seeking to adopt are aware of the possibility that any one adoption might not be actualized, they often prefer to keep the possibility secret until they actually have the child. Thus, traditional support systems, such as family and friends, may not even be aware that the parents are seeking a child. In addition, there is no routine 'maternity leave' for adoptive mothers, and 'child showers' and even baby showers are not common."[4] Those familiar steps of validation that bolster a woman before her child's birth are frequently absent in adoptive families.

In the next stage, when the child enters the home, the mother is expected to be an active participant in the process. She has the chance for contact with her child in the presence of others. These "significant others" support the mother and respond to the child. The experience is one of support for the mother—from the father, the family, friends, and professionals who may be involved.

The experiences that two families shared with me, however,

illustrate just how stressful a child's "entry" may be.[5] Carol recalls: "Our daughter arrived from Korea when she was fifteen months old. She was very weak and had pneumonia; impetigo; scabies; and herpes in her mouth and in her throat. She couldn't even crawl. The first night she had to be held in my lap the whole time. We were shocked."

Betty, a single mother, remembers their airport scene: "We entered the country covered with shit. She had diarrhea. She had exploded. At the airport, all I wanted to do was get out of there, go with my parents, go to a hotel room and take off my clothes. I didn't want to stand around an airport and celebrate. I needed to get to a private place."

How the child looked and how the child acted must surely have influenced these mothers' feelings. It's hard to feel loving toward a child who is smelly, weak, covered with sores, and generally unappealing. Illness can have a dual effect: It fosters togetherness between parent and child, but it also creates strain because of the demands and the worries put on the parents. Travel to the foreign country, where the parent or parents are alone, without supports, coping with a new culture and travel, may also increase the stress.

Barbara Berg's account of the adoption of her newborn daughter in *Nothing to Cry About* gives us a sense of the equally stressful conditions under which independent placements can occur. Berg and her husband learned about the possibility of adopting their daughter at the time of her birth and just a few days later flew out to California to pick her up. It was a joyous occasion. Berg tells us about her strong feelings of attachment right then. We also know about her own lack of preparation. We have a sense of the stress of the time and the place—caring for their daughter in a hotel room, waiting impatiently for papers to be processed in New York so that they can return home. She writes:

All of a sudden I felt very insecure. I was three thousand miles away from home, in a city where I hardly knew a soul. No doctor, no refrigerator, no way of sterilizing, with a newborn baby totally dependent upon me. For the first time since Alison was born, I worried about how well I'd manage. Other women "in waiting" worried about how well they'd cope with formula and schedules and croup. I hadn't. I had only worried about whether or not I'd have anyone to worry about. Now that I did, I worried about what everyone else worried about.[6]

In the third stage, after the placement, the mother gets into her new role, touching and exploring the child, communicating —both verbally and nonverbally—and identifying with her new son or daughter. The child interacts with the mother, responding to her nurturing behaviors. Write Smith and Sherwen: "Physical closeness and nurturing activities directed toward the child seem to be the cornerstones of bonding in both biological and adoptive situations."[7]

Yet newly adopted children may not want the closeness that the mother offers. Christine describes her first months with her eighteen-month-old daughter: "I was not prepared for the anger. She wasn't able to accept comforting for four months. She'd wake up at night and be frightened. I'd pick her up and she'd stiffen and I'd have to wait until she'd worn herself out crying."

This behavior is referred to as a "distancing factor" and it can form a part of the bonding process as it goes on. For many parents, closeness and distancing interplay—the parents wanting to make the attachment; the stress of the new parenting role and the child's actions making it difficult. Put yourself in this mother's, and her children's, place:

Sleeping: What's that? Why is Kendra inconsolably sobbing NIK-O-YAH for three hours? A call to our Korean friend at 11 P.M. fails to resolve this tiny question. Oh, she wants to sleep with her little picture book we had sent to her in Korea. How could we be so stupid? But, at least Kendra, aged four, liked to sleep. With Lisa, aged two, nothing worked. She screamed, raged, rolled all over until one night, in desperation, I spanked her legs. INSTANT silence. So, that's what they must do in Korea. Well, it may work for a few nights but forget it. One night, we let her follow me around the house. I walked in a circle for 45 minutes from 10 o'clock to nearly 11. Was she tired? Of course not.[8]

This mother's tale raises another basic issue in adoptive parenthood: How does it feel to take on the role of instant mother or father? Despite having read all the parenting books you could find, you are confronted with a child—your child, not a hypothetical child—whose habits, likes, and dislikes you barely know. All parents must come to terms with their children. The parents of newborns can follow some basic advice: If the baby's wet, change him; if he's hungry, feed him. Parents who adopt non-newborns may grope around for answers.

Two new adoptive mothers describe how it felt to take on their new roles:

He was two years old when he arrived from Korea. The day after he came, we were in a restaurant. I got ready to order breakfast for my two kids—Carol, my two-year-old birth daughter; and John, my new son. I knew what to order for Carol, but I had no idea what to order for him. I felt terribly inadequate. Since he spoke Korean, there was no way to communicate with him. Because I had become his "mother," I felt that there was something inborn that I should have had but I didn't have it.

What is a mom? You feel like you're going through the closet looking for the right "mother" role to wear. One day you reach your limit and spank your child, or you yell, or you are unkind, or you are simply an intolerable grouch. You try a role on—say, spanking—and it either suits you or it doesn't. But it takes time to change your clothes. You are instantly faced with several parenting choices; no time to reflect on them; and you feel waves of guilt on top of your overwhelming exhaustion.[9]

Mothers of infants can have these same feelings. "When I started to talk with other mothers about my son," says Paula, "I felt terribly unsure of myself. I was, after all, the two-week mother of a nine-week-old infant. We had a lot to learn about each other."

The First Days

The questions always come up: When you bring your child to your house, who should be with you? Should you celebrate? Should you take your child around to meet family, neighbors, and friends immediately? Or should you stay at home for a while just to acclimate yourselves?

This is a time of transition. Your family may profit from some private time. If you are adopting an infant and feel that you'd like a more experienced hand around, such as a grandparent, then go ahead. An older child may appreciate the time to become acquainted with you and your house before being asked to relate to the larger family network and neighborhood. There is, after all, a lifetime ahead.

You may even want to ask people to write, not call or drop by. While your child is settling in, you may not want to feel obliged to entertain company.

Postadoption Stress

Before Adam came I had read everything I could get my hands on about cerebral palsy. I was prepared for his not walking and his speech difficulties. However, reading about a disability and living with a child on a daily basis who has that disability are two different things. All of a sudden I was overwhelmed with it all—not overwhelmed with joy and happiness; instead I was overwhelmed with fear and guilt and tremendous feelings of failure. The last thing in the world I felt like celebrating was "Mother's Day" when I was feeling so inadequate as a mother (or anything else for that matter).[10]

That's not the way it's supposed to be. Or is it? Most people have heard about postpartum depression, but postadoption blues? You haven't gone through the hormonal changes associated with pregnancy that might trigger this, but you're feeling depressed, irritable, fatigued, tense, inadequate, and overwhelmed. Everything seems up in the air, in turmoil. And why not?

Your family is changing. It's disorganized. New relationships are being established. The waiting, and the tension surrounding the wait, are gone. But now you wonder when things will ever settle back to normal. What is normal? Not the way it used to be. A new family constellation is emerging, but you don't yet know how it will work. You're unsure of yourself and your child.

Recognize what is happening. Seek out supports. Be sure to leave some time for yourself. Do what you feel you can; leave what can wait until tomorrow.

Children Talk About Their Feelings

In their study of bonding, Smith and Sherwen asked thirty-three older children about their bonding experiences. They found that many of the children had not fantasized about their mothers in advance. Several of the Asian children, however, had fantasized that their mothers would look like them. Said one: "I felt sad. She was not my Korean mommy." They then had to cope with the gap between their fantasy and the reality of their parents' appearance.

The happiness that parents often feel on a child's arrival was not shared by some of the children. Some reported feeling scared, shy, mad, strange: "I cried all night." Write Smith and Sherwen: "Adults who have worked very hard and incurred great expense to arrange for the adoption may find it hard to realize that the actual placement is frequently not a joyful experience for the child. Talking about the naturalness of fearing a new environment and a new family can help the child avoid feeling guilty or ungrateful toward those who are trying to help him."[11]

For her book *How It Feels to Be Adopted*, Jill Krementz spoke with nineteen boys and girls, ages eight to seventeen years, about their experiences as adoptees. One girl talked about her fears: "I guess the hardest thing for me in the first year was when I had to go back to the agency for follow-up visits. I was always terrified that I would see my other mother there and she would want to take me home with her again. That's because when I was in foster care we had monthly visits—my mother and I—in the playroom at the agency." An eight-year-old Korean adoptee, who arrived at age three, reports: "When I was littler I always asked my Mom, 'Did they send me away because I was bad?' And she would show me a letter from the Korean agency that says, 'Soo Mee is a lovely child who brings lots of joy to all of us.' That always made me feel better."[12]

Even Infants Have Adjustments to Make

> When I held my nine-month-old daughter for the first time at the agency, she burst into tears and wouldn't let me hold her. She stopped crying when her foster mother picked her up.
>
> For our next visit, her foster mother brought her to our house. She didn't want to be held. She let herself be on the floor. She still cried almost the whole time.
>
> So, for the next visit to our house, her ten-year-old foster sister brought her. She still cried every time I picked her up.

Amanda reacted just as you would expect an infant to react to strangers: She cried. But these strangers were her new adoptive parents. After placement she did form a strong attachment to her new mother. In fact, for the next two years, she had major difficulty separating from her mother, and she slept fitfully, frequently tossing and turning, crying in her sleep, waking up and wanting to be held. "We did not sleep through the night," reported JoAnn, "until she was past two." Her pediatrician suggested it might be teething. When her teeth came in, he gave the explanation that many one-year-olds had trouble sleeping. JoAnn feels, however, that Amanda grieved for her foster mother.

Jane, born in Korea, was four months old when she joined her new family. Reported her mother:

> At first her parents were delighted that she did not cry or appear frightened. They became concerned, however, when she failed to respond to them or to anything around her. She neither laughed nor cried for several weeks. Alert and watchful, she indicated awareness by stiffening up when she was moved or spoken to. After about two months she smiled at her brother, Joe, then two years old. Shortly thereafter she began to respond to her mother, but it was about a year before she responded to her father. This withdrawal and isolation concerned and frustrated her parents and caused tensions between them.[13]

Her mother feels that the disruption in her care—and the need to adjust to new patterns of child care—caused deep feelings of insecurity that continued for several years. She feels that she underestimated the adjustment needs of her daughter "because of the myth of the adaptability of infants." She had expected her baby "to be happy and to trust" her. Instead, her first year was "unsettled and difficult."

Theresa has a different story to tell about her daughter, who was seven months old when the agency placed her.

> Tara's foster mother had told us that Tara was a light sleeper. For the first six months after Tara came to our home, she slept almost all the time, waking up for short periods to eat and play. She never really laughed and smiled. She was a glum little girl. When Tara was a little over a year old, her sleeping patterns altered dramatically. Her sleep became fitful and she would cry for several hours during the night. She'd fall back asleep when she'd worn herself out. She's three years old now and she still sleeps lightly and her sleep is sometimes still disturbed.

The burgeoning field of infant studies is revealing that infants can perceive a lot at a very young age. *Time* magazine reported the discovery by an Israeli neurologist that infants just twelve hours old show a positive reaction to tasting a drop of sugar water and grimace when tasting a drop of lemon juice. Works such as Dr. T. Berry Brazelton's *Infants and Mothers: Differences in Development* (New York: Dell, 1969) and Frank Caplan's *The First Twelve Months of Life: Your Baby's Growth Month by Month* (New York: Grosset & Dunlap, 1971) chronicle the stages of infant development. We learn how infants develop a sense of their identity separate from that of their parents, and along with that, fears of strangers and separation; how, as they develop physically, they explore their environment but periodically come back to their caretaker for nurturance and support. Says psychologist Rose Caron of George Washington University's Infant Research Laboratory: "We are learning that everything will have an impact on an infant, but we still need to know exactly what happens."[14]

Adopted infants can be expected to grieve. They have suffered a major dislocation in their lives. They cannot verbalize their feelings, but they can vocalize them. Their feelings are there. They may cry; they may withdraw; they may refuse to smile. They are reacting normally to the changes going on in their lives. As parents, you will need to help them work through their grieving.

Adjustments and the Foreign-Born Adoptee

Foreign-born children must cope with moving from one country and one culture to another. Korean children travel through many time zones and may have sleeping problems because, for them, days and nights are reversed. The child's schedule may straighten out in a week, but his sleep may remain troubled. Korean infants, who have been carried on their mothers' backs, may have a tendency to catnap rather than lie down to nap as American babies do. If the child has been malnourished, then food and eating may be very important. Recalls one mother:

There was a period of time after he came from Korea when our two-year-old son would wake up at night and hold his stomach and talk about the ghost in his stomach. He also typically hid food. We'd find rotten oranges around the house. And he guarded his food. One night he dove onto the table to prevent us from taking his plate away. Kind of a flashback. Talk about two grown-ups dancing around the kitchen showing him that there was food all over.

This child's preoccupation with food lasted many years, and now, seven years later, his mother is careful to pack a snack whenever he goes out.

Children may cling to one parent and reject the other. Often the parent who traveled abroad to pick up the child will be the person to whom the attachment is formed. But the opposite may also take place: A child whose first contact was with the adoptive mother might choose, nevertheless, to attach to the father, because of the painful memory of the loss of the birth or foster mother. One parent is then put in the "odd-man-out" position, while the other is the round-the-clock caretaker. It hurts, exhausts, and causes tension.

Cheryl Markson of FCVN points out that the foreign-born child may also communicate more in physical terms. Since language creates a barrier, the child will have to show you through his actions how he feels. One older child tried to run away several times in the first days after he arrived from Korea—a graphic statement about how unhappy he felt.

The Adjustment Process of the Older Child

In 1974 Laurie Flynn and her husband adopted two youngsters, ages fourteen and twelve. The children came with a history of many foster homes and needed love and security. Writing about her experiences in an article entitled "Why Would Anyone Adopt a Teenager?" Flynn notes: "We knew they would resist much closeness for quite a while. After all, they had no reason to trust adults. The traditional concept of family held little meaning to them."[15]

During the next few years, her son experimented with drugs and alcohol, ran away from home repeatedly, and was arrested for theft and vandalism. He was eventually ordered by the juvenile court to a residential treatment facility. Her daughter also had a difficult time adjusting to the family. "Sometimes she withdrew," writes Flynn, "and wouldn't speak to us for days at a time." Flynn balances her description by saying that they also had many "great times"—taking their son to his first real restaurant, throwing the first party for their daughter, having family picnics and camping trips. Affection did develop and "once in a while, they would open up a little and share some of their deepest feelings. And slowly and gradually, trust and caring grew between us."

The "adoption of the older child is a lot like marriage," Flynn writes. "If we are lucky, maybe the child will choose to change. But the changes belong to him, not to us. What matters most is that he have the chance to learn and grow through what we have to offer. To be effective parents, we must learn to accept risks and approach them as challenges. That essentially is how we made it with our teenagers."

Children who move into adoptive situations need to work through their experience of separation. Whether they are separated from their foster parents, birth parents, or a caretaker in an orphanage, they will have to come to terms with what has happened to them before they can fully make new attachments. They will need help to open up, to talk about and share their feelings. The process of separation, and building new attachments, will be gradual and can take years. Barbara Tremitiere says that "many children never bond." Can a family parent a child they don't feel love for? Tremitiere is adamant: Yes —by providing commitment and support. "This is your kid. This is not returnable merchandise."

Experts liken the child's grieving and attachment process to the experience that we have when a loved one dies.[16] The adjustment process may begin with an attempt to deny that this has happened. Or it may start with what is called the "honeymoon" period. The child and the parents are on their best behavior. Things are calm. This is the time when parents are likely to report that the child made a rapid adjustment to the family.

However, the calm is deceptive. You might compare it to your response to an extended vacation. At some point the exhilaration wears off. You feel frightened, overwhelmed, tired. You say to yourself, "I want to be where I can relax, where I can understand my world." You long for the familiar. In the child, you may see two responses: withdrawal and rage. These are normal reactions to a new situation.

Be it two weeks or two months after the child enters the home, the "testing" period will begin. The child will show his anger, often violently, and stop being obedient. He will exhibit a range of behaviors, both good and bad, and see how the parents react and deal with the behavior. It is not uncommon for children to have behavioral problems, acting out through temper tantrums, running away, stealing, lying, or setting fires. The children are testing you, seeing how bad they have to be before you will throw up your hands and say, "Enough," and throw them out. According to Tremitiere, "the majority of kids have learned not to trust anybody and know how to get negative attention. They will come in and challenge your biggest value. The more secure a child feels, the less he'll act out."

Children will also regress. Their behavior will tell you, "I need attention; I am insatiable." They may have eating and sleeping problems. They may wet the bed or soil themselves. They may have difficulty separating and will have fears. Bedtime may be particularly trying.

Adoptive parents often report that their children want to go through the stages of childhood that they have missed. One parent reports: "When I put my eight-year-old daughter to sleep at night, she wanted to try to nurse on my lap. She needed to sit on my lap and cuddle. She needed this so badly."

According to Claudia Jewett, an older child entering a family can act several different ages at one time. Parents may find it difficult to respond to the child, because they may not recognize what age a child is being at any given moment. She writes: "It's almost as if your kid has to crawl back into the womb and act through all of the time that you haven't shared together. So if you get an eight year old, he's going to go through parts of being 1, 2, 3, 4, 5, 6, and 7 with you." The child may act like a four-year old for one week, for example—but, writes Jewett, "you're going to have that week, if that's what it takes him."[17]

Many parents will be upset by such behavior. But it is part of the child's need for parenting—to relive pieces of his life. One mother who refused to cuddle her ten-year-old daughter at the time reflects now: "I should have given her the comfort that she missed from that part of her life." Adjustment and bonding take place as these stages occur.

Life usually settles down. But over the years the parent may find that certain events can trigger a child's behavior and the family may go through a mini–adjustment process again. When a youngster reaches adolescence, for example, he may act out long-repressed experiences from his childhood.

Parents must also recognize that a child may have been physically or sexually abused. Barbara Tremitiere says that "we have come to the conclusion that about 70% of the children that we place have been sexually used." A child's sexual experiences may vary from having slept with his foster parents to having been sexually used by older children in a group home. Tremitiere points out that "to these children sex is not sick, wrong or horrible. For many this may be the only time they felt good. They don't know that what they are doing is wrong."

An older child adopted from abroad may also have had sexual experiences. Sexual interaction may have been a culturally acceptable way of life for children who have spent time on the streets, in orphanages, and in prisons (where some societies will keep children).

As a parent, you must deal with your child's sexual reality. A few suggestions:

- Try to get whatever sexual information you can about the child. You want this information so you can work with your child. Be aware that caseworkers may not know, or may not record this information in a child's record.
- Talk to others about their experiences.
- Do some reading about sexual abuse.
- Be very aware of your new children. Don't leave teenagers alone. Don't put children in double beds.
- Talk with the other children in your household about the new sibling.
- Help your child find appropriate ways to express himself sexually.

Much is involved in the integration of older or special-needs children into a family. Parents and children may have to deal with issues of health, school, siblings, change of birth order, and the acceptance of the family and community. I have touched briefly on a few of these issues in this book. The reading you should be doing and the contact you have with other adoptive parents will help you identify issues. By the time your child enters your home, you should have made extensive preparations, including identifying support services in your community. Claudia Jewett says that "parents often come out of the adjustment period feeling that the older child's adoption has been one of the most significant experiences of their lives. They talk about a sense of enormous personal growth, of satisfaction at having sought a meaningful challenge and met it, and of the privilege of having shared something of lasting value with another human being. Most are convinced that the rewards of their adoptions were well worth the hard times, and that they wouldn't have missed out on their experiences for anything."[18]

Postadoption Support

The adjustment process may take months, but it can also take years. Just because a family "finalizes" an adoption in court doesn't mean that the adjustment process is ended. Children's and families' timetables are different from those of agencies and courts.

As the following chapter makes clear, there will also be special issues that adoptive families must deal with. Building a family by adoption is different from building a family by birth, and adoptive families must meet those issues head-on.

You may have joined a parent group before you ever identified your child. Now that your child is in your house, the temptation may be strong to let your membership lapse as your family settles in. Don't. Parent groups are not for plucking information from and discarding once you achieve the goal of a child. Groups with an intercountry focus often sponsor cultural events for families (see Chapter 12). A parent group gives you the chance to talk with people who've had similar experiences, to share with them your knowledge, and to draw upon them for support. You can raise the questions that vex you (for example, "What do you say when another mother of an infant asks you 'How was your labor?' "). Your child also needs to know and interact with other adopted children.

If you are experiencing any adjustment problems, a parent group can be indispensable. Some groups have developed a buddy system, pairing experienced adoptive families with new families so that the buddy family provides insight and moral support. Others provide respite families, who, when a family is experiencing difficulty with a child, will take the child to their home to give the adoptive parents and the child some breathing space. Some offer postadoption workshops, described as follows:

> [It's] where you come when your husband has "peeled you off the ceiling" at the end of the day; after you've been on the phone to the social worker, your kid's teacher and the police, all in one day.

It's the place to come to tell those awful things you can't tell your neighbor, that your nine year old has to wear diapers and tried to set fire to the house . . . or wrote four letter words all over the wall in black ink . . . or won't eat his meals with the family.

Post-Adopt is where it's safe to say you're not sure it's going to work, you don't even like the kid sometimes . . . where it's safe to say you have violent feelings . . . that you may become a child abuser any moment. . . . You can't say those things to the social worker (at least you think you can't).

Post-Adopt is where you can see things in their proper perspective. The things your child does that really bug you may very well be normal kid stuff . . . not some bizarre behavior requiring psychiatric care.[19]

Still other programs might offer "listening ears"—telephone hot lines for adoptive parents to talk with more-experienced adoptive parents—and discussion groups formed around such topics as single parenting, intercountry adoption, or older-child adoptions.[20]

Some agencies provide extensive postadoption support services. At Tressler-Lutheran Service Associates, parents are encouraged to develop supports from the day they first set foot in the agency inquiring about adoption. Tressler-Lutheran funds a local parent-group newsletter so that families are kept on the mailing list even if they fail to pay dues. Families receive the newsletter at no charge for years to come. Says Tremitiere: "Many people don't need support services for a number of years. What has happened, traditionally, is that when they need help, they don't have somewhere to connect." Getting the newsletter gives them a way to reconnect. Tressler-Lutheran also produces a special newsletter, *Because We Care So Much*, for families with more than five children. (If you have a large family, you can write the agency and ask to be added to the mailing list even though your child was not placed through Tressler.) Funding newsletters and supporting the parent group, Parents and Adopted Children Organization (PACO), are just two of the many services Tressler-Lutheran provides.

Vista Del Mar Child-Care Services in Los Angeles, California, is another agency that has developed an array of community services. According to Director of Community Services Reuben Pannor, "adoption is only the first step. You're just starting on the road. We view adoption as a lifelong process. It is a very special way of building a family. Unless one understands that, one is going to be in for a lot of heartache over the years."

Vista Del Mar offers several postadoption workshops to the general community. A specialized workshop for families who have recently adopted children examines basic issues: how to begin to tell a child he's adopted; how to handle adoption with the school. Pannor has found that many of the couples and singles attracted to the group have adopted infants independently and never talked about these issues. In this workshop they can read, role-play, and explore their feelings with others. Pannor believes that "every adoptive family should go through this type of workshop."

Since adolescence is a rocky time for most families (and often particularly stressful for adolescent adoptees and their parents, with the youth informing the parents that they are "not my real parents" and fantasizing extensively about birth parents), Vista Del Mar offers a special workshop. Parents and teenagers meet separately (until the final session) to delve into their feelings about birth parents, identity, and searching. The adolescents come to the workshop asking fundamental questions tied to their identities: Why did my birth mother give me up? Did she care about me? If she cared about me, why did she give me up? Pannor says that the adolescent adoptees who attend these workshops often have poor self-images and suffer from feelings of loss and abandonment. An adolescent who expresses a need to search out a birth parent is encouraged to go back to the agency or person who arranged his adoption and leave information about himself, including photographs and a notation in his file that he'd be willing to have contact. "I do not encourage adolescents to search [for birth parents]," says Pannor. "It overloads an already overloaded system." He emphasizes that "once adolescents have gone through the workshop with us, they're on the right track."

Vista Del Mar also offers assistance to adult adoptees who seek a reunion with their birth families. If the adoptive parents, adoptees, and birth parents waive their right to confidentiality under California law, Vista Del Mar extends counseling services. The agency's involvement in reunion, says Pannor, "is a very important service."

The number of agencies that see adoption services as extending throughout the lifetime of the adoptee is still small, but it is likely to grow in the years ahead as attitudes toward adoption continue to evolve. In the meantime, says Pannor, "I worry about the people who are out there on their own."

If you are out there on your own but want help, check with the agency that placed your child or another local agency about the postadoption services they provide. Following are some other organizations that have developed postadoption services.

Post-Adoption Center for Education and Research
860 Bryant Street
Palo Alto, California 94301 (415)654-3099.
    This educational outreach program offers a variety of support groups, including one in which adoptive parents, birth parents, and adult adoptees get together (the triad group). Their videotape "Adoption Is a Lifelong Process" and their book *Dialogue for Understanding* are available through them.

Family Building Associates, Inc.
11419 Rokeby Avenue
Kensington, Maryland 20895 (301)942-1218.
    They have offered courses in metropolitan Washington on such topics as "Building Positive Self-Concepts in Adopted Children." Class sessions explore telling the child about adoption, encountering bias (including "brainstorming" about what to say back), dealing with schools, and adoptees and their search. According to Marlene Ross, this course—and other programs that she and Joyce Kaser have designed—"provide educational and informational counseling."

Center for Adoptive Families, Inc.
67 Irving Place
New York, New York 10003 (212)420-8811.
    The center provides support and counseling services for families in stress.
Their treatment approach focuses on short-term family therapy as well as
adoptee peer-support groups. Says Judith Schaffer, one of the founders: "In
a way the center is an extension of the adoptive-parent movement. In the
Seventies, we successfully advocated legislative changes. Now we are seeking better psychological services and adoption research."[21]

You may also want to subscribe to *Adopted Child* (P.O. Box
9362, Moscow, Idaho 83843), a monthly newsletter that has
covered topics ranging from adjustment and bonding to citizenship and siblings' reactions to adoption. Subscriptions are $18
for one year.

Disruption

By summertime, we hoped that a major adjustment time was passed
and that after six months our living pattern was familiar and secure
to Ken. However, each day it was as though it was Ken's first day in
our family routine.
    It was one thing after another. Ken talked out loud to himself
continuously at school, at home and everywhere. We talked about
how to act every place we went. Ken could not seem to remember
from one time to the next how to act, whether it was at the store,
at church, or just visiting. Day after day, there was no significant
change.
    We became so disheartened, guilty, and frustrated. My life be-
came a see-saw of hope and despair. I became very afraid of what
would happen to us during those critical adolescent years. I began
to realize that the uncertainty of Ken's behavior was more than I
could cope with. I knew he needed time, but I had invested so much
of my life and self in trying to help us make it so far, I had no further
resources left to give him. This handsome, kind child whom we
loved was so confused and fearful within himself. Could we finalize
this adoption and make it?[22]

Ken's family chose to disrupt the adoption. His parents felt
that the toll the placement was taking on their family life and

on their other children was more than they could handle. They had tried for a year and a half, had gone for counseling, but the family had still not begun to fit together. They talked with their social worker and their adoption counselor and learned that Ken, a seven-year-old, would be able to find another placement. A new adoption plan was made; Ken's new family met with him several times; and finally he left. Ken's first adoptive mother continues: "We experienced a mixture of sadness and relief: sadness that our hopes for this adoption had not worked out; relief that Ken was moved and was settled with another family. We had come to realize that we were not a family who could survive the continuous emotional upheavals."

Not all adoptive placements proceed to finalization; some disrupt. Barbara Tremitiere, however, believes that parents who have been properly prepared will not disrupt their adoptions. Says she: "Commitment and support must be built in from the beginning. If you take your kid, that's your kid." Tressler-Lutheran tells its families, "We expect you to make it. We're going to be there to help you." Very few of Tressler-Lutheran's families fail to finalize and the agency will do its utmost to preserve the placement. Other agencies do not hold the same view, and at some agencies the disruption rate can be as high as 30 percent of all older-children placements. When disruption occurs, it is extremely painful for everyone concerned.

12

Raising the Adopted Child

There is nowadays a substantial literature written by adult adoptees about growing up adopted—for example, Florence Fisher's *The Search for Anna Fisher*, Betty Jean Lifton's *Twice Born* and *Lost and Found*, and Katrina Maxtone-Graham's *An Adopted Woman*. These books convey the disconnectedness, the anomie, felt by some adoptees, and they dramatize the strong need some adoptees feel to search for their biological roots. Some adoptive parents may have difficulty understanding or sympathizing with these books, for they touch on the issue of shared parenthood—one that many adoptive parents would like to forget.

Consider these books instead as ones that parents can use to help them understand some of their children's needs. Katrina Maxtone-Graham tells us in her memoir, *An Adopted Woman*, that she always knew she had been adopted when she was three and a half. She knew that in those few years before her final placement, she had been in foster care and had had one adoption disruption. What she could not integrate were her memories—a name by which she had previously been called, images and feelings from those early years that she could not pin down. She writes: "I thought of my origins as a vacuum. I possessed a birthdate: March 9, 1935; a birthplace: Borough of Manhattan,

New York City; and a beginning: July 1938." For her, this information was not enough:

> I had thought of my loss at all times, and since as long ago as I can remember. Every moment, every breath, I was consumed with wondering and longing and searching. Each stranger on the street, each house along the road, posed the same questions: Where? Why? Who? There were no answers; and so my yearnings were without resolution, a confirmation of my inadequacy.

At the age of thirty-eight, Maxtone-Graham sets out to fill that vacuum. It is a long struggle for knowledge that begins with a search for basic information and includes meeting her birth mother, learning about her deceased birth father, and visiting a foster parent. It is a struggle that pits her against the agency that placed her and now takes her to court. One of the first pieces of information that she gains, on the day that she meets the agency's social worker, tells us exactly how isolated she has been:

> It is a remarkable experience to sit across from a person who knows who your parents are when you do not; to hear, at the age of thirty-eight, someone tell you simple facts about your own private spectres. "Your father was six foot one, brown hair, blue eyes, a college graduate."
> Just like that you *know* something. Not six foot two, not six foot even. Six foot one. "Brown hair." Your own hair is brown, too—what a glorious coincidence! You try to imagine what a man with brown hair and blue eyes and six foot one *looks* like. You had not even expected to hear anything about your father; you had not thought his identity was even known. And now, "six foot one." I could go home, mark a spot on the wall six feet and one inch from the floor and proclaim a victory, "There, there is my *father.*"

Many adult adoptees live with this thirst for knowledge. They are missing the "who, what, where, when, why, and how" about their lives that people born into a family take for granted. What prompts them to start pushing for the answers? One fifty-year-old adoptee says his search started when he was sitting in a new doctor's office, confronted once again with a questionnaire asking him for his family's medical history. As he kept writing "Don't know," he decided, "I want to know." Others say that it was the birth—or impending birth—of a child that made them wonder about their own genealogical history. Or a contemplated marriage and the fear of inadvertently marrying a birth sibling. Or the death of a parent.

But the need to know is not limited to the adult. Wondering about birth parents is a theme that echoes through Jill Krementz's interviews with youngsters in *How It Feels to Be Adopted*. Reports one twelve-year-old: "There is one time when I do always think about my biological mother, and that's on my birthday. How does she feel on this day? Does she think of me, or does she just pretend that I was never born and it's any other day? Is she sad, or is she happy?"[1] A seventeen-year-old adoptee writes to Betty Jean Lifton:

> I think that I have always wanted to know about my roots but pushed it out of my mind. I became aware of this about two years ago when my grandfather was visiting. We had one of those big family dinners and he kept talking about relatives that did great things. Everyone started to trace our ancestry. It struck me then that I really needed to know about myself. I want to be able to tell my children and grandchildren about their ancestors. I don't want to leave my parents or go back to my natural parents. I just want to ask them a million questions.[2]

Sharing Information

All parents have to come to grips with some basic questions:

- When and what do you tell your child generally about adoption?
- How do you tell your child about adoption?
- If your child does not ask questions, do you initiate them?
- How much information do you share with your child about his past?

- How old should your child be when you tell him about his adoption?
- If there are unpleasant facts, do you reveal them?
- How should you present the birth parents?
- Should you tell the whole truth and nothing but the truth?
- If your child has memories of his birth parents, do you encourage him to share them with you?

There are some other questions that parents will also face—those that their children ask them:

- Did I grow in your tummy?
- Whose tummy did you grow in?
- Why didn't I grow in your tummy?
- Why didn't my mother keep me?
- Is my mother dead?
- Where is my mother now?
- What about my father?
- What did my parents look like?
- What were my parents' names?
- Did I have another name when I was born?
- Who is my real mother?
- What does it mean that I was adopted?
- Did you buy me?
- Why did you adopt me?
- What did the social worker, adoption agency, or lawyer do?

Not all the questions will be asked at one time; rather, they are likely to come up at different times—sometimes at odd moments—and at different stages of development in your child's life.

While the questions asked are straightforward, figuring out the answers that you will give is not. For you'll soon discover that people concerned with adoption—psychologists, counselors, agency workers, parents—disagree about what you should do and say. There is general agreement, however, that children must be told about their adoption and must be helped to understand it in order to grow. Parents must be open and accepting of adoption. They must acknowledge that their family is built by adoption, and that the process of building a family by adoption is different from that of building families by birth.

Families have found that it helps to participate in some discussion with others about postadoption issues. This might be through your parent group, your agency, or another organization (see Chapter 11).

The following suggestions should also prove helpful.[3]

- Be aware of how a child develops. What he asks, what he understands, how he sees himself relate to his stage of growth. Whether your child is a preschooler, a child in middle years, or a teenager will affect how he feels about himself and how he sees the world.

- Listen to your child's questions. A young child who asks "Where did I come from?" may be asking "Where was I born —Chicago or Detroit?" not "Tell me about adoption."

- Answer your child's questions at his age level. Don't assault him with information that he can't process. If a young child asks "Was I adopted?" say yes. If he asks "What's adoption?" give a simple explanation such as "That's the way we built our family."

- Use the word *adopted* in your home, and from an early age —but appropriately. Looking at photographs in a scrapbook that show your child's arrival, you can mention adoption just as you might use the word *born* when looking at a photo of your child at the hospital on the day he was born. Perhaps you've been told to look at your baby and say, "Oh, my beautiful adopted baby." Would you look at a birth child and say, "Oh, my beautiful birth baby?"

- Accept that you are involved in a shared parenthood experience. Your child has a set of parents, whether known or unknown, who gave him life. Your child may also have had foster parents with whom he formed attachments. Don't deny him these other parents.

- Accept that your child's interest in his other parents is natural. He will fantasize about them.
- Be aware that your child must deal with rejection, since his birth mother, no matter how loving, relinquished him. Don't place the burden of that rejection on his shoulders, however; don't let your child believe that some flaw in him led his parents to relinquish him. Saying "Your mother couldn't take care of you" suggests that he wasn't worthy of care. Better to say, "Your mother couldn't take care of any child at that time."
- Recognize that your child is likely to be angry at some point about his adoption. You and he will have to deal with that anger.
- Give real answers to real questions. Don't make up stories. Don't tell your child that his mother made a loving "plan" for him if she abandoned him on an empty road in India. And don't say that she gave him up because she loved him so much; your child may get the idea that being loved leads to being given away.
- Answer your child's questions. If he's capable of asking them, you're capable of answering them. If he asks you what his birth parents looked like, tell him. If you have any pictures, share them. Don't save all the information until he's eighteen.
- Be prepared for the fact that your child may ask questions when you least expect them. One parent was driving on an interstate highway when her three-year-old son asked, "Did I grow in your tummy?" She said no and waited for the next question. It was "Mommy, did you see that dump truck?"
- Recognize that children and parents have different tasks: Yours is to tell him about adoption; his is to understand. As your child grows up, he may ask the same questions again and

again, plus many new ones, but what he needs and wants to know, and what he understands, will deepen with age.

• Make openness and communication an integral part of your adoption telling.

Telling a child about adoption is not something you save up until a child reaches a certain magical age. Nor is it something you reveal in one fell swoop at a very young age, thereby getting the "telling" over with and behind you. You are involved in a lifetime process of sharing information about family building.

Reading

What about those adoption books for children? Can they help you, and your child, talk about adoption? Parents use a picture book like Ezra Jack Keats's *Peter's Chair* to help young children focus on feelings about a new baby. *Peter's Chair* is a sensitive, interesting book with pictures that a child can savor. Any child will enjoy it. That cannot be said about most children's books about adoption. Whereas *Peter's Chair* is a story about having to share, adoption books seem often to be written only for the specialized audience—the adopted child—and seem often to be preaching. Why don't all children need information about adoption? If authors focused on making their books interesting to all children, rather than on purveying a message, perhaps the crop of books that parents find at the bookstore would be more appealing.

There are some books you can turn to as tools to help you convey information about family building. They cannot, however, provide the answers to all your child's questions. If you're seeking a book to read with a preschooler, keep in mind that the graphics are as important as the words. If the message is terrific but the child won't look at the book, then the book will not be read. Preview a book and decide whether you want it for your children. If it's in your bookstore or library, you can spend some time reading it. If not, ask your library to order a book or obtain it from interlibrary loan. If you decide on a book, try to buy it instead of borrowing it from a library. A two-week loan does not give much time for reflection, and since you will be sharing information about adoption over a period of time, your child may want to reread the book periodically. The time when your child wants to read the book again may be the time when someone else has it out of the library.

The directory at the back of this book lists some books that you should be able to order from a bookstore. Not all are "adoption books"; some are books that touch upon related topics. All are enjoyable reading for anyone.

Preserving Your Family Story

Family stories and photographs are special ways in which people preserve their joint history. If you have a camera, have it ready the day your child arrives (or as soon after as possible) and use it. Ask for photographs from your agency or foster family. Keep drawings, mementos, and other things for your child. One child's scrapbook starts with photographs of the two-week-old infant in Colombia (the first photograph his parents received), some postcards and coins that the parents kept from their trip abroad, and a photograph of the adoptive mother stepping off the airplane with the baby in her arms. The home-made arrival announcement shows the infant in a car seat with the message "I'm all buckled in at the Jones house. I arrived on ———from Bogotá, Colombia, where I was born on ———. Please come and see me." There's also a clipping from the local newspaper announcing his arrival and, of course, more photographs chronicling his infancy.

You might want to buy one of the special memory books created for adopted children. Hallmark offers *Our Baby,* which has the feeling of a traditional baby book and would probably work best for families who have adopted young infants through an agency. (It starts: "We first applied for adoption on ———— at ———— agency.") There's space for information about baby showers, the hospital birth record, the adoption announcement, the day of final adoption, and "our baby's birth certificate." The C. R. Gibson Company of Norwalk, Connecticut, has produced *Your Very Own Book* ("Memories of Childhood"), which can be used for infants and older children. It begins with "We belong together," and provides space for "How we found you" and "Our feelings at this joyous time." The Gibson book asks for much of the same information as the Hallmark book (there are two pages for important documents) but is not infant-oriented.

Some families will celebrate a child's joining their family with a party or a religious ceremony sometime after the child has settled in. Jews may perform a circumcision on a male and a ritual bath. Girls also undergo the ritual bath and are named at the synagogue with a prayer. Christians often baptize or rebaptize their adopted children. Some churches have a special service of adoption. These are formal ways of linking the child with the family, and they are events that a family can remember and talk about in the future. Parents of foreign-born children may commemorate their children's naturalization by asking their congressmen to arrange for a flag to be flown over the U.S. Capitol on that day. (You pay for the flag and get it as a souvenir.) Family stories about the adoption itself are also cherished. Says one mother:

> The older they get, the more they want to hear their story. Thomas likes to hear about our going in a taxi to pick him up at the agency. We tell him how I held him in my lap and he smiled at me. It's important to Sandra that we changed her into certain clothing. That we painted her crib. She wants to know what people said about her when they first saw her. Each child has his own story. They hear their story. They are beginning to retell their story. It's folklore.

Folklore is important for families. But there's a side to the adoption folklore that parents must guard against. For as parents emphasize the adoption story, children may lose the sense that they were ever born. Betty Jean Lifton tells us:

> Sometimes when I'm with nonadopted friends, I will spring the question "Did you ever think you weren't born?" I get quizzical looks as to my seriousness or sanity, but always the reply "Of course I was born." For without knowing it, while they were growing up, they heard random fragments about how they kicked in the womb, how Mama almost didn't make it to the hospital, and without understanding it, they were receiving direct confirmation about their entrance into the universe and their place in the flow of generations.
>   But the Adoptee says: "I'm not sure I ever was born."[4]

The focus in adoption stories is on children's entering into their families, not on their entrance into the world. In order for children to understand how they entered the world, they need to know about their birth families. Chapter 10 discussed the importance of getting background information for your child. How can you respond to your child's questions if you have not tried to get the answers?

The Smith family in Wisconsin has a large safe-deposit box at the bank "chock-full of information about each of the birth parents." According to Jill, "We can look at the photos and say that our daughter has her father's nose." The Smiths have been involved in a more open adoption and although they are not now in direct contact with the birth mother, the agency continues to pass on information to them about the birth parents. When their son's birth mother married, they received a newspaper clipping describing the wedding.

Jeannette had never met the birth mother of her three-year-old son, but she did have her name. After the adoption of her second child, which has been a fully open adoption including postplacement meetings, she felt the need for more contact with her first child's birth parents. "One night," she says, "I got on the telephone and called his birth mother. She was just dumbfounded. She was really glad to hear about him. She asked questions about him. I sent her photos and now she's sent photos. I may get in touch with her at least once a year."

Another mother decided to travel to Korea to search for information about her children because "what would their chances be after almost twenty years had passed to find records, addresses, and people halfway around the world?"[5] In the agency records, she found out more about her daughter's birth date and name. The agency also arranged for her to meet one of her children's foster mothers. But the high point of her trip came when, using her son's documents, which gave the names and addresses of the people who had signed his relinquishment, she located her son's grandmother (who had cared for her son after his birth) and visited her at her house. She writes:

> My son's grandmother told me that she had met him often in her dreams and that she worried about him greatly, even whether or not he had lived. She told me he was so sick when she gave him away, she thought he would die. She lives in peace now, for she always had thought she would die not knowing if he was happy. When she got out the family album, there in a place of honor were pictures of our son. Mark, also, now has invaluable pictures of his grandparents, aunt, and father.

For your child to build a strong identity, he needs to have the basic building blocks. In families formed through birth ties, children have a family and a genetic history to link up with. As they grow up, they may choose to affirm or deny that history. They have the knowledge, and thus can make the choice. Should not children of an adoptive family have the same opportunities? Writes Lifton: "Adoptive parents can help their children by returning to the agencies or professionals who arranged the adoption and requesting all missing information. By preparing in advance, they can give their children the feeling they are working on their side, not against them, that as parents they care about them in the deepest sense possible—which means having empathy for their needs."[6]

Updating Information

As your child grows, you may want to inform the agency, the intermediary, or the other people who were involved with your child's adoption about his development. If your child develops a medical condition that has a possible genetic link (e.g., allergies or diabetes), be sure to let them know. You are providing this information because it should be passed on to the birth mother (she might like to know this if she has other children), not because you're upset with the placement.

You should also let your agency know that you would like any updated information that might be provided by the birth mother.

If you are vacillating about whether to update information or request it, consider the story of adolescent Jane, in Jill Krementz's *How It Feels to Be Adopted:*

> When I was five, I developed epilepsy and the specialists were always asking questions about my medical history. My father and my doctor both wrote to the adoption agency requesting additional medical data, but the agency people never responded. We had very little information and it was extremely frustrating.

Jane's birth mother, independent of the agency, later tracked her down. Jane reports:

> The most upsetting part of our conversations was learning that she had written to the adoption agency in Rochester several times asking if my parents wanted any more medical information. They always told her no, even though my doctors had been asking—and begging—for updates because of my epilepsy.[7]

Try to put yourself also in the birth mother's shoes. One woman whose social worker contacted the adoptive parents of the girl that she had relinquished eighteen years earlier says: "Just knowing that she's alive and well and happy is quite a relief, but I shouldn't have had to wait eighteen years to find out so small a fact."[8]

Sharing Information Beyond the Family

Dave and Katherine Wilcox happily announce the adoption of a baby daughter estimated to have been born on March 5, 1978 (she was discovered, abandoned, on a road in Korea on March 8, 1978).

That arrival announcement was sent to friends of the joyful adoptive parents. How would they have felt when several years later the daughter of one of these friends, who was having a fight with their daughter, told her, "You were dumped in the street. My mommy told me."

Before your child arrives, you should sit down and think about whom you will tell the details about your child's adoption and exactly what. The background information that you have about your child is his and yours. It is information for you and your child. If there is information that you want to share with your child alone, then don't discuss it with others. Even people with the best of intentions may choose at a later date to discuss your child—with your child or with others.

In the beginning, everyone who has known you since before your child arrived will know that you have adopted a child. But as time passes, as you meet new people, move, or enter new situations, not everyone will necessarily know that your child is adopted. You'll have to decide whom you should tell, when, and for what reason. Does your baby-sitter need to know? Does your mailman need to know? When someone who doesn't know you well comments on your child's curly, red hair (and yours is straight and blond), what do you say? Do you automatically say, "That's because he's adopted?" Why not say that "curly hair runs in the family"?

What exactly do you tell the school? If you have adopted an older child, you have probably worked closely with the school in getting him established in your community. But if your child entered your family as an infant, the school may not know about his adoption. Some parents are reluctant to tell the school because they feel that some people associate adopted children with problems. If openness is a part of your life, however, not telling the school will present you with quite a dilemma.

School presents challenges in other ways. There seem to be certain universal school assignments that cause adoptive families discomfort. "Our son came home one day and said, 'How can I do my homework?' " reported one father. The assignment was to look at his parents and decide from which parent he inherited his eye and hair color, his height, and other physical characteristics. Lessons about genetics and heredity, and family-tree assignments, are difficult for adopted children to do. Do they talk about their adoptive families, their birth families, or whom? Reports one adoptee: "Often I would get upset when we would talk about heredity in school, because I couldn't answer the questions."

Each family's solution may be different. One parent wrote the teacher a note saying that her son could not complete the assignment. Another child did the assignment by writing about his birth parents. Another child chose to write about the racial characteristics of Koreans. What would you have your child do?

Prejudice

Another six-year-old said to Jason, "You don't have a mother; you're adopted." Jason did not say anything. His teacher overheard the conversation and said, "Why do you think he doesn't have a mother? Who do you think is standing outside waiting to take him home?"

Doesn't have a mother . . . adopted. The words ring in your ears. Jason's teacher handled the situation by stepping in and speaking out. She also called Jason's mother and asked her to bring in a book about adoption for the class to read. And Jason's mother also worked with him on a "cover story"—a simple, basic explanation about adoption.

Your family is likely to have such experiences. H. David Kirk reports in *Shared Fate*, a provocative book published in 1964, that more than half of the adopters he surveyed had encountered the following statements:

• Isn't it wonderful of you to have taken this child? (92%)
• This child looks so much like you, he (she) could be your own. (92%)
• He (she) is certainly lucky to have you for parents. (87%)
• Tell me, do you know anything about this child's background? (82%)
• He (she) is a darling baby, and after all, you never know for sure how even your own will turn out. (55%)[9]

Kirk includes the story of one couple who returned their questionnaire with the note "You will probably be amused to know that when I first scanned your questionnaire I found these questions anachronistic. Adoptions, I said to myself, are accepted in our community. Those questions are not in good taste or ever asked. Yet when my wife and I carefully reviewed them I was surprised that we had been asked at least five of them." These questions and others are still being asked.

Has someone referred to your child's birth parents as the "natural" parents or "real" parents? Does that make you "unnatural" or "unreal" or "not his mother"? If you have children by birth, how do people refer to them? Are they your "real" children or "your own" as distinguished from your "adopted children"? If people use phrases that you don't like about adoption, tell them. Often they are just repeating what they've heard and are unaware of the implications of their remarks.

In 1983, birth parents, adoptive parents, and adoptees had to come to grips with the "Cabbage Patch dolls" mania that hit the United States as people stampeded the stores to buy these homely-looking dolls. Each of the Cabbage Patch Kids (so named because they were reputedly found in a cabbage patch) came with a birth certificate and a set of adoption papers. The owner recited an "oath of adoption" in which he or she pledged to take care of the doll. As national attention focused on the dolls, some psychologists claimed that the phenomenon was a healthy one because it permitted children to work through their adoption fantasies.[10] Others felt differently. A member of Concerned United Birthparents said, "I resent people taking [adoption] lightly."

Adoptive parents had to decide whether or not to buy the dolls. Some welcomed the dolls in the hope that they would foster positive feelings in their children and others about adoption and would lead to more open discussion. Others worried about throwaway kids and throwaway dolls. John Tepper Marlin, a member of the parent group Gathering International Families Together (GIFT) in New York, expressed his feelings in a letter to the editor of the *New York Times:* "What would the public reaction be to a 'child-bearing' mama doll, complete with a baby and snap-apart umbilical cord? Wouldn't most parents feel that the trivialization of birth outweighed the possible educational value of such a doll?" Have the promoters of the Cabbage Patch Kids trivialized adoption by using it as a selling gimmick, apparently without a thought to the fact that many people could be hurt and offended?

In addition to coping with the society's sometimes thoughtless attitudes about adoption, some adoptees must also confront the prejudices that people may hold against their ethnic group. "I can recall being teased constantly about my slanted eyes and flat little nose. I even heard the words 'chop chop' and 'aw so' and all the degrading rhymes associated with Orientals," recalled one adult Korean adoptee.[11]

According to adoption activist Holly van Gulden Wicker, who lectured about parenting issues at the 1983 Project Orphans Abroad Conference, parents of transracially adopted children must be especially sensitive to the racial prejudices their children may encounter. Wicker believes that even preschoolers "know that there are differences and can tell the hierarchical differences in our society." Within the community, school, and perhaps within their own family, they may hear racial slurs, or at least unfeeling comments about different groups. At school a child may refuse to play with your child or even to hold your child's hand because he's been told to stay away from those "chinks." One parent tells the story of the day when her son, a black Amerasian, excitedly invited a girl to his junior prom. The girl, a close school friend, eagerly accepted. Three days later, however, she declined the invitation because "my dad won't let me go out with blacks." Imagine if this were your child. Or consider this letter sent to columnist Eda LeShan: "My youngest son has been dating a Korean girl for three years. She was adopted by Anglo parents and raised in Iowa. She is a lovely girl in every sense of the word, but I just don't want her in my family. Perhaps I am very biased, but that is how I feel."[12]

Helping Children Build Their Special Identities

"I wish that I was white, because everybody else in this family is white."

Barbara's four-year-old Korean daughter told her this as she stared at the white, blond, blue-eyed child on the Cheerios box. Had Barbara failed as a mother? Was her daughter seriously disturbed? If you look at the daughter's situation from her vantage point, her comment shouldn't stun you. Young children want to be like the adults around them, so it's natural for Barbara's daughter to wish that she looked like the rest of her family. Most of her friends probably look like their parents (and she's probably heard comments about her cousins like "Oh, he's got the Jones family nose"). Why shouldn't she want this? Children at whatever age do not like difference. Said one transracially adopted black youth: "It's hard enough growing up.

Growing up as a black child in a white family is harder. Being 'other' isn't funny."[13]

At the 1982 North American Conference on Adoptable Children, a panel of black adolescent adoptees who had been raised by white parents discussed their feelings about transracial adoption. They felt that families who chose to adopt transracially should live in integrated neighborhoods and participate in interracial groups. The parents should have black friends and help the child explore the black community and his black heritage. The adoptee should also be able to spend time with other adopted children, particularly with others who are growing up in racially mixed families. Parents and children must talk about how it feels to be black in a white family.

Families with children adopted from Asia or Latin America will also want to consider issues of identity. In one of its pre-adoption pamphlets, Holt International Children's Services touches on how children may feel growing up in an interracial home:

> *Preschool years:* The people he loves the most look different from him. It will be natural for him to want to resemble those he loves, or else understand why he is different, and to learn that difference is not a bad thing.
>
> *School age:* The child will need help in understanding his heritage and background so he can explain and feel comfortable about his status with his pals. He needs to be able to answer their question: "What are you?"
>
> *Adolescence:* This is the time he tries to figure out "Who am I?" Curiosity about his original parents or background may become stronger. We share with adoptive families everything that is known to us about the child. At best the information on family background is limited, and for abandoned children there is none. The child will need help in accepting this lack of factual information. Questions about dating arise, and you should look at your community and try to guess how many of your friends or neighbors would wholeheartedly accept their children dating your child. How would you feel if your child developed a special interest in his homeland, identified himself as a foreigner, and got

involved in a group for Asian, Indian, black or Latin-American teens, or wanted to visit his original country?

Moving into adulthood: "Whom will I marry?" This is sometimes a different answer than "Whom will I date?" as dating is not seen as serious or permanent. Do you have an idea now that your child would probably marry a white person, or a person of his own background? Why? Would you recommend for or against an inter-racial marriage for your child?[14]

Transracially adopted children who grow up in small communities can feel particularly isolated. "I spoke, ate, lived American," recalled a nineteen-year-old who was adopted when she was two years old, "but I definitely looked Korean. This had bothered me since I was a little girl."[15] To help their children feel less isolated, some parent groups around the U.S. sponsor summer culture camps for younger foreign-born adoptees. At these camps children can learn about their birth countries and meet with other adoptees. OURS in Minnesota, in conjunction with the Korean Institute of Minnesota, holds an annual weeklong Korean culture camp that draws families from states as far away as California. During the week, children learn about the language, culture, holidays, customs, and life-style of Koreans. Camp programs have included an introduction to the Korean language (some Korean greetings, counting, words for body parts), crafts, songs, dances, and the martial art tae kwon do. The children eat Korean food such as *kim chi* (pickled cabbage). Says OURS member LaVon Fonck: "Camp gives the children a good image of themselves because for one week they're in the majority, not the minority."

The culture camps that have been held around the country include:

- Heritage Camp in Oregon sponsored by Holt International Children's Services (503-687-2202).
- Korean Culture Day Camp in Melville, New York, sponsored jointly by Concerned Persons for Adoption (222 Marcus Avenue, New Hyde Park, New York 11040); Friends of Children

Everywhere (516-593-5459), GIFT (212-369-0300); Love the
Children of Long Island, Inc. (516-821-0090); and the Open
Door Society of Long Island (516-587-4899).

- Korean Culture Camp sponsored by OURS (612-535-4829), a
weeklong event held in the summer. OURS also has sponsored a sleepover camp. Both are designed for school-age
children.
- Latin American Culture Camp (La Semana), organized by
Parents of Latin American Children in Minnesota (612-471-
7105) and held at the Science Museum of Minnesota.

Holt International Children's Services in Oregon has also designed a program for older teens and adult adoptees—its annual
Motherland Tour. Participants spend time in Korea at Holt's Il
San Orphanage and also live with Korean families. They sight-
see around the country. "Everything I saw and experienced,
heard and tasted, felt and smelled," wrote one adoptee afterward, "served to be the sources to gain the knowledge and
pride I had so badly desired."[16] Yet the tour was more than just
an adoptee's chance to look at his cultural heritage; on the
return trip, the tour members escorted children coming to the
United States for adoption.

Central Connecticut State University holds an annual spring
conference for Koreans and Korean Americans. In 1983 there
was a panel discussion on the education of Korean-born
adopted children—the issues and perspectives of multicultural
families. For further information, contact Professor Kwang Lim
Koh at the Center for International and Area Studies, Central
Connecticut State University, New Britain 06050 (203)827-
7465.

A booklet entitled *International Youth Exchange* describes
numerous youth exchange programs. Your family can host a
student from abroad, or your preadolescent or teenager might
live with a family abroad or attend a multinational summer

camp. (Available from the Advertising Council, 825 Third Avenue, New York, New York 10022.)

There are many other resources that your family can tap. Among them:

Information Center on Children's Cultures
United States Committee for UNICEF
331 East 38 Street
New York, New York 10016 (212)686-5522.
    They will send you book lists, information sheets, and teaching units. There are bibliographies for various countries, as well as lists for a variety of other topics, including food and cookbooks, games from around the world, sources of children's books from other countries. The U.S. Committee for UNICEF also sells books, games, puzzles, and records.

Korean Cultural Service
5505 Wilshire Boulevard
Los Angeles, California 90036.
    A subscription to their quarterly illustrated magazine, *Korean Culture,* is available free upon request, but you should indicate that your family includes a Korean-born child. Focuses on modern and historical Korean culture.

Organization of American States
19th Street and Constitution Avenue
Washington, D.C. 20006.
    Their illustrated magazine, *Americas,* covers Latin America (subscription $15).

Amerasia Bookstore
321 Towne Avenue
Los Angeles, California 90013 (213)680-2888.
    Adult and children's books for Chinese Americans, Hawaiian Americans, Japanese Americans, Filipino Americans, and Vietnamese Americans. Some of the books are bilingual. Write them for a catalog.

Some families purchase ethnic dolls for their children. Manufacturers now create dolls with black skin and dolls with an Asian or Hispanic look. Many of the international dolls are of the "show doll" or "collector's" variety—delicate dolls dressed in elaborate costumes and not intended for everyday play. Others, however, are meant to be handled by children. Check with your specialty toy store or with department stores about their selections. Don't be surprised if some of these specialty dolls carry price tags upwards of $50. Among the dolls that you might consider:

- BARBIE International Collection (Spanish, India, Oriental) and "Malibu Ken" and "Christie" dolls manufactured by Mattel.
- "Soo Ling" (girl), "Ling Ling" (girl), and "Chin Ling" (boy), authentic-looking Chinese dolls with jet-black hair and almond-shaped eyes. Created by Dolls by Pauline (14 Pelham Parkway, Pelham Manor, New York 10803). If you cannot order the dolls through your department store, contact them directly.
- "Little Tiger" and "Lotus Blossom," a Chinese boy and girl, by Effanbee (200 Fifth Avenue, Room 420, New York, New York 10010). If you cannot order the dolls through your department store, contact them directly.
- Lakeshore MultiEthnic School Dolls. Asian, black, and Native American dolls, all vinyl, seventeen inches tall with movable arms and rooted hair. Available from Lakeshore Curriculum Materials Company, 2695 Dominguez Street, P.O. Box 6261, Carson, California 90749 (800-421-5354) or from OURS.

Your family might also enjoy looking at Loretta Holtz's *How-To Book of International Dolls* (New York: Crown, 1980). This heavily illustrated book surveys dolls around the world and is filled with information about costumes, crafts, traditions, and holidays. Holtz discusses, for example, the bread-dough dolls of Ecuador and the chain-stitch dolls of Peru, and shows you how to create your own.

The Search

Some adoptees' need for information goes beyond their desire to know as much factual information as possible about their birth families. It evolves into a need to search out and arrange for a reunion with their birth parents, birth siblings, and other members of their birth families. Although many adoptive parents are comfortable with their childrens' need to search, others fear that their children are seeking to forge new families centering on their birth parents. They may see the search as a rejection, as a symbol of their failure as parents. If those are your fears, consider the explanation of Jayne Askin, author of *Search*. She points out that

> adoptees have been taken as son or daughter by adoptive parents who provide them a home and family where they are loved. The adoptive families have loved and cared for the child they've adopted and have earned the right to be called Mother and Father. What many people do not understand is that adoptees aren't searching for new families. Adoptees already have one, thank you. All that an adoptee doesn't have is a complete sense of connectedness with the past.[17]

Reunion with birth parents may, in fact, lead to stronger bonds between the adoptee and his adoptive parents. Arthur D. Sorosky, Annette Baran, and Reuben Pannor reported in *The Adoption Triangle* that most adoptees emerged from the search and reunion experience with "a deeper sense of their love and appreciation for their adoptive parents, whom they viewed as their true 'psychological' parents."[18]

What should you do if your son or daughter expresses a desire to search? If honesty has been a cornerstone in building your family, you should share whatever information you have. If you have not previously contacted the agency or the person who handled the adoption, then you will want to help your son or daughter do so now. If there is a state adoption registry that requires your signature to release records (see Chapter 5), be sure that you give your permission.

Just as there are adoptive-parent groups, there are adoptee support groups. The **Triadoption Library** (P.O. Box 5218, Huntington Beach, California 92646; 714-892-4098) can direct your family to a local group and other resources. Take a look also at Jayne Askin's book *Search* (New York: Harper & Row, 1982).

This book began with information about how to get started on the road to adoptive parenthood and how to find the children who will complete your family. It has come full circle with information about seeking out birth parents.

Your family will have its own special history. As adoptive parents, we all share important rights and crucial responsibilities that we must exercise for the sake of our children. If this book has given you a clearer perspective on adoption today, and if it has set out some guideposts that will point you toward your own informed decisions, then it will have done its job.

Domestic Adoption Directory—
A *State-by-State Guide*

This list gives basic information about adoption in each of the states and the District of Columbia. It starts with the state agency that oversees adoptions in each state. You'll probably want to begin, however, by contacting the county, district, or city agency that is the local representative of the state office. This agency is usually listed under "adoption" or "child welfare" or "public welfare" or "social services" in your telephone book. Your state agency can answer your questions about adoption in your state, and in some states is eager to provide you with information.

The state exchanges do not place children but help waiting parents

---

This directory has been based upon a variety of sources. All of the state adoption units were sent a questionnaire in 1983 to fill out. Many of them responded and sent lists of agencies in their state. I have relied also on the *Region I Resource Directory,* 1982; *Region III Adoption Resource Directory, 1982;* Region IV Adoption Resource Center, *1982 Directory of Adoption Resources; Region V Adoption Resource Directory;* Adoption Resource Center, Region VI, *Directory of Adoption Resources for the States of Arkansas, New Mexico, Oklahoma, Louisiana and Texas,* ca. 1982; *Region VII Adoption Resource Center's Adoption Service Directory,* 1981; Region VIII *1982 Adoption Resource Center Directory;* ARC 9, *Adoption Resource Directory,* 1982; and Region X *Adoption Resource Directory,* 1982. NACAC supplied me with a list of its "TEAM Programs Reported in Post-Training Survey," September 1982, and its state representatives. Many parent groups have also sent me information about the agencies in their area. I have also consulted the Child Welfare League's *Directory of Member and Associate Agencies* and the member-agency directory of the National Committee for Adoption. Telephone numbers were checked with a local telephone company information operator in December 1983.

find waiting children. You or your worker can contact them. Check with them to find out if you can list your family with them. States that do not have their own exchanges often list children with the regional exchanges (see Chapter 8). If you are having trouble getting help at the state level, you may also want to contact the regional exchange, and perhaps list your family with that exchange.

The directory also gives the names of state photolisting books. If you are hoping to adopt a waiting child, you will want to consult your state's photolisting book frequently, and quite possibly the photolisting books of other states.

This directory also indicates for each state whether independent adoption is permitted and any special restrictions. In some states independent adoption is legal, but using an intermediary to make a link between the birth parents and the adoptive parents is not.

To find a local parent group, you can contact the national office of the **North American Council on Adoptable Children** (810 18th Street N.W., Washington, D.C. 20006; 202-466-7570). The directory also lists NACAC's representatives. These representatives can answer many of your basic questions about adoption and will put you in touch with a local parent group. If you are single, you will want to contact the **Committee for Single Adoptive Parents** (P.O. Box 15084, Chevy Chase, Maryland 20815).

Finally, the directory lists private agencies in each state. Remember, some agencies place children of all ages; some have specialties. Some agencies will have geographic or religious restrictions; others will not. Start with your local or neighboring agencies. But if you need to, don't hesitate to check with other agencies in your state, or possibly out of state. If you are interested in an intercountry adoption, you will want to study the Intercountry Adoption Directory that follows.

Although this directory strives to be comprehensive and as up-to-date as possible, keep in mind that state agencies frequently reorganize, shuffle personnel, and change their telephone numbers. Local agencies may move or change their programs. An agency may have been inadvertently omitted. Some of this information may already be outdated, but persistence will reward you with the correct address or phone number. If you call for information and are rebuffed, try again. Turn to others for help and advice.

ALABAMA
State Agency: State Department of Pensions and Security, Bureau of Family and Children's Services, 64 North Union Street, Montgomery 36130 (205)261-3409

State Exchange: Alabama Adoption Resource Exchange (see above)
State Photolisting Book: *Alabama Adoption Resource Exchange*
Independent Adoption: Permitted/no intermediaries
NACAC Representative: Kathy Casler, 220 Dexter Avenue, Birmingham 35212 (205)879-7008
Private Agencies:
AGAPE of North Alabama, Inc., 2733 Mastin Lake Road, Huntsville (205)859-4481
AGAPE of South Alabama, Inc., P.O. Box 16414, Mobile (205)660-5002
AGAPE of Central Alabama, Inc., P.O. Box 11558, Montgomery (205)272-9466
Catholic Family Services, P.O. Box 3284, Birmingham (205)324-6561
Catholic Family Services, P.O. Box 745, Huntsville (205)536-0041
Catholic Social Services, P.O. Box 454, Montgomery (205)269-2387
Children's Aid Society, 3600 8th Avenue, South, Birmingham (205)251-7148. TEAM program.
Lifeline Children's Services, 2908 Pump House Road, Birmingham (205)967-0811

ALASKA
State Agency: Alaska Department of Health and Social Services, Division of Family and Youth Services, Pouch H-05, Juneau 99811 (907)465-3631.
State Exchange: No
State Photolisting Book: No
Independent Adoption: Permitted
NACAC Representative: Pam Stratton, 1728 Logan, Anchorage 99504 (907)277-9627
Private Agencies:
Adoption Services of WACAP (see Washington)
Catholic Community Services, 529 Gold Street, Juneau (907)586-2534.
Catholic Social Services, 3925 Reka Drive, Anchorage (907)277-2554. Serves state.
Fairbanks Counseling and Adoption, P.O. Box 1544, Fairbanks (907)456-4729
Church of Jesus Christ Latter Day Saints (LDS) Social Services (see Washington). Serves state. Religious requirement.

ARIZONA
State Agency: Arizona Department of Economic Security, State Adoption Registry, 1717 West Jefferson Street, P.O. Box 6123, Phoenix 85005 (602)255-3981
State Exchange: Arizona State Adoption Registry (see above)
State Photolisting Book: *Arizona Adoption Exchange Book*
Independent Adoption: Permitted
NACAC Representative: Melanie James, 4704 South McAllister, Tempe 85282 (602)839-0756
Private Agencies:
Arizona Children's Home, 2700 South 8th Avenue, Tucson (602)622-7611
Catholic Social Service of Flagstaff, 9 West Cherry Street, Flagstaff (602)774-1911
Catholic Social Service of Phoenix, 1825 West Northern Avenue, Phoenix (602)-997-6105

Catholic Social Service of Tucson, 155 West Helen Street, Tucson (602)623-0344

Catholic Community Services of Yuma, 301 South Second Avenue, Yuma (602)-783-3308

Catholic Social Service Tri-City Agency, 610 East Southern, Mesa (602)964-8771

Catholic Social Services, Yavapai County, 533 West Gurley, Prescott (602)778-2531

Family Service of Phoenix, 1530 East Flower Street, Phoenix (602)264-9891

Globe International Adoptions, Inc., 6220 West Monte Vista Road, Phoenix (602)-247-3038

Jewish Family and Children's Service of Phoenix, 2033 North 7th Street, Phoenix (602)257-1904

Jewish Family Service of Tucson, 102 North Plumer Avenue, Tucson (602)792-3641

LDS Social Services, 235 South El Dorado, Mesa (602)968-2995

LDS Social Services, P.O. Box 856, Snowflake (602)536-4118

LDS Social Services, 2501 West Anklam Road, Tucson (602)822-0889.

ARKANSAS

State Agency: Arkansas Department of Human Services, Division of Social Services, Seventh and Main Streets, P.O. Box 1437, Little Rock 72203 (501)-371-2207. *Specialized unit:* Black Family Adoption Outreach, 1512 Izard, Little Rock (501)371-5526

State Exchange: No

State Photolisting Book: *Portfolio*

Independent Adoption: Permitted

NACAC Representative: Contact National Headquarters of NACAC.

Private Agencies:

Children's Home, Inc., 22 East 22, North Little Rock (501)758-9270. Serves state

Shady Acres Children's Home (see Missouri)

The Edna Gladney Home (see Texas)

Volunteers of America, Shreveport (see Louisiana)

CALIFORNIA

State Agency: Adoptions Branch, State Department of Social Services, 744 "P" Street, Sacramento 95814 (916)322-5973

State Exchange: Adoption Resource and Referral Center, State Department of Social Services, 744 "P" Street, Sacramento (916)323-0591

State Photolisting Book: *ARRC Album*

Independent Adoption: Permitted

NACAC Representative: Martha Shaw Howell, 14802 Delfbush, Sunnymead (714)656-5011

Private Agencies:

Adoption Horizons, P.O. Box 247, Arcata (707)822-2660

Adoptions Unlimited, 4479 Riverside Drive, Chino (714)591-0391

Aid to the Adoption of Special Kids (AASK), 3530 Grand Avenue, Oakland (415)-451-1748. Focuses on waiting children.

Bal Jagat, Inc., 9311 Farralone Avenue, Chatsworth (213)709-4337

Bethany Christian Services, 115D Mark Randy Place, Modesto (209)522-5121

Catholic Social Service of San Francisco, 2045 Lawton Street, San Francisco (415)665-5100

Children's Bureau of Los Angeles, 2824 Hyans Street, Los Angeles (213)384-2515

Children's Home Society of California, 5429 McConnell Avenue, Los Angeles (213)306-4654. Serves state. Branch offices.

Christian Adoption and Family Services, 17150 Norwalk Boulevard, Cerritos (213)-860-3766

Family Builders by Adoption, P.O. Box 9202, North Berkeley Station, Berkeley (415)531-5913. Part of the Family Builders Agency Network. Serves waiting children. No fees.

Family Connections, 1528 Oakdale Road, Modesto (209)524-8844

Holy Family Services, 357 South Westlake Avenue, Los Angeles (213)484-1441

Infant of Prague Adoption Service, 3520 East Ventura, Fresno (209)237-0851

LDS Social Services, 333 North Glenoaks Boulevard, Burbank (213)841-2640

LDS Social Services, 1003 E. Cooley Drive, Colton (714)824-5191

LDS Social Services, 37541 Blacow Road, Fremont (415)790-1800

LDS Social Services, 5171 East Illinois Avenue, Fresno (209)251-8077

LDS Social Services, 3000 Auburn Boulevard, Sacramento (916)971-3555

LDS Social Services, 5821 Lindo Paseo, San Diego (619)287-4410

Partners for Adoption, P.O. Box 2791, Santa Rosa (707)-578-0212

Sierra Adoption Services, Mount Saint Mary's School, Church and Chapel Streets, P.O. Box 361, Nevada City (916)272-3476

Vista Del Mar Child-Care Service, 3200 Motor Avenue, Los Angeles (213)836-1223. Open adoptions possible. Postadoption services.

For people interested in intercountry adoption, the Department of Social Services offers an excellent and thorough handbook of general information, *Intercountry Adoption in California and Abroad.* It was created because "persons considering intercountry adoption have a right to accurate information about these adoptions and the processes involved. Such information will help them make informed decisions about initiating and completing such an adoption, the kind of child they can best parent, and whether they want to make the lifetime commitment required."

COLORADO

State Agency: State Department of Social Services, 1575 Sherman Street, Denver 80203 (303)866-5270

State Exchanges: Colorado State Pool, Colorado Adoption Resource Registry (see above)

Photolisting Book: *Colorado Adoption Resource Registry* (CARR book)

Independent Adoption: Permitted/no intermediaries

NACAC **Representative:** Violet Pierce, 6660 South Race Circle West, Littleton 80121 (303)795-2890

Private Agencies:

Adoption Option, 7529 West 5th Avenue, Lakewood (303)233-2463. Uses TEAM home-study concept.

Bethany Christian Services, 2150 South Bellaire, Denver (303)758-4484. Serves state. Religious requirement. Places infants.

Catholic Community Services, Social Services of Pueblo United, 302 Jefferson, Pueblo (303)544-4234

Christian Home for Children, Inc., 6 West Cheyenne Road, Colorado Springs (303)632-4661

Colorado Baptist Family Services, 1653 York Road, Colorado Springs (303)598-1101. Serves state. Religious requirement.

Colorado Christian Service, 4796 South Broadway, Englewood (303)761-7236. Serves state. Religious requirement.

Denver Catholic Community Services, 200 Josephine Street, Denver (303)388-4411

Family Builders by Adoption, 5800 Cody Court, Arvada (303)425-1667. Part of Family Builders Agency Network. Serves waiting children. No fees.

FCVN, 600 Gilpin Street, Denver (303)321-8251

Hand in Hand International, 4965 Barnes Road, Colorado Springs (303)596-1588

Jewish Family and Children's Service of Colorado, 300 South Dahlia Street, Denver (303)321-3115.

LDS Social Services, 9590 West 14 Avenue, Lakewood (303)238-8169

Lutheran Social Services of Colorado, 2695 Alcott Street, Denver (303)433-6371

Methodist Mission Home of Texas (see Texas)

Youth Behavior Program, Inc., P.O. Box 2764, Evergreen (303)674-1910

The parent group, Colorado Parents for All Children (c/o Leslie Coffman, 9625 West 35th Avenue, Wheatridge), has put out an informative booklet, *How to Adopt in Colorado.*

CONNECTICUT

State Agency: Department of Children and Youth Services, Centralized Home-finding-Recruitment and Training Unit, 170 Sigourney Street, Hartford 06105 (203)566-8742 or in Ct: (800)842-6348

State Exchange: Connecticut Adoption Resource Exchange (see above)

State Photolisting Book: CARE book

Independent Adoption: Not permitted

NACAC **Representative:** Linda Cotter, 73 Mather Street, Manchester 06040 (203)-649-8115

Private Agencies:

Casey Family Program East, 102 Bank Street, Bridgeport (203)334-6991 and 60 Lorraine Street, Hartford (203)233-9643

Catholic Charities, Inc., Diocese of Norwich, 11 Bath Street, Norwich (203)889-8346

Catholic Family and Community Service, 238 Jewett Avenue, Bridgeport (203)-372-4301

Catholic Family Services, Archdiocese of Hartford, 896 Asylum Avenue, Hartford (203)522-8241

Child and Family Agency of Southeastern Connecticut, Inc., 255 Hempstead Street, New London (203)443-2896

Child and Family Services, Inc., 1680 Albany Avenue, Hartford (203)236-4511

The Children's Center, 1400 Whitney Avenue, Hamden (203)248-2116

Chosen Children Adoption Services (see Kentucky)

Family and Children's Aid of Greater Norwalk, Inc., 138 Main Street, Norwalk (203)846-4203

Family and Children's Services, Inc., 60 Palmer's Hill Road, Stamford (203)324-3167

The Family Life Center, 79 Birch Hill, Weston (203)222-1468

Family Service, Inc., 92 Vine Street, New Britain (203)223-9291. Serves state.

Franciscan Life Center, Finch Avenue, Meriden (203)237-8084. Serves state.

The Edna Gladney Home (see Texas)

International Adoptions, Inc. (see Massachusetts)

International Alliance for Children, 23 South Main Street, New Milford (203)354-3417

Jewish Family Service, Inc., 2370 Park Avenue, Bridgeport (203)366-5438

Jewish Family Service of Greater Hartford, 740 North Main Street, West Hartford (203)236-1927

Jewish Family Service of New Haven, Inc., 152 Temple Street, New Haven (203)-777-6641. Serves state.

LDS Social Services (see New Hampshire)

Lutheran Service Association of New England, Inc., 74 Sherman Street, Hartford (203)236-0679. Serves state.

Professional Counseling Center, 79 South Benson Road, Fairfield (203)335-7666

Thursday's Child, Inc., 227 Tunxis Avenue, Bloomfield (203)242-5491

DELAWARE

State Agency: Division of Child Protective Services, 1901 North DuPont Highway, New Castle 19720 (302)421-6786

State Exchange: No

State Photolisting Book: *Delaware Children Needing Homes*

Independent Adoption: Not permitted

NACAC Representative: Nancy McKenna, 24 Arthur Drive, R.D. 1, Hockessin, Delaware 19707 (302)239-7340

Private Agencies:

Catholic Social Service of Delaware, 1200 North Broom Street, Wilmington (302)-655-9624

Child and Home Study Associates, 101 Stone Crop Road, Wilmington

Children's Bureau of Delaware, 2005 Baynard Boulevard, Wilmington (302)658-5177. Serves state.

LDS Social Services (see Maryland)
Methodist Board of Child Care (see Maryland)

DISTRICT OF COLUMBIA
Public Agency: Adoption and Placement Resources Branch, Department of Human Services, 500 First Street N.W., Washington 20001 (202)727-3161
Exchange: No
Photolisting Book: No
Independent Adoption: Permitted
NACAC Representative: Contact National office.
Private Agencies:
Adoption Service Information Agency (ASIA), 7720 Alaska Avenue N.W., Washington (202)726-7193
American Adoption Agency, 1611 Connecticut Avenue N.W., Washington (202)-797-3756
The Barker Foundation, 4545 42nd Street N.W. (202)363-7751. Places infants.
Catholic Charities–Archdiocese of District of Columbia, 2800 Otis Street N.E. (202)526-4100
Children's Adoption Resource Exchange, 1039 Evarts Street, N.E., Washington (202)526-5200. Focuses on special-needs children.
Family and Child Services of Washington, D.C., 929 "L" Street N.W. (202)289-1510. Special program: Homes for Black Children.
International Adoption Agency, 1100 17th Street N.W., Washington (202)466-2088
Lutheran Social Services of the National Capital Area, 2635 16th Street N.W. (202)232-6373. Serves metropolitan Washington.
Peirce-Warwick Adoption Service, 5229 Connecticut Avenue N.W., Washington (202)966-2531. Part of Family Builders Agency Network. Serves waiting children. No fees. Serves metropolitan Washington.
Saint Sophia Greek Orthodox Adoption Services, 3601 Massachusetts Avenue N.W., Washington (202)333-4730
World Child, Inc., 2000 "K" Street N.W., Washington (202)429-8885

FLORIDA
State Agency: Department of Health and Rehabilitative Services, Children, Youth and Families, 1317 Winewood Boulevard, Tallahassee 32301 (904)488-1060
State Exchange: Florida Adoption Exchange (see above)
State Photolisting Book: *Florida's Waiting Children*
Independent Adoption: Permitted
NACAC Representative: Debbie Griggs, 209 McVay Drive, Sanford 32771 (305)-321-1061
Private Agencies:
Catholic Charities Bureau, P.O. Box 14375, Gainesville (904)372-0294
Catholic Charities Bureau, P.O. Box 8161, Jacksonville (904)725-6911
Catholic Charities Bureau, 218 East Government Street, Pensacola (904)438-8564

Catholic Charities Bureau, P.O. Box 543, St. Augustine (904)829-6300
Catholic Community Services, 1300 South Andrews Avenue, Ft. Lauderdale (305)-522-2513
Catholic Service Bureau, Inc., 1010 Windsor Lane, Key West (305)296-8032
Catholic Social Service, 3190 Davis Blvd., Naples (813)774-6483
Catholic Social Services, 319 Riveredge Boulevard, Cocoa (305)636-6144
Catholic Social Services, Inc., 40 Beal Parkway S.W., Ft. Walton Beach (904)-244-2825
Catholic Social Services, Inc., 215 Lemon East, Lakeland (813)686-7153
Catholic Social Services, 3191 Maguire Boulevard, #135, Orlando (305)894-8888
Catholic Social Services, 714 North Cove Boulevard, Panama City (904)763-0475
Catholic Social Services, 6533 Ninth Avenue North, St. Petersburg (813)345-9126
Catholic Social Services, Sterling Avenue, Tampa (813)870-6220
Catholic Social Services, 532 Avenue "M" N.W., Winter Haven (813)299-7983
The Children's Home, Inc., 10909 Memorial Highway, Tampa (813)855-4435
Children's Home Society, 3027 San Diego Road, Jacksonville (904)396-2641.
    Serves state. Branch offices throughout state. Utilizes TEAM program.
Christian Family Services, 2720 Southwest Second Avenue, Gainesville (904)-378-1471
Christian Home and Bible School, P.O. Box 1017, Mt. Dora (904)383-2155
Florida Baptist Children's Home, P.O. Box 1653, Lakeland (813)687-8811
Florida United Methodist Children's Home, P.O. Box 8, Enterprise (305)668-4486
Jewish Family and Children's Services, Inc., 1416 LaSalle Street, Jacksonville
    (904)396-2941
Jewish Family and Children's Services, Inc., 1790 Southwest 27th Avenue, Miami
    (305)445-0555
Jewish Family and Children's Services, 2411 Okeechobee Boulevard, West Palm
    Beach (305)684-1991
Jewish Family Services, Inc., of Broward County, 4517 Hollywood Boulevard,
    Hollywood (305)966-0956
LDS Social Services, 2300 Maitland Center Parkway, Maitland (305)660-2471
Project CAN, Family Service Centers, 2960 Roosevelt Boulevard, Clearwater
    (813)531-0481. Part of Family Builders Agency Network. Serves waiting chil-
    dren. No fees.
Slaughter Cottage, Route 1, Box 149, Wildwood
Suncoast International Adoptions, Inc., 1016 Ponce de Leon Boulevard, Belleaire
    (813)586-5015(813)855-4435
United Family and Children's Services, 2190 Northwest 7th Street, Miami (305)-643-5700
United Methodist Children's Home, 4711 Scenic Highway, Pensacola (904)433-1790
Universal Aid for Children, Inc., 1175 Northeast 125th Street, Suite 202, North
    Miami 33161 (305)893-1535

GEORGIA

State Agency: Georgia Department of Human Resources, Family and Children's Services, 878 Peachtree N.E., Atlanta 30309 (404)894-5294

State Exchange: Georgia State Adoption Exchange (see above; telephone: 404-894-2641)

State Photolisting Book: *Be My Parent*

Independent Adoption: Permitted

NACAC Representative: Elizabeth Rowe, 1041 Oakdale Road N.E., Atlanta 30307 (404)378-5358

Private Agencies:

Child Service and Family Counseling Center, Inc., 1105 West Peachtree Street N.E., Atlanta (404)873-6916

Children's Services International, 3098 Piedmont Road N.E., Atlanta (404)261-6992

Georgia Association for Guidance, Aid, Placement and Empathy, Inc., 790 Church Street, Smyrna (404)432-0063

Illien Adoptions International Ltd., 1254 Piedmont Avenue, Atlanta (404)872-6787

Jewish Family and Children's Bureau, 1753 Peachtree Road N.E., Atlanta (404)-873-2277

LDS Social Services, 4843 North Royal Atlanta Drive, Tucker (404)493-7795

Parent and Child Development Services, 312 East 39th Street, Savannah (912)-232-2390. Utilizes TEAM program.

HAWAII

State Agency: Department of Social Services and Housing, Family and Children's Services, P.O. Box 339, Honolulu 96809 (808)548-2211

State Exchange: No

State Photolisting Book: No

Independent Adoption: Permitted

NACAC Representative: Contact National Office at NACAC.

Private Agencies:

Catholic Social Services, 250 South Vineyard Street, Honolulu (808)537-6321

Child and Family Service, 200 North Vineyard Boulevard, Honolulu (808)521-2377

Hawaii International Children Placement, P.O. Box 13, Hawi (808)889-5122

LDS Social Services, 1500 South Beretania Street, Honolulu (808)945-3233

Liliuokalani Children's Center, 1300 Halona Street, Honolulu (808)847-1302

IDAHO

State Agency: Department of Health and Welfare, Division of Adoption, Statehouse Mail, Boise 83720 (208)334-4085

State Exchange: Idaho Adoption Exchange (see above)

State Photolisting Book: No

Independent Adoption: Permitted

NACAC Representative: Susan Smith, North 3431 Pleasant Lane, Post Falls 83854 (208)773-5629

Private Agencies:

Adoption Services of WACAP (see Washington)

Adoptions in Idaho, Adoption Agency, Inc., P.O. Box 742, Post Falls (208)773-0526. Serves state.

LDS Social Services, 1010 North Orchard, Boise (208)376-0191

LDS Social Services, 255 Overland Avenue, Burley (208)678-8200

LDS Social Services, 1420 East 17th Street, Idaho Falls (208)522-0061

LDS Social Services, 920 Deon Drive, Pocatello (208)323-7780

North Idaho Children's Home Adoption Services, P.O. Box 319, Lewiston (208)-743-9404

ILLINOIS

State Agency: Department of Children and Family Services, Office of Adoptions, 510 North Dearborn Street, Chicago. However, for all adoption information, contact the state exchange (see below).

State Exchange: Adoption Information Center of Illinois, 201 North Wells Street, Suite 1342, Chicago 60606 (312)346-1516 or, in state, (800)572-2390

State Photolisting Book: *Adoption Listing Service*

Independent Adoption: Permitted

NACAC **Representative:** Barbara Hearn, 515 West Maple Street, Hinsdale 60521 (312)323-0530

Private Agencies:

The Baby Fold, 108 East Willow Street, Normal (309)452-1170

Bensenville Home Society, 331 South York Road, Bensenville (312)766-5800

Bethany Home, 220 11th Avenue, Moline (309)797-7700

Catholic Charities of Chicago, 126 North Des Plaines, Chicago (312)236-5172

Catholic Charities of Lake County, 1 North Genessen, Waukegan (312)249-3500

Catholic Charities–Joliet Diocese, 411 Scott Street, Joliet (815)723-3405

Catholic Social Service, Diocese of Belleville, 220 West Lincoln Street, Belleville (618)277-9200

Catholic Social Services, 413 North East Monroe Street, Peoria (309)671-5700

Catholic Social Services, 921 West Galena Boulevard, Aurora (312)892-4366

Catholic Social Services–Springfield Diocese, 108 East Cook Street, Springfield (217)523-4551

Central Baptist Family Services, 201 North Wells, Chicago (312)782-0874

Chicago Child Care Society, 5467 South University Avenue, Chicago (312)643-0452. Primarily places black children.

The Children's Home, 2130 North Knoxville, Peoria (309)685-1047

Children's Home and Aid Society of Illinois, 1002 College Avenue, Alton (618)-462-2714

Children's Home and Aid Society of Illinois, 1122 North Dearborn, Chicago (312)-944-3313. Serves state. Branch offices. Special office: Homes Now for Black Children, 2151 West 95 Street, Chicago (312)238-3203

Children's Home and Aid Society of Illinois, 730 North Main Street, Rockford (815)962-1043

Counseling and Family Service, 1821 North Knoxville Avenue, Peoria (309)685-5287

The Cradle Society, 2049 Ridge Avenue, Evanston (312)475-5800. Places infants.

Evangelical Child and Family Agency, 1530 North Main Street, Wheaton (312)-653-6400

Family Care Services of Metropolitan Chicago, 234 South Wabash Avenue, Chicago (312)427-8790. Focuses on waiting children.

Family Counseling Clinic, Inc., 19300 West Highway 120, Grayslake (312)223-8107

Family Service Center of Sangamon County, 1308 South 7th Street, Springfield (217)528-8406

Family Service of Decatur, 151 East Decatur Street, Decatur (217)429-5216

Jewish Children's Bureau of Chicago, 1 South Franklin, Chicago. Serves state. Religious requirement.

Lake/Bluff/Chicago Homes for Children, 1661 North Northwest Highway, Park Ridge (312)298-1610.

LDS Social Services, 1809 North Mill Street, Suite H, Naperville (312)369-0486

Lutheran Child and Family Services, 7620 Madison Street, P.O. Box 186, River Forest (312)287-4848 (Chicago) and (312)771-7180 (suburban). Serves state. Part of Family Builders Agency Network. Serves waiting children. No fees.

Lutheran Social Services of Illinois, 4840 West Byron Street, Chicago (312)282-7800. Serves state. Branch offices.

St. Mary's Services, 5725 North Kenmore Avenue, Chicago (312)561-5288. Places infants.

Sunny Ridge Family Center, 2 South 426 Orchard Road, Wheaton (312)668-5117. Serves state. Places infants.

Travelers and Immigrants Aid, 327 South LaSalle Street, Room 1500, Chicago (372)435-4561

The Junior League of Chicago, Inc. (1447 North Astor Street, Chicago), has produced an informative handbook, *Adoption: A Guide to Adoption in Illinois*, 1981. It provides detailed information about Illinois agencies and their requirements.

INDIANA

State Agency: Department of Public Welfare, Child Welfare–Social Services Division, 141 South Meridian Street, Indianapolis 46225 (317)232-5613

State Exchange: Indiana Adoption Resource Exchange

State Photolisting Book: *Indiana Adoption Resource Exchange*

Independent Adoption: Permitted/court must waive agency approval prior to placement.

NACAC Representative: Bonnie Henson, 0516 East 400th Street, La Porte 46350 (219)393-3259

Private Agencies:

Adoptions Unlimited, Inc., 218 South 3rd Street, Elkhart (219)295-8985

Baptist Children's Home and Family Ministries, 354 West Street, Valparaiso (219)-462-4111. Serves state. Religious requirement. Places out of state.

Catholic Charities Bureau, 603 Court Building, Evansville (812)423-5456

Catholic Charities–Diocese of Lafayette, 100 North Street, Kokomo (317)457-1172. Places infants.

Catholic Family Service, 524 Franklin Street, Michigan City (219)879-9312

Catholic Social Services, 919 Fairfield Avenue, Fort Wayne (219)422-7511

Catholic Social Services, 120 South Taylor Street, South Bend (219)234-3111

Catholic Social Services of Lake and Porter County, 5252 Hohman Avenue, Hammond (219)933-0696

Children's Bureau of Indianapolis, Inc., 615 North Alabama Street, Indianapolis (317)634-6481. Utilizes TEAM program.

Chosen Children Adoption Services, Inc., 305 Bank Street, New Albany (812)-945-6021

Family and Children's Service, 305 South Third Avenue, Evansville (812)425-5181. Places infants.

Homes for Black Children, 3131 East 38th Street, Indianapolis (317)545-5281. Serves state. Seeks to find homes for black children. Recruitment of black families. Everyone considered.

Jewish Family and Children's Services, 1717 West 86th Street, Indianapolis (317)-872-6641

LDS Social Services, 51515 West 84th Street, Indianapolis (317)875-0046

LDS Social Services, 100 West Court Avenue, Jeffersonville (812)288-9779

Lutheran Child and Family Services, 1525 North Ritter, Indianapolis (317)359-5467. Serves state.

Lutheran Family Services of Northwest Indiana, 7101 Broadway, Merrillville (219)-769-3521

Lutheran Social Services, 330 Madison Street, Fort Wayne (219)426-3347

St. Elizabeth's Home, 2500 Churchman Avenue, Indianapolis (317)787-3412. Serves state.

Shults-Lewis Children and Family Services, P.O. Box 471, Valparaiso (219)462-0513. Religious requirement.

South Central Christian Children's Home, Inc., 2420 Highway 62, Jeffersonville (812)282-8248. Serves state. Religious requirement.

Suemma Coleman Agency, 1100 West 42nd Street, Indianapolis (317)926-3891. Serves state. Places infants.

The Villages, Inc., P.O. Box 994, Bedford (812)275-7539.

IOWA

State Agency: Iowa Department of Social Services, Hoover Building, Des Moines 50319 (515)281-5658 or 281-6074

State Exchange: Iowa Adoption Exchange

State Photolisting Book: *Iowa's Waiting Children*

Independent Adoption: Permitted

NACAC **Representative:** Beverly Chartier, R.R. 1, Prole 50229 (515)462-3428

Private Agencies:

American Home Finding Association, 217 East 5th, Ottumwa (515)682-3449

Bethany Christian Services, 322 Central Avenue N.W., Orange City (712)737-4831. Serves state. Religious requirement.

Catholic Charities of Dubuque, 1229 Mt. Loretta Street, Dubuque (319)556-2580

Catholic Charities of Sioux City, 1812 Jackson Street, Sioux City (712)252-4547

Catholic Social Services–Des Moines Diocese, 818 5th Avenue, Des Moines (515)-244-3761

Children's Home of Cedar Rapids, 2309 "C" Street Southwest, Cedar Rapids (319)365-9164

Family and Children's Services, 115 West 6th Street, Davenport (319)323-1852

Florence Crittenton Home, 1105 28th Street, Sioux City, Iowa (712)255-4321

Hillcrest Family Services, 1727 First Avenue S.E., Cedar Rapids (319)362-3149. Serves state.

Iowa Children's & Family Services, 1101 Walnut, Des Moines (515)288-1981. Serves state.

Jewish Family Services, 910 Polk Boulevard, Des Moines (515)277-6321

Keys to Living, 5300 North Park Place N.E., Cedar Rapids (319)373-1301

Lutheran Family Service, 230 9th Avenue North, Fort Dodge (515)573-3138. Serves state.

Lutheran Social Services of Iowa, 3116 University Avenue, Des Moines (515)-277-4476. Serves state. Branch offices.

KANSAS

State Agency: Division of Children in Need of Care, State Department of Social and Rehabilitation Services, 2700 West 6th Street, Topeka 66606 (913)-296-4661

State Exchange: (see above)

State Photolisting Book: No

Independent Adoption: Permitted/no intermediaries

NACAC **Representative:** Contact National office of NACAC.

Private Agencies:

Adult and Child Services Assoc., Inc., 445 North Dellrose, Wichita (316)681-3840

Catholic Charities–Diocese of Kansas City, 229 South 8th, Kansas City (913)-621-1504

Catholic Charities–Diocese of Salina, 137 North 9th Street, Salina (913)825-0208

Catholic Social Services, 2546 20th Street, Great Bend (316)792-1393

Catholic Social Services, P.O. Box 659, Wichita (913)264-8344

Christian Family Services, Inc., 10300 Antioch, Overland Park (913)383-2456. Serves state.

Family and Children's Services of Kansas City, Inc., 63 West 95th, Overland Park (913)642-4300

Highlands Child Placement Services (see Missouri)

Jewish Family and Children's Services, Inc. (see Missouri)

Lutheran Social Services, 1855 North Hillside, Wichita (316)686-6645. Serves
state.
Kansas Children's Service League, P.O. Box 517, Wichita (316)942-4261. Serves
state. Focuses on special needs.
LDS Social Services (see Missouri)
Lutheran Social Services (see Oklahoma)
St. Vincent's Home, 1800 Stone, Topeka (913)272-4950. Serves state. Places
older and special-needs children.
Spaulding Midwest, 1855 North Hillside, Wichita (316)686-9171. Part of Family
Builders Agency Network. Serves waiting children. No fee.
The Villages, Inc., 2209 West 29th, Topeka (913)267-5900

KENTUCKY
State Agency: Cabinet for Human Resources, Bureau for Social Services, 275
East Main Street, Frankfort 40601 (502)564-2136
State Exchange: Kentucky Adoption Resource Exchange; contact also Special
Needs Adoption Program; in-state (800)432-9346
State Photolisting Book: *Kentucky's Special Needs Adoption Program* (SNAP)
Independent Adoption: Permitted
NACAC **Representative:** Contact National office of NACAC.
Private Agencies:
Catholic Charities Agency, 2911 South 4th Street, Louisville (502)637-9786
Catholic Social Services, 3629 Church Street, Covington (606)581-8974
Chosen Children Adoption Services, 4010 Dupont Circle, Louisville (502)897-
0318. Places infants.
Christian Church Children's Center, P.O. Box 45, Danville 40422 (606)236-5507
Jewish Family Services (see Ohio)
Kentucky Baptist Home for Children, 10801 Shelbyville Road, Middletown (502)-
245-2101
Hope Hill Children's Home, Inc., Hope
LDS Social Services (see Ohio)
Lutheran Social Services of the Miami Valley (see Ohio)
Midwestern Children's Home (see Ohio)
SUMA (see Ohio)

LOUISIANA
State Agency: Louisiana Department of Health and Human Resources, Office of
Human Development, Division of Evaluations and Services, Adoption Pro-
grams, 333 Laurel Street, Baton Rouge 70502 (504)342-4040
State Exchange: Louisiana Adoption Resource Exchange (LARE), P.O. Box
3318, Baton Rouge (504)342-4041
State Photolisting Book: LARE
Independent Adoption: Permitted

258   DOMESTIC ADOPTION DIRECTORY

NACAC **Representative:** Royann Avegno, 9500 Abel Lane, Riverridge 70186
(504)737-7778

Private Agencies:

Associated Catholic Charities of New Orleans, Inc., 1231 Prytania Street, New
Orleans (504)523-3755

Catholic Charities, Diocese of Alexandria-Shreveport, P.O. Box 5003, 2417 Texas
Avenue, Alexandria (318)445-2401

Catholic Community Life Office of Catholic Social Services, Inc., P.O. Box 1668,
Baton Rouge (504)344-0427

Catholic Community Services, 3718 Uree Drive, Shreveport (318)869-3241

Catholic Social Services, 1220 Aycock Street, P.O. Box 883, Houma (504)876-
0490

Catholic Social Services of the Diocese of Lafayette, Louisiana, Inc., 1408 Carmel
Drive, Lafayette (318)235-5218

Children's Bureau of New Orleans, 226 Carondelet, New Orleans (504)525-2366.
Serves state.

Jewish Children's Regional Service of Jewish Children's Home, 5342 St. Charles
Avenue, P.O. Box 15225, New Orleans (504)899-1595.

Jewish Family and Children's Services, Inc., 2026 St. Charles Avenue, New Orleans (504)524-8475. Places infants.

Latter Day Saints Social Services, 2000 Old Spanish Trail, Pratt Center, Slidell
(504)649-2774. Religious requirement.

Louisiana Child Care and Placement Services, Inc., 9080 Southwood Drive,
Shreveport (318)686-2243

Lutheran Social Services of the South, Inc., 4430 Bundy Road, New Orleans
(504)241-1337

Protestant Home for Babies, 1233 Eighth Street, New Orleans (504)895-0920

Sellers Baptist Home and Adoption Center, 2010 Peniston Street, New Orleans
(504)895-2088. Religious requirement.

Volunteers of America, 3720 Prytania Street, New Orleans (504)895-7791

Volunteers of America, 354 Jordan Street, Shreveport (318)221-2669

MAINE

State Agency: Department of Human Services, Bureau of Social Services, 221
State Street, Augusta 04333 (207)289-2971 or in Maine (800)452-4640

State Exchange: The Maine-Vermont Exchange

State Photolisting Book: *The Maine-Vermont Exchange*

Independent Adoption: Permitted/no intermediaries

NACAC **Representative:** Judy Collier, 281 Parkmur Avenue, Bangor 04411 (207)-
947-3178

Private Agencies:

Community Counseling Center, 622 Congress Street, Portland (207)799-7339

Good Samaritan Agency, 160 Broadway, Bangor (207)942-7211

Growing-Thru-Adoption, P.O. Box 7082, Lewiston (207)786-2597. Serves Maine except Aroostook and Washington counties.

International Christian Adoption Agency, 60 West River Road, Waterville (207)-872-2156. Serves state.

Maine Adoption Placement Services, P.O. Box 772, Houlton (207)532-9358

The Maine Children's Home for Little Wanderers, 34 Gilman Street, Waterville (207)873-4253. Serves state except Aroostook and York.

St. Andre Home, Inc., 283 Elm Street, Biddeford (207)282-3351. Serves state. Places infants and toddlers.

MARYLAND

State Agency: Maryland Adoption Resource Exchange, Social Services Administration, 300 West Preston Street, Baltimore 21201 (301)576-5313

State Exchange: Maryland Adoption Resource Exchange (see above)

State Photolisting Book: *Maryland Adoption Resource Exchange*

Independent Adoption: Permitted/no intermediaries

NACAC Representative: Sherry Simas, 6902 Nashville Road, Lanham 20706 (301)551-1888

Private Agencies:

Adoption Associates, Inc., 300 East Joppa Road, Towson (301)296-6334. Serves state.

American Adoption Agency (see District of Columbia)

Associated Catholic Charities, 320 Cathedral Street, Baltimore (301)547-5508. Serves state.

Barker Foundation (see District of Columbia)

Church of Christ Children's Home (see Virginia)

Bethany Christian Services, 114 Annapolis Street, Annapolis (301)263-7703. Places infants. Serves state. Religious requirements.

Family and Children's Society, 204 West Lanvale Street, Baltimore (301)669-9000. Has done identified adoptions.

Jewish Family and Children's Service, 5750 Park Heights Avenue, Baltimore (301)-466-9200

Jewish Social Service Agency, 6123 Montrose Road, Rockville (301)881-3700

LDS Social Services, 198 Thomas Jefferson Drive, Frederick (301)428-4988. Religious requirement.

Lutheran Social Services of National Capital Area (see District of Columbia)

Maryland Children's Aid and Family Service Society, 303 West Chesapeake Avenue, Towson (301)825-3700

Methodist Board of Child Care, 3300 Gaither Road, Baltimore (301)922-2100. Serves state.

Peirce-Warwick Adoption Service (see District of Columbia)

MASSACHUSETTS

State Agency: Department of Social Services, 150 Causeway Street, Boston 02114 (617)727-0900

State Exchange: Massachusetts Adoption Resource Exchange, 25 West Street, Boston (617)451-1460 or in Massachusetts (800)882-1176 or (617) 451-1472

State Photolisting Book: MARE Manual

Independent Adoption: Not permitted

NACAC **Representative:** Mary Lou Robinson, 96 Rick Drive, Florence 01060 (413)584-8459

Private Agencies:

Alliance for Children, P.O. Box 557, Needham (617)449-1277

Berkshire Center for Families and Children, 472 West Street, Pittsfield (413)-448-8281. Places infants.

Boston Adoption Bureau, Inc., 14 Beacon Street, Boston (617)227-1336

Boston Children's Service Association, 867 Boylston Street, Boston (617)267-3700. Does legal-risk adoptions.

Cambridge Adoption and Counseling Associates, Inc., P.O. Box 190, Cambridge (617)491-6245. Serves state.

Cambridge Family and Children's Service, 99 Bishop Richard Allen Drive, Cambridge (617)876-4210

Catholic Charitable Bureau, 49 Franklin Street, Boston (617)523-5165. Does legal-risk adoptions.

Catholic Charities Center, 430 North Canal Street, Lawrence (617)685-5930

Catholic Charities Center, 70 Lawrence Street, Lowell (617)452-1421

Catholic Charities Centre of Old Colony Area, 686 North Main Street, Brockton (617)587-0815

Catholic Charities–Diocese of Worcester, Inc., 15 Ripley Street, Worcester (617)-798-0191

Catholic Charities, Family and Children's Services, 79 Elm Street, Southbridge (617)765-5936

Catholic Charities, Family and Children's Services, 16 Main Street, Uxbridge (617)-278-2424

Catholic Family Services of Greater Lynn, 55 Lynn Shore Drive, Lynn (617)593-2312

Catholic Social Services of Fall River, Inc., 783 Slade Street, Fall River (617)-674-4681

Children's Aid and Family Service, 47 Holt Street, Fitchburg (617)345-4147

Children's Aid and Family Service, 8 Trumbull Road, Northampton (413)584-5690

Concord Family Service, Old Road to 9 Acre Corner, Concord (617)369-4909

DARE, 3 Monument Square, Beverly (617)927-1674

Downey Side, Inc., 999 Liberty Street, Springfield (413)781-2123. Places adolescents.

ECHO, 29 Devonshire Road, Cheshire (413)743-9240

Family and Children's Service of Greater Lynn, Inc., 111 North Common Street, Lynn (617)598-5517

Family Service Association of Greater Lawrence, 430 North Canal Street, Lawrence (617)683-9505. Places infants.

Fitchburg Family and Children's Service, 53 Highland Avenue, Fitchburg (617)-422-6718

Florence Crittenton League, 201 Thorndike Street, Lowell (617)452-9671. Intercountry adoption programs.

International Adoptions, Inc., 218 Walnut Street, Newton (617)965-2320. Serves state. Has done identified adoptions. Intercountry adoption programs.

Italian Home for Children, 1125 Centre Street, Jamaica Plain (617)524-3116

Jewish Family and Children's Service, 31 New Chardon Street, Boston (617)-227-6641. Will do identified adoptions.

Jewish Family Service, 646 Salisbury Street, Worcester (617)755-3101

Jewish Family Service of the North Shore, 564 Loring Avenue, Salem (617)-745-9760. Serves state.

Jewish Family Services, 184 Mill Street, Springfield (413)737-2601

Nazareth Child Care Center, 420 Pond Street, Jamaica Plain (617)522-4040

New Bedford Child and Family Service, 141 Page Street, New Bedford (617)-996-8572. Does legal-risk adoptions.

New England Home for Little Wanderers, 161 South Huntington Avenue, Boston (617)232-8600. Places special-needs children.

North Shore Catholic Charities Centre, 3 Margin Street, Peabody (617)532-3600

Our Lady of Providence Center, 2112 Riverdale Street, West Springfield (413)-788-7366

Project IMPACT, 25 West Street, Boston (617)451-1472. Part of Family Builders Agency Network. Serves waiting children.

Protestant Social Service Bureau, Inc., 776 Hancock Street, Quincy (617)773-6203. Does legal-risk adoptions.

Roxbury Children's Service, 22 Elm Hill Avenue, Roxbury (617)445-6655. Serves state.

Southeastern Adoption Services, P.O. Box 356, Marion (617)748-2979

Worcester Children's Friend Society, 21 Cedar Street, Worcester (617)753-5425

World Adoption Services, Inc., 161 Auburn, Newton (617)332-3307

The Open Door Society of Massachusetts, Inc. (25 West Street, Boston 02111), has produced an informative booklet, *Adoption Today,* (1982) which is a general guide to adoption as well as a close look at adoption in Massachusetts.

MICHIGAN
State Agency: Michigan Department of Social Services, Office of Children and Youth Services, 300 South Capitol Avenue, P.O. Box 30037, Lansing 48909 (517)373-3513

State Exchange: Michigan Adoption Resource Exchange (see above)

State Photolisting Book: MARE

Independent Adoption: Not permitted

NACAC Representative: Edie Hoyle, 1222 Broadway, Bay City 48706 (517)892-4776

Private Agencies:

Americans for International Aid and Adoption, 877 South Adams, Birmingham (313)645-2211

Bethany Christian Services, 6995 West 48th, Box 173, Fremont (616)924-3390

Bethany Christian Services, 901 Eastern Avenue N.E., Grand Rapids (616)459-6273 or nationwide (800)-BETHANY.

Bethany Christian Services, 135 North State Street, Zeeland (616)772-9195

Bethany International Adoptions, 32500 Concord, Suite 353-West, Madison Heights (313)588-9400

Catholic Family Service of Bay City, 1008 South Senona, Bay City (517)892-2504

Catholic Family Service of the Thumb Area, 592 North Port Crescent, Bad Axe (517)269-7931

Catholic Family Services, 1819 Gull Road, Kalamazoo (616)381-9800

Catholic Family Services, Diocese of Saginaw, 710 North Michigan, Saginaw (517)753-8446

Catholic Social Services, 117 North Division Street, Ann Arbor (313)662-4534

Catholic Social Services, 202 East Boulevard Drive, Flint (313)232-9950

Catholic Social Services, 300 North Washington, Lansing (517)372-4020

Catholic Social Services, 347 Rock Street, Marquette (906)228-8630

Catholic Social Services, 6 South Monroe Street, Monroe (313)242-3800

Catholic Social Services, 235 Gratiot Avenue, Mt. Clemens (313)468-2616

Catholic Social Services, 313 West Webster Avenue, Muskegon (616)726-4735

Catholic Social Services, 2601 13th Street, Port Huron (313)987-9100

Catholic Social Services of Wayne County, 9851 Hamilton, Detroit (313)883-2100

Catholic Social Services of the Diocese of Grand Rapids, 300 Commerce Building, Grand Rapids (616)456-1443

Catholic Social Services of Oakland County, 29625 Inkster Road, Farmington Hill (313)851-7180

Child and Family Service of Bay County, Van Buren Street, Bay City (517)895-5932

Child and Family Service of Saginaw County, 1226 N.W. Michigan Street, Saginaw (517)753-8491

Child and Family Service of Washtenaw County, 2301 Platt Road, Ann Arbor (313)971-6520

Child and Family Services of Michigan, Inc., 3075 East Grand Avenue, Brighton (517)546-7530. Serves state. Branch offices.

Child and Family Services and Muskegon Children's Home, 202 Frauenthal Building, Muskegon (616)726-3582

Children's Aid and Family Service of Macomb County, Inc., 57 Church Street, Mt. Clemens (313)468-2656

Children's Aid Society, 7700 Second Avenue, Detroit (313)875-0020

Community, Family and Children Services, Diocese of Gaylord, 1000 Hastings Street, Traverse City (616)947-8110. Has used open adoptions.

Christian Family Services, 17105 West 12 Mile Road, Southfield (313)557-6420

The Cradle Society (see Illinois). Serves Detroit

D. A. Blodgett Homes for Children, 805 Leonard Street N.E., Grand Rapids (616)-451-2021

Family and Child Services of the Capitol Area, Inc., 300 North Washington Avenue, Lansing (517)484-4455

Family and Children's Service, 182 West Van Buren, Battle Creek (616)965-3247

Family and Children's Service of Midland, 116 Harold Street, Midland (517)631-5390

Family and Children's Services of the Kalamazoo Area, 1608 Lake Street, Kalamazoo (616)344-0202

Family and Children's Services of Oakland, 50 Wayne Street, Pontiac (313)332-8352

Family Counseling and Children's Service of Lenawee County, 213 Toledo Street, Adrian (517)265-5342

Family Service and Children's Aid of Jackson County, 906 West Monroe Avenue, Jackson (517)787-7970

Homes for Black Children, 2340 Calvert, Detroit (313)869-2316. Specializes in the placement of black children. Has developed programs that are used nationwide.

Jewish Family Service, 24123 Greenfield Road, Southfield (313)559-1500. Religious requirement. Has developed an identified-adoption program known as "referred adoption."

LDS Social Services, 30700 Telegraph Road, Birmingham (313)645-6122. Serves state. Religious requirement.

Lutheran Adoption Service, 10811 Puritan Avenue, Detroit (313)864-4200

Lutheran Child and Family Service of Michigan, 522 North Madison, Bay City (517)892-1539

Lutheran Social Services of Michigan, 484 East Grand Boulevard, Detroit (313)-579-0333

Lutheran Social Services of Northwest Ohio (see Ohio)

Methodist Children's Home Society, 26645 West Six Mile Road, Detroit (313)-531-4060. Serves state.

Spaulding for Children, 3660 Waltrous Road, Chelsea (313)475-8693. Part of Family Builders Agency Network. Serves waiting children. No fees.

MINNESOTA

State Agency: Adoption Unit, Minnesota Department of Public Welfare, Centennial Building, St. Paul 55155 (612)296-3740

State Exchange: Minnesota State Adoption Exchange (see above)

State Photolisting Book: *Minnesota's Waiting Children*

Independent Adoptions: Not permitted

NACAC **Representative:** Judith Anderson, 9125 West Bush Lake Road, Minneapolis 55438 (612)941-5146

Private Agencies:

Bethany Christian Services (see Michigan). Serves state.

Caritas Family Services, 305 7th Avenue N., St. Cloud (612)252-4121

Catholic Charities of the Archdiocese of Minneapolis/St. Paul, 404 South 8th Street, Minneapolis (612)340-7500. For St. Paul; 215 Old 6th Street (612)-222-3001

Catholic Social Service Association, P.O. Box 610, 1200 Memorial Drive, Crookston (218)281-4224

Catholic Social Service Diocese of Winona, Inc., P.O. Box 829, Winona (507)-454-2270

Children's Home Society of Minnesota, 2230 Como Avenue, St. Paul (612)646-6393. Serves state.

Crossroads, Inc., 7703 Normandale Road, 100B, Edina (612)831-5707. Serves state.

Hope International Family Service, Inc., 421 South Main Street, Stillwater (612)-439-2446

Jewish Family Service of St. Paul, 1546 St. Clair Avenue, St. Paul (612)698-0767

LDS Social Services (see Illinois). Works throughout state.

The Lutheran Home, 611 West Main Street, Belle Plain (612)873-2215. Serves state.

Lutheran Social Service of Minnesota, 2414 Park Avenue, Minneapolis (612)-871-0221. Serves state.

New Life Homes and Family Service, 6121 Excelsior Boulevard, St. Louis Park (612)920-8117.

Wilder Foundation Children's Placement Service, 919 Lafond, St. Paul (612)642-4008

MISSISSIPPI

State Agency: Mississippi State Department of Public Welfare, Adoption Unit, P.O. Box 352, Jackson 39205 (601)354-0341

State Exchange: Mississippi Adoption Resource Exchange (see above)

State Photolisting Book: *Mississippi Adoption Resource Exchange*

Independent Adoption: Permitted

NACAC **Representative:** Linda West, 430 Forest Avenue, Jackson 39202 (601)-982-9149

Private Agencies:

Catholic Charities, Inc., 748 North President Street, Jackson (601)355-8634

Catholic Social and Community Services, P.O. Box 1457, Biloxi (601)374-8316

LDS Social Services (see Louisiana)

Mississippi Children's Home Society, 1801 North West Street, Jackson (601)-352-7784

MISSOURI

State Agency: Department of Social Services, Division of Family Services, P.O. Box 88, Jefferson City 65103 (314)751-2981 or in Missouri (800)554-2222

State Exchange: Adoption Exchange of Missouri (see above)

State Photolisting Book: *Adoption Exchange of Missouri Photo-Listing*
Independent Adoption: Permitted
NACAC Representative: Pat Krippner, 301 North Bompart, St. Louis 63119 (314)-725-2955
Private Agencies:
APLACE, P.O. Box 28036, St. Louis (314)965-5600
Bethany Christian Services, 7750 Clayton Road, St. Louis (314)644-3535
Catholic Charities, 4532 Lindell Boulevard, St. Louis (314)367-5500
Catholic Charities–Diocese of Kansas City, 1112 Broadway, Kansas City (816)-221-4377
Child Placement Services, Inc., 201 West Lexington, Independence (816)461-3488. Religious requirement.
Children's Home Society of Missouri, 9445 Litzsinger Road, Brentwood (314)-968-2350
Christian Family Services, 8812 Manchester, St. Louis (314)968-2216. Serves state. Religious requirement.
Edgewood Children's Center, 330 North Gore Avenue, Webster Groves (314)-960-2060
Evangelical Children's Home, 8240 St. Charles Rock Road, St. Louis (314)427-3755
Family Adoption and Counseling Services, Inc., 2 Bon Price Terrace, St. Louis (314)567-0707
Family and Children's Services of Greater St. Louis, 2650 Olive Street, St. Louis (314)371-6500
Family and Children's Services of Kansas City, Inc., 3515 Broadway, Kansas City (816)753-5280
Highlands Child Placement Services, 5506 Cambridge Avenue, Kansas City (816)-924-6565. Serves state. Religious requirement. Places out of state.
Homecrest Children's Home, 611 Homecrest Avenue, Kennet (314)888-5974. Serves state.
Jewish Family and Children's Services, 1115 East 65th Street, Kansas City (816)-333-1172. Office in St. Louis (314)993-1000.
LDS Social Services, 517 Walnut, Independence (816)461-5512. Serves state. Religious requirement.
Love Basket, Inc., 8965 Old LeMay Ferry Road, Hillsboro (314)789-4368. Religious requirement.
Lutheran Family and Children's Service, 4625 Lindell Boulevard, St. Louis (314)-361-2121. Serves state.
Missouri Baptist Children's Home, 11300 St. Charles Rock Road, St. Louis (314)-739-6811
National Benevolent Association, 11780 Borman Drive, St. Louis (314)993-9000
St. Louis Christian Home, 3033 North Euclid Avenue, St. Louis (314)381-3100

MONTANA
State Agency: Community Services Division, S.R.S., Box 4210, Helena 59604 (406)444-3865

State Exchange: No
State Photolisting Book: No
Independent Adoption: Permitted/no intermediaries
NACAC **Representative:** Mel and Lois Ann Jones, P.O. Box 485, Anaconda 59711 (406)563-5077
Private Agencies:
Catholic Social Services for Montana, Inc., 530 North Ewing, Helena (406)442-4130. Serves state. Branch offices.
Confederated Salish and Kootenai Tribes, Tribes of the Flathead Reservation, Family Assistance Division, Pablo (406)675-4600. Native American placement agency.
LDS Social Services, 2001 11th Avenue, Helena (406)443-1660
Lutheran Social Services, 7 Park Drive, Great Falls (406)761-4341
Lutheran Social Services, 202 Brooks Street, Missoula (406)549-0147
Lutheran Social Services, 100 North 24th Street, Billings (406)652-1310
Montana Children's Home and Hospital, Division of Children's Services, 840 Helena Avenue, Helena (406)442-1980. Serves state.

NEBRASKA
State Agency: Department of Social Services, 301 Centennial Mall S., P.O. Box 95026, Lincoln 68509 (402)471-3121
State Exchange: Adoption Exchange Services of Nebraska (see above)
State Photolisting Book: No
Independent Adoption: Permitted/no intermediaries
NACAC **Representative:** Penny Winfield, 2320 North 56th Street, Omaha 68135 (402)551-7951
Private Agencies:
Catholic Social Service Bureau, P.O. Box 2723, Lincoln (402)423-6555. Serves state.
Child Saving Institute, 115 South 46th Street, Omaha (402)553-6000. Serves state. Has done open adoption.
Jewish Family Service, 333 South 132d Street, Omaha (402)334-8200
LDS Social Services (see Missouri). Serves state.
Lutheran Family and Social Services, 120 South 24th Street, Omaha (402)342-7007. Serves state.
Nebraska Children's Home Society, 3549 Fontenelle Boulevard, Omaha (402)-451-0787. Serves state. Branch offices.
United Catholic Social Services of the Archdiocese of Omaha, Inc., 2132 South 42d Street, Omaha (402)558-3533

NEVADA
State Agency: Nevada State Welfare Division, Department of Human Resources, 251 Jeanell Drive, Carson City 89710 (702)885-4771
State Exchange: No
State Photolisting Book: *Nevada Adoption Exchange Book*

Independent Adoption: Permitted/no intermediaries
NACAC Representative: Contact National Office of NACAC.
Private Agencies:
Catholic Community Services of Nevada, 808 South Main Street, Las Vegas (702)-385-2662
LDS Social Services, 1906 Santa Paula Drive, Las Vegas (702)735-1072
LDS Social Services, 907 Casazza Drive, Reno 89502 (702)323-7376

NEW HAMPSHIRE
State Agency: New Hampshire Division of Welfare, Adoption Unit, Hazen Drive, Concord 03301 (603)271-4419
State Exchange: No
State Photolisting Book: No
Independent Adoption: Permitted
NACAC Representative: Contact National Office of NACAC.
Private Agencies:
Adoptive Families for Children, 26 Fairview Street, Keene (603)357-4456
Child and Family Services of New Hampshire, 99 Hanover Street, Manchester (603)668-1920
LDS Social Services, 491 Amherst Street, Nashua (603)889-0148. Serves state. Religious requirement.
New Hampshire Catholic Charities, Inc., 215 Myrtle Street, P.O. Box 686, Manchester (603)669-3030. Serves state.
Vermont Children's Aid Society, Inc. (see Vermont). Serves border towns.

NEW JERSEY
State Agency: State of New Jersey, Division of Youth and Family Services, Adoption Services Unit, CN 717, 1 South Montgomery Street, Trenton 08625 (609)-633-6902
State Exchange: No
State Photolisting Book: No
Independent Adoption: Permitted/no intermediaries
NACAC Representative: Phyllis Tusler, 223 Logan Street, Woodbury (609)853-1381
Private Agencies (many have fees as high as 10 percent of a family's income, with a maximum of $4,000 or $5,000):
Associated Catholic Community Services, 17 Mulberry Street, Newark (201)596-4100
Association for Jewish Children of Philadelphia (see Pennsylvania)
Bethany Christian Services, 475 High Mountain Road, North Haledon (201)427-2566
Catholic Family and Community Services, 10 Jackson Street, Paterson (201)-279-7100
Catholic Guardian Society of New York (see New York)
The Catholic Home Bureau for Dependent Children (see New York)

Catholic Social Services (see Pennsylvania)

Catholic Social Services of the Diocese of Camden, Inc., 1845 Haddon Avenue, Camden (609)541-2100

Catholic Welfare Bureau, Diocese of Trenton, 47 North Clinton Avenue, P.O. Box 1423, Trenton (609)394-5181

Child and Home Study Associates (see Pennsylvania)

Children's Aid Society (see New York)

Children's Aid and Adoption Society of New Jersey, 360 Larch Avenue, Bogota (201)487-2022

Children's Aid Society of Pennsylvania (see Pennsylvania)

Children's Bureau of Delaware (see Delaware)

Children's Home Society of New Jersey, 929 Parkside Avenue, Trenton (609)-695-6274. Serves state.

Chosen Children Adoption Services, Inc. (see Kentucky)

The Cradle Society (see Illinois)

The Edna Gladney Home (see Texas)

Edwin Gould Services for Children (see New York)

Family and Children's Services, Inc., of Monmouth County, 191 Bath Avenue, Long Branch (201)222-9100

The Family and Children's Society, 40 North Avenue, P.O. Box 314, Elizabeth (201)352-7474

Goodwill Home and Missions, Inc., 79 University Avenue, Newark (201)621-9560

Graham-Windham Child Care (see New York)

Harlem-Dowling Children's Service (see New York)

LDS Social Services (see New York)

Louise Wise Services (see New York)

Lutheran Social Services of New Jersey, 489 West State Street, Trenton (609)-393-3440

New York Foundling Hospital (see New York)

St. Joseph's Children's and Maternity Hospital (see Pennsylvania)

Sheltering Arms Children's Service (see New York)

Spaulding for Children, 36 Prospect Street, Westfield (201)233-2282. Part of Family Builders Agency Network. Serves waiting children. No fees.

Spence-Chapin Services to Families and Children (see New York)

Talbot-Perkins Children's Services (see New York)

Texas Cradle Society (see Texas)

United Family and Children's Society, 305 West 7 Street, Plainfield (201)755-4848

Women's Christian Alliance (see Pennsylvania)

The New Jersey Adoption Services Unit has produced a most informative booklet, *Directory of Adoption Agencies Serving New Jersey,* which outlines each agency's eligibility requirements.

NEW MEXICO

State Agency: New Mexico Department of Human Services, Adoption Services, PERA Building, P.O. Box 2348, Santa Fe 87503 (505) 827-4058 or in New Mexico (800)432-2075

State Exchange: New Mexico State Exchange, P.O. Box 2348, Santa Fe (505)-827-2285

State Photolisting Book: *Life Book*

Independent Adoption: Permitted/obtain from court prior to placement an order waiving placement by a licensed agency.

NACAC Representative: Judy McDaniel, 4004 Camino de la Sierra N.E., Albuquerque 87111 (505)292-1976

Private Agencies:

Catholic Social Services of Santa Fe, P.O. Box 443, Santa Fe (505)982-0441

Chaparral Home and Adoption Services, 4401 Lomas N.E., Albuquerque (505)-266-5837. Serves state.

Christian Placement Services, West Star, Route Box 48, Portales (505)356-4232. Serves state.

LDS Social Services, 7800 Marble N.E., Albuquerque (505)262-2639

LDS Social Services, 925 West L.E. Murray Thruway, Farmington (505)337-6123

Methodist Mission Home (see Texas)

NEW YORK

State Agency: New York State Department of Social Services, Adoption Services, 40 North Pearl Street, Albany 12243 (518)473-1509 or (212)488-5290 or (800)342-3715

State Exchange: (see above)

State Photolisting Book: *New York State's Waiting Children* (often referred to as the "Blue Books")

Independent Adoption: Permitted

NACAC Representatives: Virginia Butler, P.O. Box 771, Brooklyn 11202; and Judith Ashton, 105 McIntyre Place, Ithaca 14850 (607)257-2477

Private Agencies:

Abbott House, 100 North Broadway, Irvington (914)591-7300. The overwhelming majority of the children served are minority.

Angel Guardian Home, 6301 12th Avenue, Brooklyn (212)232-1500

Astor Home for Children, 36 Mill Street, Rhinebeck (914)876-4081

Brooklyn Bureau of Community Service, 285 Schermerhorn Street, Brooklyn (212)-875-0710

Brookwood Child Care, 363 Adelphi Street, Brooklyn (212)783-2610. Places primarily black children.

Cardinal Hayes Home, North Avenue, Millbrook (914)677-6363

Cardinal McCloskey School/Home, 2 Holland Avenue, White Plains (914)997-8000

Catholic Adoption Office, 27 North Main Avenue, Albany (518)438-2322

Catholic Charities of Buffalo, 525 Washington Street, Buffalo (716)856-4494

Catholic Family Center, 50 Chestnut Street, Rochester (716)546-7220

Catholic Family Service, 1654 West Onondaga Street, Syracuse (315)424-1800

Catholic Family Service, 37 First Street, Troy (518)272-2383

Catholic Family Services, 816 Union Street, Schenectady (518)372-5667

Catholic Home Bureau, 1011 First Avenue, New York City (212)371-1000

270   DOMESTIC ADOPTION DIRECTORY

Child and Family Services, 330 Delaware Avenue, Buffalo (716)842-2750
Child and Family Services, 678 West Onondaga Street, Syracuse (315)474-4291
The Children's Aid Society, 150 East 45th Street, New York City (212)949-4800
Children's Home of Kingston, 26 Grove Street, Kingston (914)331-1448
Children's Home of Poughkeepsie, 91 Fulton Street, Poughkeepsie (914)452-1420
Children's Village, Dobbs Ferry (914)693-0600
The Cradle Society (see Illinois). Serves Manhattan and Westchester counties.
Chosen Children Adoption Services (see Kentucky)
The Edna Gladney Home (see Texas)
Edwin Gould Services for Children, 109 East 31st Street, New York City (212)-
    679-5520
Episcopal Mission Society, 1331 Franklin Avenue, Bronx (212)589-1434
Evangelical Adoption and Family Services, 201 South Main Street, North Syracuse
    (315)458-1415
Family and Children's Services of Albany, 12 South Lake Avenue, Albany (518)-
    462-6531
Family and Children's Society of Broome County, 257 Main Street, Binghamton
    (607)729-6206
Family and Children's Services of Ithaca, 315 North Tioga Street, Ithaca (607)-
    273-7494
Family and Children's Services of Niagara Falls, 826 Chilton Avenue, Niagara Falls
    (716)285-6984
Family and Children's Service of Schenectady, 246 Union Street, Schenectady
    (518)393-1369
Family Resources, 165 Main Street, Ossining (914)762-6550. Focuses on special-
    needs children.
Family Service of Chemung County, 500 Walnut Street, Elmira (607)733-5696
Family Service of Greater Utica, 239 Genesee Street, Utica (315)735-2236
Family Service of Westchester, Inc., 470 Mamaroneck Avenue, White Plains (914)-
    948-8004
Goodwill Home and Missions, Inc. (see New Jersey)
Graham-Windham Services, Inc., 1 Park Avenue, New York City (212)889-5600
Green Chimneys, Putnam Lake Road, Brewster (212)892-6810
Greer-Woodycrest Services, Hope Farm, Millbrook (914)677-5041. Places primar-
    ily black adolescents.
Harlem-Dowling Children's Services, 2090 Seventh Avenue, New York City (212)-
    749-3656. Places primarily black children.
Hillside Children's Center, 1183 Monroe Avenue, Rochester (716)473-5150
    Serves state. Utilizes TEAM program.
Infants Home of Brooklyn, 2950 West 25th, Brooklyn (212)266-5050
Jewish Child Care Association, 345 Madison Avenue, New York City (212)490-
    9160. Places special-needs children.
Jewish Family Service, 70 Barker Street, Buffalo (716)883-1914
Jewish Family Service Bureau, 4101 East Genesee Street, Syracuse (315)445-
    0820

LDS Social Services, 105 Main Street, Fishkill (914)896-8226

Leake and Watts Children's Home, 463 Hawthorne Avenue, Yonkers (914)963-5220. Places black children.

Little Flower Children's Service, 200 Montague Street, Brooklyn (212)858-1212

Louise Wise Services, 12 East 94th Street, New York City (212)876-3050

Lutheran Community Services, 33 Worth Street, New York City (212)431-7470

Lutheran Service Society, 2500 Kensington Avenue, Buffalo (716)839-3391

McMahon Services for Children, 225 East 45th Street, New York City (212)986-3418. Places black and Hispanic children.

Malone Catholic Charities, 105 West Main Street, Malone (518)483-1460

Mercy Home for Children, 273 Willoughby Avenue, Brooklyn (212)622-5842

Mishkon Children's Home, 4106 16th Avenue, Brooklyn (212)851-6570

New York Foundling Hospital, 1175 3rd Avenue, New York City (212)472-2233

New York Spaulding for Children, 22 West 27th Street, New York City (212)-696-9560. Part of Family Builders Agency Network. Serves waiting children. No fees.

Ohel Children's Home, 4423 16th Avenue, Brooklyn (212)851-6300

Parsons Child and Family Center, 60 Academy Road, Albany (518)447-5211

Rome Catholic Social Services, 212 West Liberty Street, Rome (315)337-8600

St. Cabrini Home, West Park (914)384-6720. Primarily places adolescents.

St. Christopher's Home, Park Avenue, Sea Cliff (516)671-1253

St. Christopher's, 71 Broadway, Dobbs Ferry (914)693-3030

St. Dominic's, 535 East 138th Street, Bronx (212) 993-5765

St. John's Residence for Boys, 150 111th Street, Rockaway (212)945-2800

St. Vincent's Hall, 66 Boerum Place, Brooklyn (212)522-3700

Salvation Army Social Services for Children, 50 West 23d Street, New York City (212)255-9400. Places primarily black children.

Sheltering Arms Children's Service, 122 East 29th Street, New York City (212)-679-4242

Society for Seamen's Children, 26 Bay Street, Staten Island (212)447-7740

Spence-Chapin Services to Families and Children, 6 East 94th Street, New York City (212)369-0300

Talbot Perkins Children's Services, 342 Madison Avenue, New York (212)697-1420

Catholic Charities, 1408 Genesee Street, Utica (315)724-2158

Vermont Children's Aid Society, Inc. (see Vermont). Places in border towns.

Watertown Catholic Charities, 380 Arlington Street, Watertown (315)788-4330

Wyndham Lawn Children's Home, 6395 Old Niagara Road, Lockport (716)433-4487

The New York Junior League (130 East 80th Street, New York City) has produced a helpful guide, *Adoption: A Guide to Adopting in the New York Area,* 1980, which discusses agencies in the New York metropolitan area and outlines their programs. Some of the information may be outdated, but it is worthwhile reading.

The New York State Citizens' Coalition for Children, Inc., has also produced a helpful booklet, *New York State's Adoptive and Foster Parent Support Groups,* 1983. Contact Nancy Foss, 3 Lee Drive, Saratoga Springs 12866 (518)587-9959.

NORTH CAROLINA

State Agency: Division of Social Services, Department of Human Resources, 325 North Salisbury Street, Raleigh 27611 (919)733-3801

State Exchange: North Carolina Adoption Resource Exchange (see above)

State Photolisting Book: *Photo Adoption Listing Service* (PALS)

Independent Adoption: Permitted/no intermediaries

NACAC Representative: Jan Chadwick, Route 2, Box 56, Apex 27502 (919)362-7066

Private Agencies:

Catholic Social Services, Inc., 1524 East Morehead Street, Charlotte (704)333-9954

Catholic Social Services, Diocese of Raleigh, Inc., 300 Cardinal Gibbons Drive, Raleigh (919)821-0350

The Children's Home Society of North Carolina, Inc., 740 Chestnut Street, Greensboro (919)274-1538. Works throughout state. Branch offices.

Family Services, Inc., 610 Coliseum Drive, Winston-Salem (919)722-8173

LDS-Social Services, 5624 Executive Center Drive, Charlotte (704)535-2436

NORTH DAKOTA

State Agency: Children and Family Service Division, North Dakota Department of Human Service, Bismarck 58505 (701)224-2316

State Exchange: No

State Photolisting Book: No

Independent Adoption: Not permitted

NACAC Representative: Contact National Office of NACAC.

Private Agencies:

Catholic Family Services, Box 686, Fargo (701)235-4457

LDS Social Services, 2900 Broadway, Bismarck (701)222-4179

Lutheran Social Services of North Dakota, 1325 South 11th Street, Fargo (701)-235-7341

Lutheran Social Services, 227 West Broadway, Bismarck (701)223-1510

SAME Christian Resource Center, Inc., P.O. Box 2344, Bismarck (701)222-3960

The Village Family Service Center, 420 North 4th Street, Bismarck (701)255-1165. Focuses on special-needs adoption.

The Village Family Service Center, 1721 South University Drive, Fargo (701)-235-6433. Focuses on special-needs adoption.

The Village Family Service Center, 610 South Washington, Grand Forks (701)-746-4584. Focuses on special-needs adoption.

The Village Family Service Center, 400 22d Avenue N.W., Minot (701)852-3328. Focuses on special-needs adoption.

OHIO

State Agency: Division of Social Services, Bureau of Children Services, 30 East Broad Street, Columbus 43215 (614)466-8510

State Exchange: Ohio Adoption Resource Exchange (see above)

State Photolisting Book: No

Independent Adoption: Permitted

NACAC Representative: Beth Frank, 518 Carrol Avenue, Sandusky 44870 (419)-625-6149

Private Agencies:

Catholic Charities Service Bureau, Inc., 234 West Highland, Ravenna (216)296-2803

Catholic Service Bureau of Columbiana County, 964 North Market Street, Lisbon (216)424-9509

Catholic Service Bureau of Lake County, 8 North State Street, Painesville (216)-352-6191

Catholic Service League, 640 North Main Street, Akron (216)762-7481

Catholic Service League, 4631 Main Avenue, Ashtabula (216)998-7221

Catholic Service League, 5385 Market Street, Youngstown (216)788-8726

Catholic Social Service Bureau, 124 West Washington Street, Medina (216)725-4923

Catholic Social Service of Geauga County, 10762 Mayfield Road, Chardon (216)-285-3537

Catholic Social Services, 641 High Street, Springfield (513)325-8715

Catholic Social Services Bureau (see Kentucky)

Catholic Social Services Diocese of Toledo, 1933 Spiebusch Avenue, Toledo (419)244-6711.

Catholic Social Services of Cuyahoga County, 3409 Woodland Avenue, Cleveland (216)881-1600

Catholic Social Services Diocese of Columbus, 197 Gay Street, Columbus (614)-221-5891

Catholic Social Services of Hamilton, 140 North 5th Street, Hamilton (513)863-6129

Catholic Social Services of the Miami Valley, 922 West Riverview Avenue, Dayton (513)223-7217

Catholic Social Services of Southwest Ohio, 100 East 8th Street, Cincinnati (513)-241-7745

Child and Family Service, 616 South Collett Street, Lima (419)225-1040

Children's and Family Service Agency, 535 Marmion Avenue, Youngstown (216)-782-5664

Children's Home of Cincinnati, 5051 Duck Creek Road, Cincinnati (513)272-2800

Children's Services, 1001 Huron Road, Cleveland (216)781-2043

Family Counseling and Crittenton Services, Inc., 185 South 5th Street, Columbus (614)221-7608

Family Counseling Services of Western Stark County, Inc., 11 Lincoln Way West, Massillon (216)832-5043

Family Service Association, 184 Salem Avenue, Dayton (513)222-9481

Family Service Association, 1704 North Road S.E., Warren (216)856-2907

Family Services of Summit County, 212 East Exchange Street, Akron (216)376-9494

Franklin County Children's Adoption Services Board, 1951 Gantz Road, Columbus (614)275-2511

Greene County Children Services Board, 651 Dayton-Xenia Road, Xenia (513)-376-5222. Focuses on special-needs adoption.

Jewish Children's Bureau, 22001 Fairmount Boulevard, Cleveland (216)932-2800. Has done identified adoptions.

Jewish Family and Children's Service, 505 Gypsy Lane, Youngstown (216)746-3251

Jewish Family Service, 1175 College Avenue, Columbus (614)231-1890

Jewish Family Service, 1710 Section Road, Cincinnati (513)351-3680

Jewish Family Service, 6525 Sylvania Avenue, Toledo (419)885-2561

LDS Social Services, 4431 Marketing Place, Groveport (614)836-2466. Serves state.

Lutheran Children's Aid and Family Services, 4100 Franklin Boulevard, Cleveland (216)281-2500

Lutheran Social Services of Central Ohio, 57 East Main Street, Columbus (614)-228-5209. Focuses on special-needs adoption. Serves state.

Lutheran Social Services of the Miami Valley, 6451 Far Hills Avenue, Dayton (513)433-2140

Lutheran Social Services of Northwestern Ohio, 2149 Collingwood Boulevard, Toledo (419)243-9178

Midwestern Children's Home, 4581 Long Spurling Road, Pleasant Plain (513)-877-2141. Serves state.

Northeast Ohio Adoption Services, 8031 East Market Street, Warren (216)856-5582. Focuses on special-needs children.

Spaulding for Children (Beech Brook), 3737 Lander Road, Cleveland (216)464-4445. Part of Family Builders Agency Network. Serves waiting children. No fees. Serves state.

SUMA (Services for Unmarried Mothers and Specialized Adoption), 1216 East McMillan, Cincinnati (513)221-7862. Focuses on special-needs children.

The United Methodist Children's Home, P.O. Box 68, Worthington (614)885-5020.

OKLAHOMA

State Agency: Department of Human Services, Attn: Adoptions, P.O. Box 25352, Oklahoma City 73125 (405)521-2475

State Exchange: Oklahoma Children's Adoption Resource Exchange (OK CARE), 227 N.W. 23rd, Oklahoma City (405)524-6920

State Photolisting Book: *Oklahoma Childrens Adoption Resource Exchange*

Independent Adoption: Permitted

NACAC **Representative:** Suzanne Joyce, Route 1, Box 137, Dewey 74029 (918)-534-2237

Private Agencies:

Baptist General Convention, 1141 North Robinson, Oklahoma City (405)236-4341

Catholic Social Ministries, 425 N.W. 7th, P.O. Box 1516, Oklahoma City (405)-232-8514

Catholic Social Services, 739 North Denver, Tulsa (918)585-8167

Cookson Hills Christian School (see Arkansas)

Deaconness Hospital and Home, 5501 North Portland, Oklahoma City (405)946-5581. Infants only.

Dillon International, 7615 East 63d Place South, Tulsa (918)250-1561

The Edna Gladney Home (see Texas)

Family and Children's Services, 650 South Peoria, Tulsa (918)587-9471

LDS Social Services of Oklahoma, 2005 South Elm Place, Broken Arrow (918)-451-3090

Lutheran Social Services, 227 N.W. 23d, Oklahoma City (405)528-3124. Serves state.

Neighborhood Services, Inc., 1613 North Broadway, Oklahoma City (405)236-0413. Serves state.

Oakcrest Church of Christ, 1111 S.W. 89th Street, Oklahoma City (405)631-5534

Turley Children's Home, 6101 North Cincinnati (918)428-2557

United Methodist Placement Counseling, 2617 North Douglas, Oklahoma City (405)528-1906

OREGON

State Agency: Adoption Services, Children's Services Division, 198 Commercial Street S.E., Salem 97310 (503)378-4452

State Exchange: No

State Photolisting Book: *CSD Special Needs Bulletin*

Independent Adoption: Permitted

NACAC Representative: Harriet Gahr, Route 3, Box 267B, McMinnville 97128 (503)472-6960

Private Agencies:

Adventist Adoption and Family Services Program, 6040 S.E. Belmont Street, Portland (503)232-1211

Albertina Kerr Center for Children, 424 N.E. 22d Avenue, Portland (503)239-8101. Serves state.

The Boys and Girls Aid Society of Oregon, 2301 N.W. Glisan Street, Portland (503)222-9661. Serves state.

Catholic Services for Children, 319 S.W. Washington Street, Portland (503)228-6531

Holt International Children's Services, P.O. Box 2880, Eugene (503)687-2202

Jewish Family and Child Service, 1130 S.W. Morrison Street, Portland (503)-226-7079

LDS Social Services, 2900 Junipero Way, Medford (503)779-2391

LDS Social Services, 3000 Market Street N.E., Salem (503)581-7483

Plan Loving Adoptions Now, P.O. Box 667, McMinnville (503)472-8452. Serves state.

PENNSYLVANIA

State Agency: Pennsylvania Adoption Cooperative Effort, P.O. Box 2675 Harrisburg 17105 (717)787-5010

State Exchange: Pennsylvania Adoption Cooperative Effort (see above)

State Photolisting Book: *Pennsylvania Adoption Cooperative Effort*

Independent Adoption: Permitted

NACAC **Representatives:** Jan Reitnauer, 208 East Edison Avenue, New Castle 16101 (regional coordinator); Pam Grabe, 233 West Fulton Street, Butler 16001 (412)283-1971 (western Pennsylvania); Marcia Siegel, 20 Lansdowne Court, Lansdowne 19050 (215)259-3934 (eastern Pennsylvania)

Private Agencies:

Aid for Children International, 1516 Ridge Road, Lancaster (717)393-0296

Association for Jewish Children, 1301 Spencer Street, Philadelphia (215)549-9000

Bair Foundation, 241 High Street, New Wilmington (412)946-8711

Bethany Christian Services, 906 Bethlehem Pike, Erdenheim (215)233-4626

Catholic Charities Agency, Inc., 115 Vannear Avenue, Greensburg (412)837-1840

Catholic Family Services, 222 North 17th Street, Philadelphia (215)587-3812

Catholic Family Services, P.O. Box 1349, Altoona (814)944-9388; Sharon (412)-346-4332

Catholic Social Agency of the Diocese of Allentown, 928 Union Boulevard, Allentown (215)435-1541

Catholic Social Services, 300 Wyoming Avenue, Scranton (717)346-8936

Catholic Social Services of Shenango Valley, 2120 Shenango Valley Freeway, Sharon (412)346-1077

Catholic Social Services of the Diocese of Erie, 329 West 10th Street, Erie (814)-452-3610

Catholic Social Services of the Diocese of Harrisburg, 4800 Union Deposit Road, Harrisburg (717)652-3934

Child and Home Study Associates, 31 East Franklin Street, Media (215)565-1544

Children's Aid Society of Franklin County, P.O. Box 353, 255 Miller Street, Chambersburg (717)263-4159

Children's Aid Society of Mercer County, 350 West Market Street, Mercer (412)-662-4730

Children's Aid Society of Montgomery County, 1314 DeKalb Street, Norristown (215)279-2755

Children's Aid Society of Pennsylvania, 311 South Juniper Street, Philadelphia (215)546-2990

Children's Home of Pittsburgh, 5618 Kentucky Avenue, Pittsburgh (412)441-4884. Places infants.

Children's Home Society of Somerset County, 574 East Main Street, Somerset (814)445-2009 and (814)443-1637

Church of Christ Children's Home (see Virginia)

Concern, 1 East Main Street, Fleetwood (215)944-0445. Utilizes TEAM program.
The Cradle Society (see Illinois). Serves Philadelphia.
Eckels Adoption Agency, 915 5th Avenue (rear), Williamsport (717)323-2520
The Edna Gladney Home (see Texas)
Family and Child Service, 110 West 10th Street, Erie (814)455-2725
Family and Children's Service, 630 Janet Avenue, Lancaster (717)397-5241
Family and Children's Service, 717 Liberty Avenue, Pittsburgh (412)261-3623
Family and Children's Service of Blair County, 2022 Broad Avenue, Altoona (814)-944-3583
Family and Children's Service of Lehigh County, 411 Walnut Street, Allentown (215)435-9651
Family Service and Children's Aid Society of Venango County, 716 East 29th Street, Oil City (814)677-4005
Golden Cradle Home, 555 East City Line Avenue, Bala Cynwyd (215)668-2136. Places infants.
Love the Children, Inc., 221 West Broad Street, Quakertown (215)536-4180
Lutheran Children and Family Service, 2900 Queen Lane, Philadelphia (215)-951-6850
The Lutheran Home at Topton, Topton (215)682-2145
Philadelphia Society for Services to Children, 419 South 15th Street, Philadelphia (215)875-3400. Focuses on waiting children.
St. Joseph's Children's and Maternity Hospital, 2010 Adams Avenue, Scranton (717)342-8379
Social and Community Services of the Diocese of Pittsburgh, 307 4th Avenue, Pittsburgh (412)471-1120
Tressler-Lutheran Service Associates, Inc., 25 West Springettsbury Avenue, York (717)845-9113. Nationally recognized agency for its work in placing waiting children. NACAC's TEAM program is modeled on Tressler-Lutheran's programs. Works within a twenty-six-county area of Pennsylvania.
Welcome House, Inc., P.O. Box 836, Doylestown (215)345-0430
Women's Christian Alliance, 1610-14 North Broad Street, Philadelphia (215)236-9911. Part of Family Builders Agency Network. Serves waiting children. No fee.

RHODE ISLAND
State Agency: Department for Children and Their Families, 610 Mt. Pleasant Avenue, Providence 02908 (401)277-3797
State Exchange: Ocean State Adoption Resource Exchange, 610 Mt. Pleasant Avenue, Providence (401)277-3444
State Photolisting Book: *OSARE Photo-Listing*
Independent Adoption: Permitted/no intermediaries
NACAC **Representative:** Contact National Office at NACAC.
Private Agencies:
Catholic Social Services, 433 Elmwood Avenue, Providence (401)467-7200. Serves state.

Children's Friend and Service, 2 Richmond Street, Providence (401)331-2900. Serves state.

International Adoptions, Inc. (see Massachusetts)

Jewish Family and Children's Services, 229 Waterman Street, Providence (401)-331-1244. Serves state.

LDS Social Services (see New Hampshire)

SOUTH CAROLINA

State Agency: Department of Social Services, Adoption Unit, P.O. Box 1520, Columbia 29202 (803)758-8740; The Children's Bureau of South Carolina, 1001 Harden Street, Columbia 29205 (803)785-2702

State Exchange: South Carolina Seedlings, Route 5, Box 242A, Pickens (803)-878-4500

State Photolisting Book: *The South Carolina Seedlings*

Independent Adoption: Permitted

NACAC Representative: Joyce Thompson, 1453 Hammond Pond Road, North Augusta 30041 (803)279-4184

Private Agencies:

Bethany Christian Services, 300 University Ridge, Greenville (803)235-2273

Catholic Charities of Charleston, 119 Broad Street, Charleston (803)722-8318

Children Unlimited, P.O. Box 11463, Columbia (803)799-8311. Part of Family Builders Agency Network. Serves waiting children. No fee.

Connie Maxwell Children's Home, P.O. Box 1178, Greenwood (803)223-8321

Epworth Children's Home, 2900 Millwood Avenue, Columbia (803)256-7394

LDS Social Services (see North Carolina)

SOUTH DAKOTA

State Agency: Department of Social Services, Adoption Unit, Kneip Building, Illinois Street, Pierre 57505 (605)773-3227

State Exchange: No

State Photolisting Book: No

Independent Adoption: Permitted/Medical and social history must be filed in court prior to placement.

NACAC Representative: Contact National Office of NACAC

Private Agencies:

Catholic Family Social Services, 3200 West 41st Street, Sioux Falls (605)336-3326

Catholic Social Services, 918 5th Street, Rapid City (605)348-6086

Child Protection Program, Sisseton Wahpeton Sioux Tribe, 409 East 1st Avenue, Sisseton (605)698-3992. Native American placement agency.

Children's Home Society, 3209 South Prairie Avenue, Sioux Falls (605)334-6004. Serves state.

LDS Social Services, 2525 West Main Street, Rapid City (605)342-3500. Serves state.

Lutheran Social Services of South Dakota, 600 West 12th Street, Sioux Falls (605)336-3347. Serves state.

TENNESSEE
State Agency: Tennessee Department of Human Services, 111 7th Avenue North, Nashville 37203 (615)741-5936
State Exchange: Tennessee Adoption Resource Exchange (see above); (615)-741-5935
State Photolisting Book: *Tennessee Department of Human Services Adoption Resources Exchange Book*
Independent Adoption: Permitted/no intermediaries
NACAC Representative: Contact National office of NACAC.
Private Agencies:
AGAPE, 2406 Parkway Place, Memphis (901)327-7339
AGAPE, 2610 Westwood Drive, Nashville (615)385-0190
Baptist Children's Home, 6896 Highway 70, Memphis (901)386-3961
Bethany Christian Services, 4706 Brainerd Road, Chattanooga (615)622-7360
Catholic Center of Tennessee, Inc., 2400 21st Avenue South, Nashville (615)-383-6393
Catholic Social Services, 114 Hinton Street, Knoxville (615)524-9896
Child and Family Services of Knox County, 114 Dameron Avenue, Knoxville (615)-524-7483
Chosen Children Adoption Services (see Kentucky)
Christian Counseling Services, 515 Woodland Street, Nashville (615)254-8341
Family and Children's Service, 201 23d Avenue North, Nashville (615)327-0833
Family and Children's Services of Chattanooga, Inc., 323 High Street, Chattanooga (615)755-2800
Greater Chattanooga Christian Services, 400 Vine Street, Chattanooga (615)-267-1114
Holston United Methodist Home, P.O. Box 188, Greeneville (615)638-4171. Branch offices.
Jewish Service Agency, Poplar Street, Memphis (901)767-8511
St. Peter's Village for Children, 1805 Poplar Avenue, Memphis (901)725-8240
Tennessee Baptist Children's Homes, Inc., P.O. Box 347, Brentwood (615)373-5707

TEXAS
State Agency: Texas Department of Human Resources, Adoption Unit, P.O. Box 2960, Austin 76769 (512)835-0440
State Exchange: Texas Adoption Resource Exchange (see above)
State Photolisting Book: *Texas Adoption Resource Exchange*
Independent Adoption: Permitted/no intermediaries
NACAC Representative: Clara Flores, Route 2, Box 177F, Edinburg 78539 (512)-383-2680.
Private Agencies:
AGAPE Social Services, Inc., 1412 Jeffries, Dallas (214)714-4244
Buckner Baptist Benevolences, P.O. Box 271189, Dallas (214)328-3141
Catholic Charities, Adoption Services, 513 East Jackson, Harlingen (512)425-3422

Catholic Charities of the Diocese of Galveston-Houston, Montrose Boulevard, Houston (713)526-4611

Catholic Counseling Services, 3845 Oak Lawn, Dallas (214)528-4870 Religious requirement. Places infants.

Catholic Family and Children Services, Inc., Archdiocese of San Antonio, 2903 West Salinas, San Antonio (512)433-3256

Catholic Family Service, Inc., 1522 South Van Buren, Amarillo (806)376-4571

Catholic Guardian Society, 3915 Lemon Avenue, Dallas (214)528-2240

Catholic Social Service, 1025 South Jennings, Fort Worth (817)877-1231

Child and Family Service, Inc., 2001 Chicon Street, Austin (512)478-1648

Child Placement Center of Texas, P.O. Box 259, 408 North 4th Street, Killeen (817)526-8872

Children's Home of Lubbock, P.O. Box 2824, Lubbock (806)762-0421. Serves state. Has accepted out-of-state applications for waiting children. Religious requirement.

Children's Service Bureau, 625 North Alamo, San Antonio (512)223-6281

Christian Child Help Foundation, 3605 North MacGregor Way, Houston (713)-522-2708

Christian Homes of Abilene, Inc., 242 Beech Street, P.O. Box 717, Abilene (915)-677-2205. Serves state.

Christian Services of the Southwest, 3330 Walnut Hill Lane, Dallas (214)351-9946

Christ's Haven for Children, P.O. Box 467, Keller (817)431-1544

The DePelchin Faith Home, Adoption Department, 100 Sandman Street, Houston (713)861-8136

The Edna Gladney Home, 2300 Hemphill, Fort Worth (817)926-3304. Serves state. Places infants.

Family Counseling and Children's Services, 201 West Waco Drive, Waco (817)-753-1509

High Plains Children's Home, 1501 West 58th Street, Amarillo (806)355-6588. Serves state. Religious requirement.

Home of the Holy Infancy, 510 West 26th Street, Austin (512)472-9251

Homes of St. Mark, 1922 North Braeswood, Houston (713)797-1791 or in Texas (800)392-3807. Serves state.

Hope Cottage-Children's Bureau, Inc., 4209 McKinney Avenue, Dallas (214)526-8721. Serves state. Places infants.

Jewish Family Service, 7800 Northaven, Dallas (214)696-6400

Jewish Family Service, 4131 South Braeswood, Houston (713)723-2807

LDS Social Services, 1100 West Jackson Road, Carrollton (214)242-2182

Lee and Beulah Moor Children's Home, 1100 East Cliff Drive, El Paso (915)-544-8777

Los Niños International Adoption Center, 3200 South Congress, Austin (512)-443-2833

Lutheran Social Service of Texas, Inc., 408 West 45th Street, P.O. Box 4736, Austin (512)459-1000. Serves the state through its various branch offices.

Lutheran Social Service in San Antonio (512)277-8142 has gained national attention through its advocacy of open infant adoptions.

Marywood Maternity and Adoption Services, 510 West 26th Street, Austin (512)-472-9251. Serves state.

Methodist Mission Home of Texas, 6487 Whitby Road, San Antonio (512)696-2410 or in-state (800)-292-5103 or out-of-state (800)255-9612. Has placed black infants and infants of mixed ethnic heritage out of state.

Methodist Home, 1111 Herring Avenue, Waco (817)753-0181. Serves state.

Pleasant Hills Children's Home, Fairfield (214)389-2641

Presbyterian Children's Home and Service Agency, 400 South Zang Street, Dallas (214)942-8674

Presbyterian Home for Children, 3400 South Bowie, Amarillo (806)352-5771

Sherwood-Myrtie Foster Home for Children, P.O. Box 978, Stephenville (817)-968-2143

Smithlawn Maternity Home and Adoption Agency, 711 76th Street, Lubbock (806)-745-2574. Serves state.

South Texas Children's Home, Box 1210, Beeville (512)375-2101

Spaulding Southwest, 4219 Richmond Avenue, Houston (713)850-9707. Part of Family Builders Agency Network. Serves waiting children. No fee.

Texas Baptist Children's Home, Drawer 7, Round Rock (512)255-3668

Texas Cradle Society, 8222 Wurzbach, San Antonio 78229 (512)696-7700. Serves state. Has placed infants of mixed ethnic background (e.g., Mexican/black) out of state.

Therapeikos, Inc., 2817 North 2, Abilene (915) 677-2216

UTAH

State Agency: Department of Social Services, Division of Family, 150 West North Temple, Salt Lake City 84103 (801)533-7123.

State Exchange: No

State Photolisting Book: No

Independent Adoption: Permitted

NACAC Representative: Contact National Office of NACAC.

Private Agencies:

Adoption Services of WACAP (see Washington)

Catholic Community Services of Salt Lake City, 333 East South Temple, Salt Lake City (801)328-8641

Children's Aid Society of Utah, 652 26th Street, Ogden (801)393-8671

Children's Service Society, 576 East South Temple, Salt Lake City (801)355-7444

LDS Social Services 718 South Main, Cedar City (801)586-4479

LDS Social Services, 95 West 100, South, Logan (801)752-5302

LDS Social Services, 7200 South 101 East Street, Midvale (801)531-2556

LDS Social Services, 349 12th Street, Ogden (801)621-6510. Utilizes a TEAM program.

LDS Social Services, 1190 North 900 East, Provo (801)378-7620

LDS Social Services, 50 East North Temple, Salt Lake City (801)531-3100

VERMONT

State Agency: Department of Social and Rehabilitation Services, Adoption Unit, 103 South Main Street, Waterbury 05676 (802)241-2150

State Exchange: No

State Photolisting Book: No

Independent Adoption: Permitted

NACAC Representative: Contact National office of NACAC.

Private Agencies:

The Elizabeth Lund Home, Inc., 76 Glen Road, Burlington (802)864-7467. Serves state.

LDS Social Services (see New Hampshire)

Vermont Catholic Charities, 351 North Avenue, Burlington (802)658-6110. Serves state.

The Vermont Children's Aid Society, 72 Hungerford Terrace, Burlington (802)-864-9883. Serves state.

VIRGINIA

State Agency: Commonwealth of Virginia, Department of Social Services, 8007 Discovery Drive, Richmond 23288 (804) 281-9403

State Exchange: Adoption Resource Exchange of Virginia (AREVA), 8007 Discovery Drive, Richmond 23288 (804)281-9149

State Photolisting Book: *Adoption Resource Exchange of Virginia Child Photolisting Book*

Independent Adoption: Permitted/no intermediaries

NACAC Representative: Barbara Smith, 2225 Dragonfly Lane, Richmond 23235 (703)320-0275

Private Agencies:

American Adoption Agency (see District of Columbia)

Barker Foundation (see District of Columbia)

Catholic Charities of the Diocese of Arlington, 10 West Boscawen Street, Winchester (703)667-7940

Catholic Charities of the Diocese of Arlington, Inc., 3838 North Cathedral Lane, Arlington (703)841-2531

Catholic Family and Children's Service, 1520 Aberdeen Road, Hampton (804)-827-0510

Catholic Family and Children's Services, Inc., of Tidewater, Virginia, 1301 Colonial Avenue, Norfolk (804)625-2568

Catholic Family and Children's Services, 4206 Chamberlayne Avenue, Richmond (804)264-2778

Catholic Family and Children's Services of Roanoke Valley and Western Virginia, Inc., 820 Campbell Avenue S.W., Roanoke (703)344-5107

Catholic Family Services, 2308 Airline Boulevard, Portsmouth (804)393-0043

Children's Adoption Services (see District of Columbia)

Children's Home Society of Virginia, 4200 Fitzhugh Avenue, Richmond (804)-353-0191. Serves state.

Church of Christ Children's Home, P.O. Box 9, Gainesville, (703)754-8516. Serves
state. Religious requirement.

De Paul Children's Services, Inc., 1701 Grandin Road S.W., Roanoke (703)982-
0120

Family and Child Services of District of Columbia (see District of Columbia)

Family Service/Travelers Aid, Inc., 222 19th Street W., Norfolk (804)622-7017

Grafton School, Inc., T/A Grafton Teaching Homes, P.O. Box 469, Berryville
(703)955-2400

Holston United Methodist Home for Children, Inc., 102 Wall Street, Abingdon
(703)628-8604

Jewish Family Service of Tidewater, Inc., 7300 Newport Avenue, Norfolk (804)-
489-3111

Jewish Family Services, Inc., 7027 Chopt Road, Richmond (804)282-5644

LDS Social Services of Virginia, Inc., 8110 Virginia Pine Court, Richmond (804)-
743-0727

Lutheran Children's Home of the South, P.O. Box 151, Salem (703)389-8646.
Serves metropolitan area.

Lutheran Social Services of the National Capital Area (see District of Columbia)

Peirce-Warwick Adoption Service (see District of Columbia)

United Methodist Family Services of Virginia, Inc., 4016 West Broad Street, Richmond (804)359-9451. Serves state.

Virginia Baptist Children's Home, Inc., Mount Vernon Avenue, Salem (703)389-
5468. Serves state. Religious requirement.

Welcome House (see Pennsylvania)

WASHINGTON

State Agency: Department of Social and Health Services, Adoptions, OB, 41-C,
Olympia 98504 (206) 753-0965

Adoption Exchange: Washington Adoption Resource Exchange (WARE), OB
41-C, Olympia (206)378-4452

State Photolisting Book: *WARE Bulletin*

Independent Adoption: Permitted

NACAC Representative: Mary Ellen Haley, 2806 34th Avenue S., Seattle 98144
(206)722-2806

Private Agencies:

Adoption Advocates International, 658 Black Diamond Road, Port Angeles (206)-
452-4777.

Adoption Services of WACAP, P.O. Box 2009, Port Angeles (206)452-2308. Places
infants through its Options for Pregnancy Program. Serves waiting children.
Active intercountry programs.

Adventist Adoption and Family Services, 1207 East Reserve Street, Vancouver
(206)693-2110

Americans for International Aid and Adoption, P.O. Box 6051, Spokane (206)-
782-4251

Catholic Children and Family Service, 418 Drumheller Building, Walla Walla (509)-525-0572

Catholic Community Services Northwest, 207 Kentucky Street, Bellingham (206)-733-5840

Catholic Community Services—Snomish County, Room 510, Commerce Building, Everett (206)259-9188

Catholic Community Services—King County, 1715 East Cherry Street, Seattle (206)323-6336

Catholic Community Services, 5410 North 44th Street, Tacoma (206)752-2455

Catholic Family and Child Service, 805 Williams Boulevard, Richmond (509)946-4645

Catholic Family Service, 611 West Columbia, Pasco (509)547-0521

Child Placement Agency of the Puyallup Tribe, 2209 East 32d Street, Tacoma (206)597-6255. Serves Native Americans.

Children's Home Society of Washington, P.O. Box 15190, Seattle (206)524-6020. Serves state. Branch offices.

Church of Christ Homes for Children, 30012 South Military Road, Federal Way (206)839-2755. Serves state. Religious requirement.

Hope Services, 424 North 130th, Seattle (206)367-4600

International Children's Services of Washington, 3251 107th S.E., Bellevue (206)-451-9370

Jewish Family Services, 1214 Boylston Avenue, Seattle (206)447-3240. Religious requirement.

LDS Social Services, 6500-B West Deschutes, Kennewick (509)735-8406. Religious requirement.

LDS Social Services, 220 South Third Place, Renton (206)624-3393. Religious requirement.

LDS Social Services, North 606 Pines Road, Spokane (509)926-6581. Religious requirement.

Lutheran Social Services of Washington, 320 North Johnson, Kennewick (509)-735-6440

Lutheran Social Services of Washington, 19230 Forest Park Drive N.E., Seattle (206)365-2700

Lutheran Social Services of Washington, North 1226 Howard, Spokane (509)-327-7761

Medina Children's Services, 123 16th Avenue, Seattle (206)324-9470. Part of Family Builders Agency Network. Serves waiting children. No fee. Black child adoption program.

Regular Baptist Child Placement Agency, P.O. Box 16353, Seattle (206)938-1487. Religious requirement.

Seattle Indian Center, 121 Stewart Street, Seattle (206)624-8700. Serves state but has placed out of state. Serves enrolled Indian families.

Travelers Aid Society, 909 Fourth Avenue, Seattle (206)447-3888

WEST VIRGINIA
State Agency: Department of Human Services, Child Welfare, 1900 Washington Street East, Charleston 25305 (304)348-7980
State Exchange: West Virginia Adoption Exchange, P.O. Box 2942, Charleston 25330 (304)346-1062
State Photolisting Book: *West Virginia Adoption Exchange* (WVAE)
Independent Adoption: Permitted
NACAC Representative: Irene Carubia, R.D. #1, Box 137-D, Core 26529 (304)-879-5752
Private Agencies:
Children's Home Society of West Virginia, 1118 Kanawha Boulevard East, Charleston (304)346-0795. Serves state.
United Methodist Child Placement Service, Inc., P.O. Box 2078, Fairmont (304)-366-0694

WISCONSIN
State Agency: Department of Health and Social Services, Office for Children, Youth and Families, Division of Community Services, 1 West Wilson Street, P.O. Box 7851, Madison 53707 (608)266-0690
State Exchange: Wisconsin Adoption Resource Exchange
State Photolisting Book: *Lives Full of Beautiful Promise*
Independent Adoption: Permitted/Birth parents and adoptive parents must file petition for court approval of placement jointly.
NACAC Representative: Kay Peña, 3409 North 46th Street, Milwaukee 53216 (414)442-5278
Private Agencies:
Catholic Charities, Inc., Diocese of LaCrosse, 128 South 6th Street, LaCrosse (608)782-0704
Catholic Social Service, Diocese of Madison, 25 South Hancock Street, Madison (608)256-2358
Catholic Social Services, Diocese of Green Bay, 1825 Riverside Drive, Green Bay (414)437-7531. Places infants. Has done open adoptions.
Catholic Social Services of the Archdiocese of Milwaukee, Inc., 207 East Michigan Street, Milwaukee (414)271-2881
Children's Service Society of Wisconsin, 610 North Jackson Street, Milwaukee (414)276-5265. Serves state. Branch offices.
Human Element, Inc., 2701 North 56th Street, Milwaukee (414)445-9111
Lutheran Children's Friend Society, 3515 North 124th Street, Wauwatosa (414)-258-4542. Serves state.
Lutheran Social Services of Wisconsin and Upper Michigan, 3200 West Highland Boulevard, Milwaukee (414)342-7175. Serves state.
Pauquette Children's Service, 304 West Cook Street, Portage (608)742-5518
Seven Sorrows of our Sorrowful Mother Infants' Home, Route 1, Box 905, Nececah (608)565-2417. Serves state.

Wisconsin Lutheran Child and Family Service, 6800 North 76th Street, Milwaukee
    (414)353-5000

If you are interested in intercountry adoption, the Division of Community Services,
    Office for Children, Youth and Families can send you its *Handbook for Persons Thinking about Adopting a Foreign Child: Intercountry Adoption.*

WYOMING
State Agency: Wyoming State Department of Social Service, Hathaway Building,
    Cheyenne 82002 (307)777-6075
State Exchange: Wyoming State Exchange
State Photolisting Book: No
Independent Adoption: Permitted
NACAC Representative: Beverly Craig, 632 23rd Street, Cody 82414 (307)587-
    2494
Private Agencies:
Catholic Social Services, 623 South Wookott, Casper (307)237-2723
Lutheran Child and Family Services, 617 East 4th Street, Casper (307)265-9000
Wyoming Children's Society, P.O. Box 105, 716 Randall Avenue, Cheyenne (307)-
    632-7619

Intercountry Adoption Directory—

A Guide to U.S. Agencies

Many agencies in the United States have developed intercountry adoption programs. Some place only within a particular metropolitan area or state. Others have programs that will accept applicants from several states or around the country.

This list is *not* all-inclusive, although it lists many adoption programs. To compile this list, I have drawn upon fact sheets from parent groups, information provided by state departments of social services, the *Report on Foreign Adoption,* and the *OURS* Magazine "Placing Agency Update." Many agencies with intercountry programs were kind enough to fill out a questionnaire and send me brochures describing their programs.

Remember that intercountry adoption programs change frequently, so that some of the information listed here may already be out-of-date —an agency may have expanded its programs and service areas or discontinued a program. This list is intended as a guide, giving you many places to start and a sense of the intercountry programs that have been developed.

In using this guide, be aware that each *agency is listed by the state in which its main office is located. Read all entries since some agencies use the interstate compact to place children out of state or have branch offices in other states.*

For the most up-to-date information, contact parent groups or the International Concerns Committee for Children (911 Cypress Drive, Boulder, Colorado 80303; 303-494-8333), which publishes the *Report on Foreign Adoption.* Singles will want to check with the Committee for Single Adoptive Parents.

If you write to an agency, be sure to include a stamped, self-addressed envelop. If you ask them to call you, say that they can call "collect."

ARIZONA
Globe International Adoptions, Inc., 6220 West Monte Vista Road, Phoenix 85035 (602) 247-3038. *Programs:* various countries in Asia and Latin America. *Area Served:* United States.

CALIFORNIA
Adoption Horizons, P.O. Box 247, Arcata 95521 (707) 822-2660. *Programs:* India and Korea. *Area Served:* certain counties of California.

Adoptions Unlimited, 4479 Riverside Drive, Chino 91710 (714)591-0391. *Programs:* several countries in Asia and Latin America. *Area Served:* southern California.

Bal-Jagat, Inc., 9311 Farralone Avenue, Chatsworth (213) 709-4337 *Program:* India. *Area Served:* Certain counties in California.

Catholic Social Service, 2045 Lawton Street, San Francisco 94122 (415)665-5100. *Programs:* various countries in Asia and Latin America. *Area Served:* greater Bay Area

COLORADO
FCVN, 600 Gilpin Street, Denver 80218 (303) 321-8251. *Programs:* Korea, Colombia, Mexico. Special interest in Amerasian children. *Area Served:* Colorado

International Mission of Hope, 10734 Tancred Street, Denver 80234 (303)-457-4206. The purpose of IMH is to find homes for lost, abandoned, and orphaned children in India. It has placed children for adoption in the United States through licensed adoption agencies. IMH works extensively with newborns (it operates its own nursery in Calcutta). Its babies are high-risk infants who rarely weigh more than five pounds at birth and often less. You can contact the Denver office to learn which U.S. agency serves your area.

Hand in Hand International, 4965 Barnes Road, Colorado Springs 80907 (303) 596-1588. *Program:* Philippines. *Area Served:* United States.

CONNECTICUT
Family and Children's Aid of Greater Norwalk, 138 Main Street, Norwalk 06841 (203)846-4203. *Program:* Korea. *Area Served:* Connecticut.

International Alliance for Children, 23 South Main Street, New Milford 06776 (203)354-3417. *Program:* Philippines. *Area Served:* Connecticut and New York.

Thursday's Child, Inc., 227 Tunxis Avenue, Bloomfield 06002 (203)242-5941. *Programs:* India and Latin America. *Area Served:* United States

DISTRICT OF COLUMBIA

Adoption Service Information Agency, Inc. (ASIA), 7720 Alaska Avenue N.W., Washington 20012 (202)726-7193. *Program:* Korea. *Area Served:* metropolitan Washington.

American Adoption Agency, 1611 Connecticut Avenue N.W., Washington 20009 (202) 797-3756. *Programs:* Chile, India. *Area Served:* United States.

The Barker Foundation, 4545 42nd Street N.W., Washington 20016 (202)363-7751. *Programs:* Colombia, Brazil, Philippines. *Area Served:* metropolitan Washington.

World Child, Inc., 2025 "I" Street N.W., Suite 521, Washington 20006 (202)-429-8885. *Programs:* various countries in Latin America. *Area Served:* United States.

FLORIDA

Suncoast International Adoptions, Inc., 1016 Ponce De Leon Boulevard, Belleaire 33516 (813)586-5015. *Programs:* various countries in Asia and Latin America. *Area Served:* Florida.

Universal Aid for Children, Inc., 1175 Northeast 125th Street, Suite 202, North Miami 33161 (305)893-1535. *Programs:* Belize, Bolivia, Chile, Costa Rica, Dominican Republic, Ecuador, El Salvador, Hong Kong, India. Its programs seem to vary continually. *Area Served:* United States for some programs; Florida and Virginia for others.

GEORGIA

Children's Services International, 3098 Piedmont Road N.E., Atlanta 30305 (404)261-6992. *Programs:* Korea and various countries in Latin America. *Area Served:* Alabama, Georgia, Florida.

Illien Adoptions International Ltd., 1254 Piedmont Avenue N.E., Atlanta 30309 (404)872-6787. *Programs:* El Salvador, India. *Area Served:* United States.

HAWAII

Hawaii International Child Placement, P.O. Box 13, Hawaii 96719 (808)889-5122. *Programs:* Korea and Philippines. *Area Served:* Hawaii.

ILLINOIS

Travelers and Immigrants Aid, 327 South LaSalle Street, Room 1500, Chicago 60604 (312)435-4561. *Programs:* Korea, Colombia, and the Philippines. *Area Served:* Illinois.

MAINE

International Christian Adoption Agency, 60 West River Road, Waterville 04901 (207)872-2156. *Programs:* El Salvador and other countries in Latin America. *Area Served:* Maine.

MARYLAND

International Children's Services, Associated Catholic Charities, Inc., 320 Cathedral Street, Baltimore 21201 (301)547-5553. *Programs:* India, Korea, Latin America, and the Philippine Islands. *Area Served:* Florida; Louisana; Maryland; Washington, D.C.; and West Virginia.

MASSACHUSETTS

The Alliance for Children, Inc., P.O. Box 557, Needham 02192 (617)449-1277. *Programs:* various countries in Latin America. *Area Served:* Massachusetts.

Cambridge Adoption and Counseling Associates, P.O. Box 190, Cambridge 02142 (617)491-6245. *Programs:* various countries in Latin America. *Area Served:* Massachusetts.

Florence Crittenton League, 201 Thorndike Street, Lowell 01852 (617) 452-9671. *Program:* Colombia. *Area Served:* Massachusetts.

International Adoptions, Inc., 218 Walnut Street, Newton 02160 (617)965-2320. *Programs:* various countries in Asia and Latin America. *Area Served:* Connecticut, Massachusetts, New Hampshire, New York, Rhode Island, and Vermont.

World Adoption Services, Inc., 161 Auburn Street, Newton 02166 (617)332-3307. *Programs:* various countries in Asia and Latin America. *Area Served:* Connecticut, Massachusetts, New Hampshire. Has a limited referral program that accepts home studies from other licensed agencies within the United States.

MICHIGAN

Americans for International Aid and Adoption, 877 South Adams, Suite 106, Birmingham 48011 (313)645-2211. *Programs:* Guatemala, India, and Korea. Special concerns are Amerasian children and special-needs children. *Area Served:* United States, with branch offices in New York State and Washington.

Bethany International Adoptions, 32500 Concord, Suite 353-West, Madison Heights 48071 (313)588-9400. *Programs:* Korea. *Area Served:* Michigan, Ohio, Illinois, Colorado, Indiana, Minnesota, North Carolina, South Carolina, Mississippi, Wisconsin.

MINNESOTA

Children's Home Society of Minnesota, 2230 Como Avenue, St. Paul 55108 (612)646-6393. *Programs:* Hong Kong, India, Korea, and Latin America. Special interest in Amerasian and waiting children. *Area Served:* Minnesota for healthy children. Its waiting-child programs—Asian Waiting Child Program, Latin-American Waiting Child Program, and India program—accept applications throughout the United States.

Crossroads, Inc., 7703 Normandale Road, Office 100B, Edina 55437 (612)831-5707. *Programs:* various countries in Asia and Latin America. *Area Served:* Minnesota.

MISSOURI

Family Adoption and Counseling Services, Inc., 2 Bon Price Terrace, St. Louis 63122 (314)567-0707. *Programs:* India and various countries in Latin America. *Area Served:* United States.

Family and Children Services of Kansas City, Inc., 3515 Broadway, Kansas City 64111 (816)753-5280. *Program:* Korea. *Area Served:* Missouri and Kansas.

Love Basket, Inc., 8965 Old LeMay Ferry Road, Hillsboro 63050 (314)789-4100. *Program:* India. *Area Served:* United States.

Worldwide Love For Children, Inc., 1031 East Battlefield, Springfield 65807 (417)881-1044. *Programs:* India, Philippines, Korean waiting children. *Area Served:* Missouri.

NEW YORK

International Social Service/American Branch, Inc., 20 West 40th Street, New York 10018 (212)398-9142. *Programs:* Hong Kong, Japan. *Area Served:* United States. One of the parents must be Japanese for the Japan program. For the Hong Kong program, one of the parents must be Chinese or the family must be interested in a special-needs child.

Spence-Chapin Services to Families and Children, 6 East 94th Street, New York 10028 (212)369-0300. *Programs:* Hong Kong, Korea. *Area Served:* Connecticut, New Jersey, New York.

NORTH DAKOTA

SAME Christian Resource Center, Inc., P.O. Box 2344, Bismarck 58502 (701)-222-3960. *Programs:* various countries in Latin America. Special interest in waiting children. *Area Served:* United States. Its information sheets state that "persons seeking the adoption of a foreign child must show evidence of their Christian convictions and their ability and intentions to rear a child as a Christian. The Christian experience of one will not necessarily be the same as that of another and the language expressing one's faith may differ, but the personal acceptance of God and Jesus as the Lord and Savior should be the same. Views regarding moral, ethical, and spiritual convictions and their place in the rearing of children are considered appropriate areas for discussion during the adoption study."

OKLAHOMA

Dillon International, 7615 East 63d Place S., Tulsa 74133 (918)250-1561. *Programs:* India, Korea. *Area Served:* For Korea, Oklahoma, Arizona, Texas, New York; for India, U.S. Branch offices in Ronkonkoma, New York and Scottsdale, Arizona.

OREGON

Holt International Children's Services, Inc., P.O. Box 2880, Eugene 97402 (503)687-2202. *Programs:* Colombia, India, Korea, the Philippines, Thailand. Special interest in waiting children and Amerasians. *Area Served:* There was a time when Holt placed Korean children throughout the United States. Changes in Korean law have caused Holt to limit placements from Korea to some states. Children have been placed in Arkansas, California, Iowa, Kentucky, Mississippi, Nebraska, New Jersey, Oregon, South Dakota, Tennessee, and Wyoming. Its other programs are open to people throughout the United States.

Plan Loving Adoptions Now, Inc. (PLAN), P.O. Box 667, McMinnville 97128 (503)472-8452. *Programs:* various countries in Asia and Latin America. *Area served:* Oregon for some; U.S. for others.

PENNSYLVANIA

Aid for Children International, 1516 Ridge Road, Lancaster 17603 (717)393-0296. *Programs:* various countries in Asia and Latin America. *Area Served:* near Lancaster.

Love the Children, Inc., 221 West Broad Street, Quakertown 18951 (215)536-4180. *Program:* Korea. *Area Served:* Massachusetts, New Jersey, New York, and Pennsylvania.

Welcome House, P.O. Box 836, Doylestown (215)345-0430. *Programs:* Hong Kong, Korea, Philippines. Special interest in Amerasians. *Area Served:* varies by the program along the East Coast. Contact them.

TEXAS

Los Niños International Adoption Center, 3200 South Congress, Austin (512)-443-2833. *Programs:* Chile, Colombia, Costa Rica, Honduras, Lebanon, Taiwan. *Area Served:* serves Texas directly and works through referral agencies in Iowa, Maryland, Nebraska, North Dakota, and Wisconsin. Contact them for details.

WASHINGTON

Adoption Advocates International, 658 Black Diamond Road, Port Angeles 98362 (206)452-4777. *Programs:* various countries in Asia and Latin America. *Area Served:* Washington.

Adoption Services of WACAP, P.O. Box 2009, Port Angeles 98362 (206)452-2308. *Programs:* various countries in Asia and Latin America. Special interest in Amerasian and waiting children. *Area Served:* Alaska, Idaho, Utah, Washington. Families with an approved home study and a supervising agency from other states may contact them about their waiting children.

Catholic Community Service—King County, 1715 East Cherry Street, Seattle 98122 (206)323-6336. *Program:* Korea, Japan. *Area Served:* Washington.

International Children's Services of Washington, 3251 107th S.E., Bellevue 98004 (206)451-9370. *Program:* Colombia. *Area Served:* United States.

Travelers Aid Society, Intercountry Adoption Service, 909 4th Avenue, Room 630, Seattle 98104 (206)447-3888. *Program:* Korea. *Area Served:* Washington.

Recommended Reading

You may find the following books and pamphlets stimulating reading. These materials focus on a variety of subjects related to adoption. This list is not comprehensive (there is a vast literature today about adoption) but rather singles out some current interesting books for both adults and children. The majority of these books are still in print. Also, consult the index of this book for additional reading suggestions mentioned in discussions of specific topics.

Adoption Information Books

Jayne Askin with Bob Oskam, *Search: A Handbook for Adoptees and Birthparents* (New York: Harper & Row, 1982). A resource book that takes interested people through the stages of the search—what's involved and how to go about it. A state-by-state compilation of helpful information covers such subjects as inheritance, the sealing and opening of records, state agencies connected to adoption, and where records are held.

Linda Cannon Burgess, *The Art of Adoption* (New York: Norton, 1981). Focuses on the feelings of birth parents, adoptees, and adoptive parents. Grapples with questions of raising children.

Families Adopting Children Everywhere, *Family Building Thru Adoption* (Bel Air, Md.: FACE, 1980). Booklet developed for this parent group's course on family building. The writings collected —e.g., a sample home study, a work sheet for evaluating your ability to parent a special-needs child—make it informative and valuable. Available from FACE, P.O. Box 102, Bel Air, Maryland.

Claudia L. Jewett, *Adopting the Older Child* (Harvard: The Harvard Common Press, 1978). A landmark book that introduces people to the adoption of older children. Jewett follows the history of several children and their adoptive families, starting before the adoption and following them through to the postplacement period.

Hope Marindin, ed., *The Handbook for Single Adoptive Parents* (Committee for Single Adoptive Parents: Chevy Chase, Md.: 1982). Although written for the single considering adoption, this book contains much valuable information for anyone contemplating adoption. There is a nice mix of practical information (the mechanics of adoption and managing single parenthood) with adoption experiences. Available through the Committee for Single Adoptive Parents, P.O. Box 15084, Chevy Chase, Maryland.

Dorothy W. Smith and Laurie Nehls Sherwen, *Mothers and their Adopted Children—the Bonding Process* (New York: Tiresias Press, 1983). Based on a survey and interviews, the book looks at how bonding takes place.

Jerome Smith, *You're Our Child: A Social/Psychological Approach to Adoption* (Washington, D.C.: University Press of America, 1981). Looks at the psychological tasks faced by adoptive parents and adoptees.

Adoption Reform

Suzanne Arms, *To Love and Let Go* (New York: Knopf, 1983). A group of profiles: birth mothers who relinquished their children; an adult adoptee's search; an adoption attorney; and prospective adoptive families. Arms vividly describes several open infant adoptions, including one in which the parents were present at the child's birth. The adoptions that she witnessed occurred through independent placement. Her book is a strong plea for more openness in adoption.

William Feigelman and Arnold R. Silverman, *Chosen Children* (New York: Praeger, 1983). A research study that examines new patterns of adoptive relationships. Among its subjects: the differences in attitudes between infertile couples and "preferential adopters" (fertile couples, singles), adjustments of black children adopted by white families, adaptation of transracially adopted Korean-born adolescents, and adjustment of Colombian-born children adopted by white families.

H. David Kirk, *Adoptive Kinship: A Modern Institution in Need of Reform* (Toronto: Butterworth, 1981). This book extends the argument that Kirk set forth in his 1964 book, *Shared Fate* (available from Ben-Simon Publications, P.O. Box 318, Brentwood Bay, B.C., Canada VOS IAO), that the adoptive situation is different from that of the family whose bonds are based on birth. People involved in adoption must acknowledge the differences as they build their family relationships.

Betty Jean Lifton, *Lost and Found: The Adoption Experience* (New York: Dial Press, 1979). Focuses on the adoptee's struggle for a sense of identity using extensive interviews with members of the adoption triangle. Her final chapter, "Rights and Responsibilities for Everyone in the Adoption Circle," is one of the most cogent statements I have seen.

Kathleen Silber and Phylis Speedlin, *Dear Birthmother* (San Antonio: Corona, 1983). Letters exchanged between adoptive parents and birth parents as well as letters from birth parents to their children form the backbone of this book. The letters are used to hammer away at four myths: (1) that birth parents don't care about their children (2) that adoption must be a strictly confidential matter, (3) that birth parents will forget about their children, and (4) that if the adoptee loved her parents, she would not have to search for her birth parents. Kathleen Silber is the director of the San Antonio office of Lutheran Social Service of Texas.

Arthur D. Sorosky, Annette Baran, and Reuben Pannor, *The Adoption Triangle* (Garden City, New York: Anchor, 1979). Examines the effect of the sealed record on adoptees, birth parents, and adoptive parents and sets forth the belief that adoption is a lifelong process. The authors call for reevaluation of current adoption practices toward more openness.

Barbara T. Tremitiere, R. Kent Boesdorfer, Joyce S. Kaser, and William C. Tremitiere, *TEAM Parent Preparation Handbook* (Washington, D.C.: North American Council on Adoptable Children, 1981). Describes the TEAM program and how groups can implement their own.

For Children and Adolescents

Catherine and Sherry Bunin, *Is That Your Sister? A True Story of Adoption* (New York: Pantheon, 1976). Illustrated with photographs of her family and narrated by six-year-old Catherine, this book tells her family's adoption story—the building of a transracial family. Presents questions that children may hear from others.

Betsy Byars, *The Pinballs* (New York: Harper & Row, 1977). The fictional tale of three children who find themselves in foster care and how they build a friendship.

Jeannette Caines, *Abby* (New York: Harper & Row, 1973). Picture book for preschoolers. Abby, who was adopted when she was an infant, likes to look at her baby book and hear the story of her arrival in her family.

Shirley Gordon, *The Boy Who Wanted a Family* (New York: Harper & Row, 1980). The fears, hopes, and experiences of seven-year-old Michael during the one-year waiting period before the finalization of his adoption. The fictional account takes him from his foster home—the last of many—to his home with his single adoptive mother.

Ezra Jack Keats, *Peter's Chair* (New York: Harper & Row, 1967). Peter is upset that his cradle has been given to his new baby sister. Story focuses on how Peter decides to share his special chair.

Jill Krementz, *How It Feels to Be Adopted* (New York: Knopf, 1982). Nineteen children, ages eight to sixteen, shared their feelings with Krementz. Photographs of the children, alone and with their parents and family, are an integral part of the book. A book for parents of young children to read and think about; for older children to read; for families to share together.

Susan Lapsley, *I Am Adopted* (Great Britain: Bodley Head, 1982). Gentle picture book designed for young children, with a simple message: "Adoption means belonging." Distributed in the United States through The Bodley Head/Merrimack, 47 Pelham Road, Salem, New Hampshire.

Betty Jean Lifton, *I'm Still Me* (New York: Knopf, 1981). The book starts out: "It may sound weird to say that your whole life was changed because of an American history assignment. But that's the way it was...." When teenaged Lori Elkins is asked to prepare a family tree, she has to deal with the issues of adoption, origins, and feelings. Lori Elkins decides to search. A book not for teenagers only.

Lois Lowry, *Find a Stranger, Say Goodbye* (Boston: Houghton Mifflin, 1978). In this novel, a teenager seeks out her birth mother. The book explores her complex emotions.

Patricia MacLachlan, *Mama One, Mama Two* (New York: Harper & Row, 1982). Simple children's picture book that tells the story of a little girl's entry into foster care.

Katherine Paterson, *The Great Gilly Hopkins* (New York: Harper & Row, 1978). Eleven-year-old Gilly has been shuffled around. When she lands in her latest foster home, she schemes against everyone who tries to befriend her.

Lila Perl, *Piñatas and Paper Flowers* (New York: Clarion, 1983). Discusses eight holidays of Latin America. Bilingual edition.

Harriet Langsam Sobol, *We Don't Look Like Our Mom and Dad*. (New York: Coward-McCann, 1984). Photo-essay about two Korean adoptees and their family.

Peter Spier, *People* (New York: Doubleday, 1980). A joyful picture book about people and how they're different and similar. Says Spier: "We come in all sizes and shapes: tall, short, and in between. But without a single exception, we all began quite small!"

Marjorie Ann Waybill, *Chinese Eyes* (Scottdale, Pa.: Herald Press, 1974). A picture book that tells the story of a first-grade Korean adoptee's encounter with prejudice—"There's little Chinese eyes!" The book looks at her feelings and her mother's explanation of differences and similarities.

Infertility

Lori B. Andrews, *New Conceptions* (New York: St. Martin's Press, 1984). Guide to infertility, treatments with emphasis on *in vitro* fertilization, artificial insemination, and the use of surrogates.

Rochelle Friedman and Bonnie Gradstein, *Surviving Pregnancy Loss* (Boston: Little, Brown, 1982). A sensitive discussion of miscarriage, stillbirth, ectopic pregnancy, and multiple losses. Includes a chapter about adoption. Gradstein has counseled people about independent-placement adoption.

Robert H. Glass and Ronald J. Ericsson, *Getting Pregnant in the 1980s* (Berkeley: University of California Press, 1982). An informative, basic guide that focuses on the newest developments in human reproduction.

Barbara Eck Menning, *Infertility* (Englewood Cliffs, N.J.: Prentice-Hall, 1977). Focuses on the experience of infertility and how it affects people. Written by the founder of Resolve, this book looks at the psychological and social toll that infertility takes.

Sherman J. Silber, *How to Get Pregnant* (New York: Scribner's, 1980). A basic guide to the problem of infertility, particularly strong in explaining the reproductive system. Silber emphasizes that infertility is a problem shared by a couple, hence treatment must be directed at both husband and wife.

Intercountry Adoption

Jean Nelson-Erichsen and Heino R. Erichsen, *Gamines: How to Adopt
    from Latin America* (Minneapolis: Dillon Press, 1981). A general
    overview.

Frances M. Koh, *Oriental Children in American Homes: How Do They
    Adjust?* (Minneapolis: East-West Press, 1981). A study of culture
    and adoption. Koh analyzes the differences between Asian and
    American society in social relations, methods of discipline, educa-
    tion, and personality development, and discusses their effects on
    the adjustment of Asian children in American homes.

Report on Foreign Adoption (International Concerns Committee for
    Children, 911 Cypress Drive, Boulder, Colorado 80303). Issued
    annually, this report takes a country-by-country, agency-by-
    agency look at intercountry adoption. Updated nine times during
    the year.

Mary Taylor, revised by Betty Laning, *A Parent's Guide to Intercoun-
    try Adoption* (Boston: Open Door Society of Massachusetts, 1981).
    Basic guide chock-full of useful information.

Personal Accounts/Family Profiles

Barbara J. Berg, *Nothing to Cry About* (New York: Bantam Books,
    1983). A moving account of the author's experiences (she suffered
    two late miscarriages before successfully giving birth). One chap-
    ter chronicles her daughter's adoption through an independent
    placement. Berg's technique involved spreading the word
    through résumés.

Joseph Blank, *Nineteen Steps Up the Mountain: The Story of the De-
    Bolt Family* (Philadelphia: Lippincott, 1976). Biography of the
    DeBolts who built a large family of special-needs children.

Lorraine Dusky, *Birthmark* (New York: Evans, 1979). A birth mother's
    account of her pregnancy, her relinquishment of her child, and
    her postpartum feelings. The book appeared some thirteen years
    after the birth of her child. Dusky searched for—and eventually
    found—her daughter.

Florence Fisher, *The Search for Anna Fisher* (New York: Arthur
    Fields, 1973). A landmark personal chronicle of an adoptee's
    search for her birth family. Fisher was instrumental in the creation
    of the adoptee group Adoptees' Liberty Movement Association
    (ALMA).

Jan de Hartog, *The Children* (New York: Atheneum, 1969). A thoroughly enjoyable, but practical, chronicle of his family's experiences in adopting two Korean girls, ages five and three.

Bertha Holt, *The Seed from the East* and *Outstretched Arms* (Eugene, Oregon: reprinted by Industrial Publishing Company, 1983). The story of the development of the Holt adoption program in Korea. If you're the parent of a child from Korea, particularly if your child came from the Holt agency in the United States or in Korea, you'll enjoy reading this family's story. Available from Holt International Children's Services.

Betty Kramer, ed., *Carry It On: A Collection of Writings on Interracial and International Adoption* (Minneapolis: OURS, 1978). Reprints of articles that originally appeared in the parent group's magazine. Helpful in capturing feelings involved in the waiting, the child's arrival, and adjustment.

Tony Kornheiser, *The Baby Chase* (New York: Atheneum, 1983). What's it like to find yourself involved in an independent-placement adoption where the go-between wants $15,000 in cash? Kornheiser describes his and his wife's difficulties in dealing with their infertility; their desire to adopt a child; and their temptation to pursue this opportunity. The book is strong in conveying their pain and anguish and also their lack of supports and basic information—the kind that comes through parent groups.

Betty Jean Lifton, *Twice-Born* (New York: McGraw-Hill, 1975). An autobiography focusing on how Lifton felt as an adoptee, her search and reunion with her birth mother, and the relationship that developed following her search. The emotional complexities of adoption, rather than any legal barriers set up in Lifton's path, form the heart of the book.

Doris Lund, *Patchwork Clan: How the Sweeny Family Grew* (Boston: Little, Brown, 1982). A portrait of John and Ann Sweeny and their seventeen children. The book is particularly good in its description of the adjustment processes of the children in this multiracial family.

Katrina Maxtone-Graham, *An Adopted Woman* (New York: Rémi, 1983). An autobiography describing the author's search and the many barriers thrown up in her path. Her account raises questions about the policy of closed records and particularly the reluctance of one agency to provide even nonidentifying information.

Diane Nason with Birdie Etchison, *The Celebration Family* (Nashville: Thomas Nelson, 1983). An autobiography focusing on the creation of a large adoptive family in which many of the children have special needs.

Grace Layton Sandness, *Brimming Over* (Minneapolis: Mini-World, 1978). Paralyzed by polio as a teenager, Sandness goes on to marry and parent a large adopted family. The book is her account of how she and her husband did it.

Poetry

Patricia Irwin Johnston, comp., *Perspectives on a Grafted Tree: Thoughts for Those Touched by Adoption* (Fort Wayne, Ind.: Perspectives Press, 1983). Poetry written by adoptive parents and birth parents that touches on parts of the adoption process—"beginnings and endings," "the grafting," "reactions," "attachments," "motherspeakings," "identities," and "reflections."

Special-Needs Adoption

Joan McNamara, *Adopting the Child with Special Needs* (Washington, D.C.: North American Council on Adoptable Children, 1982). A booklet providing basic information about special-needs children —the types of handicaps they may have and the resources that are available. If you're unfamiliar with special-needs children, the booklet is a good starting place.

Linda Dunn, ed., *Adopting Children with Special Needs: A Sequel* (Washington, D.C.: NACAC, 1983). Stories by adoptive and foster parents describing their experiences.

Notes

1. Learning About Adoption

1. This information comes from statistics provided by various states in response to a questionnaire I mailed out in 1983.
2. The statistics for the 1970s come from William Feigelman and Arnold R. Silverman, *Chosen Children* (New York: Praeger, 1983). The National Committee for Adoption gives its estimate in a letter that it mails to prospective adoptive parents. Officials at the State Department and the Children's Bureau took the time to get their statistics for me.
3. Sherman J. Silber, *How To Get Pregnant* (New York: Scribner's, 1980), p. 5.
4. Robert H. Glass and Ronald J. Ericsson, *Getting Pregnant in the 1980s* (Berkeley: University of California Press, 1982).
5. Marcia Stamell, "Infertility: Fighting Back," *New York*, March 21, 1983.
6. Ibid.
7. "The Adoptive Family: Changing Views," *Child and Adolescent Mental Health Review*, Winter 1983, published by Del Amo Hospital, Torrance, California.

2. Exploring Adoption Through an Agency

1. Barbara Joe, "Black Children Waiting," *Metropolitan Washington*, Dec. 1982–Jan. 1983, reprinted in the newsletter of the International Concerns Committee for Children.
2. Barbara Joe, "Singles: Adopting the Family Way," *Washington Post*, 25 Jan. 1982.
3. Diane Nason with Birdie Etchison, *The Celebration Family* (Nashville: Thomas Nelson, 1983), p. 80.
4. Kathleen Silber and Phylis Speedlin, *Dear Birthmother* (San Antonio: Corona, 1983), p. 1.

5. Ibid., p. 145.
6. Ibid., pp. 165–187.
7. With the cooperation of Catholic Social Services, I conducted extensive telephone interviews with birth mothers and with adoptive parents. The material that follows is excerpted from those interviews. The names used are pseudonyms.
8. Arthur D. Sorosky, Annette Baran, and Reuben Pannor talk about the birth parent's continued feelings of loss in their book *The Adoption Triangle* (Garden City, New York: Anchor, 1979). The feelings of birth parents are also poignantly conveyed in *Ours Is a Solomon's Child*, a pamphlet published by the Children's Bureau of Delaware, and Lorraine Dusky's *Birthmark* (New York: Evans, 1979).
9. Many of these questions are based on material in *How to Adopt in Colorado*, published by Colorado Parents for All Children, and Pat Shirley's "So You Want to Adopt an Older Child," *FACE Facts*, Nov. 1982.

3. The Home Study

1. Thomas Morton, "Practice Issue: The Home Study," *Adoption Report*, 1982.
2. Much of this list is derived from the helpful pointers in "How to Survive a Homestudy" by Julie Fahrer of the Adoption Research Center in Culver City, California. An adoptive parent shared this information sheet with me.
3. Barbara T. Tremitiere, R. Kent Boesdorfer, Joyce S. Kaser, and William C. Tremitiere, *TEAM Parent Preparation Handbook*, p. 1.
4. One of the sessions is actually a double session. The list is derived from the overview of the TEAM model of parent preparation given in R. Kent Boesdorfer, Joyce S. Kaser, and William C. Tremitiere, *Guide to Local TEAM Programs*, p. 40. A full discussion of the program can be found in the *TEAM Parent Preparation Handbook*.
5. Barbara Tremitiere, "Model Placement Services for Children with Special Needs—The 'Client-Centered' Approach," in T-LSA Adoption Services, *There are Children Waiting . . .*, p. 2.
6. Morton, *Adoption Report*, p. 5.
7. Pat Shirley, *FACE Facts*, Nov. 1982.
8. Ibid.
9. Based on Kenneth J. Hermann, Jr., *Adoption: Questions, Resources and Readings* (OURS of Western New York, Feb. 1983) and *What to Do if You Get Stuck* (OURS of Sonoma County,)

4. Considering Intercountry Adoption

1. William Feigelman and Arnold R. Silverman provide some data in *Chosen Children* (New York: Praeger, 1983).
2. The Immigration and Naturalization Service keeps track of the number of immigrant orphans admitted. Its most current figures were for 1981. The

Bureau of Consular Affairs of the Department of State records the number of visas issued. The Office of Public Affairs provided these figures to me. If we assume the total nonrelative adoptions to be 59,000, then intercountry adoptions accounted for 12.5 percent of adoptions in 1983.
3. Letter from Father Piergiovanni, Feb. 1983
4. From *Adoption—A family affair,* prepared by Holt International Children's Services, P.O. Box 2880, Eugene, Oregon.
5. *FACE Facts,* Jan. 1983.
6. *GIFT,* Summer 1982.
7. Excerpted from their form entitled "Family's Opinion of Possible Acceptance of Child with Special Medical Needs."

5. Paperwork

1. Based on information in *Where to Write for Birth and Death Records, United States and Outlying Areas,* and *Where to Write for Marriage Records, United States and Outlying Areas,* prepared by the U.S. Department of Health, Education and Welfare, rev. ed., 1979; Nancy D. Wright and Gene P. Allen, comps., *National Directory of State Agencies 1982–1983* (Arlington, Va.: Information Resources Press, 1982); and *State Administrative Officials Classified by Function* 1982–1983 (Lexington, KY: The Council of State Governments, 1984).
2. State Department of Social and Rehabilitation Services of Kansas, Division of Services to Children and Youth, *Kansas Statutes Relating to Adoption of Children.*

7. Searching for a Baby Independently

1. Information from questionnaires returned to me by officials in the states.
2. Grace Lichtenstein, "Babies from the Want Ads," *New York,* 28 Sept. 1981, p. 40.
3. Bonnie D. Gradstein, Marc Gradstein, and Robert H. Glass, "Private Adoption," *Fertility and Sterility* 37, no. 4 (Apr. 1982), pp. 548–51.
4. Gradstein et al. state that half of their clients had personal meetings with the mother, and nineteen attended the birth.
5. Gradstein et al., p. 549. Cynthia White Hecker tells how she successfully used this approach in "Wanted: A Baby to Love," *Wellesley,* Summer 1983. Hecker and her husband met with success within a few months; in fact they met with two birth mothers and ended up the parents of two infants!
6. See Cynthia D. Martin, *Beating the Adoption Game* (La Jolla, Calif.: Oak Tree Publications, 1980), pp. 138–49.
7. Barbara Berg in "Our Fail-safe Way to Adopt" (*Parents,* Feb. 1983) describes how she and her husband sent out résumés to people they knew. The Bergs became parents less than three months after their letters went out.

8. Adapted from Adoptive Parents Committee, Inc., *Guidelines for Independent Placement (Parent-Initiated) Adoption*, rev. ed., 1980.

8. Searching for a Waiting Child in the United States

1. Based on the *Directory of Adoption Exchanges Serving the United States*, prepared by the National Adoption Exchange (1983).
2. Barbara Tremitiere, "But I Thought It Would Be Okay," *Children and Adoptive Parents*, Apr.–Aug. 1982.
3. Ibid.
4. From the newsletter of Alabama Friends of Adoption (Birmingham, Ala., 1982).
5. Connecticut Adoption Resource Exchange, *Second Annual Report*, 1 July 1981–30 June 1982, p. 18.

9. Searching Independently for a Child Abroad

1. "Private or Agency Adoption (A Comparison)," in *Intercountry Adoption in California and Abroad* (Department of Social Services of California, 1981), p. 61.
2. This list is based on information supplied by the overseas agencies and the embassies in the United States. It also draws upon the fact sheets produced by LAPA and OURS.

10. Preparing for Your Child

1. Betsy Guinn, "Adopting: While You Wait," *HI Families*, July–Aug. 1983, p. 17.
2. Claudia L. Jewett, *Adopting the Older Child* (Harvard: The Harvard Common Press, 1978), p. 53.
3. *New York Times*, 2 Nov. 1983.
4. Caroline Gerberich, "A Survey of Working Adoptive Mothers' Employee Benefits," *FACE Facts*, Oct. 1983. The survey was sent out to readers of *FACE Facts* and of *Adoptalk*. Forty-three surveys were sent back.
5. Hewitt Associates, "Adoption Benefits," 1980.
6. Mary Ann Jones, *The Sealed Adoption Record Controversy* (New York: Child Welfare League of America, Inc., 1976).
7. Jayne Askin with Bob Oskam, *Search* (New York: Harper & Row, 1982).
8. Jewett, *Adopting the Older Child*, p. 99.
9. Ibid., pp. 99–100.
10. For a fuller discussion of breast-feeding an adopted infant, you may want to take a look at two articles that appeared in the newsletter *Adopted Child* (P.O. Box 9362, Moscow, Idaho 83843): "Breastfeeding: Goal Is Emotional, Not Nutritional Benefit" (Mar. 1983) and "Adoptive Mothers' Milk Different" (Nov. 1982).

11. Comments made by Jack Frank at the Adoptive Parents Committee adoption conference, "Adoption: Directions for the '80's," 20 Nov. 1983.
12. Jewett, p. 81.
13. *Adoptalk,* July–Aug. 1982, pp. 1–2. The entire issue focused on postplacement support.
14. *PLAN,* July–Aug. 1982. Reprinted in *FAIR,* Oct. 1982, p. 11.
15. "Don't Re-name Even a Young Child," *Adopted Child,* July 1982, pp. 1, 4.
16. Gloria Petersen, ed., "The Special Student" (Illinois Council on Adoptable Children, Inc., 1982), p. 1.
17. Comments made by Jack Frank at the Adoptive Parents Committee adoption conference, "Adoption: Directions for the '80's," 20 Nov. 1983.
18. Joyce S. Kaser and R. Kent Boesdorfer, "What Should We Name This Child?: The Difficulties of Naming Older Adopted Children," *Children Today,* Nov.–Dec. 1981, p. 8.

11. Adjustments

1. *FACE Facts,* Nov. 1983.
2. *Buena Vista,* May 1983.
3. Dorothy W. Smith and Laurie Nehls Sherwen, *Mothers and their Adopted Children—the Bonding Process* (New York: Tiresias, 1983), pp. 12–13. I have tried to summarize some of their main points in the following paragraphs.
4. Ibid., pp. 82–83.
5. Many adoptive parents talked with me about their adjustment experiences. Where the anecdote is based on a published source, I have footnoted the source. Otherwise the information comes from my interviews.
6. Barbara J. Berg, *Nothing to Cry About* (New York: Bantam Books, 1983), p. 199.
7. Smith and Sherwen, pp. 86–87.
8. *FACE Facts,* Apr. 1983.
9. Ibid.
10. *Clark Adoption Resources Newsletter,* June 1983.
11. Smith and Sherwen, p. 104.
12. Jill Krementz, *How It Feels to Be Adopted* (New York: Knopf), 1982, pp. 16 and 99.
13. "Infant Adoption: Two Family Experiences with Intercountry Adoption," *Children Today,* Nov.–Dec. 1980, pp. 2–5. All quotations about Jane are taken from this article.
14. "What Do Babies Know?" *Time,* 15 Aug. 1983, p. 59.
15. Laurie Flynn, "Why Would Anyone Adopt a Teenager," *Change,* Fall 1980, pp. 7–8. All quotations from Flynn are from this article.
16. When discussing the grieving process, experts often refer to Elisabeth Kübler-Ross, *On Death and Dying* (New York: Macmillan, 1969). You might

also want to read Claudia L. Jewett's *Helping Children Cope with Separation and Loss* (Harvard: The Harvard Common Press, 1982).
17. Claudia Jewett, *A Parent's Guide to Adopting An Older Child*, p. 21. Booklet available from the Open Door Society of Massachusetts.
18. Jewett, *Adopting the Older Child*, p. 288.
19. From the newsletter of the Open Door Society of Long Island.
20. For a full range of support services, see NACAC's *Guide to Local TEAM Programs*.
21. Adoptalk, July-Aug. 1982.
22. "Looking Back at Disruption." Materials developed at a 1975 "Disruption" workshop in conjunction with the annual meeting of Spaulding for Children. The quoted material is excerpted from a section entitled "Disruption: One Mother's Point of View."

12. Raising the Adopted Child

1. Krementz, p. 8.
2. Betty Jean Lifton, *Lost and Found* (New York: Dial Press, 1983), pp. 205–206.
3. The list that I have compiled derives from many sources—articles, books, parent newsletters, interviews. Several of the books listed in "Recommended Reading" focus on telling a child about adoption. Among the more insightful are the following: Linda Cannon Burgess, *The Art of Adoption* (New York: Norton, 1981); William Feigelman and Arnold R. Silverman, *Chosen Children* (New York: Praeger, 1983); Betty Jean Lifton, *Lost and Found;* and Arthur D. Sorosky, Annette Baran, and Reuben Pannor, *The Adoption Triangle* (New York: Anchor, 1979). David Brodzinsky has published an interesting report on his research, "Children's Understanding of Adoption: Implications for the Telling Process," in *Adoption Report,* Fall 1982. Claire Berman has also written a good overview in "Raising the Adopted Child," *Parents,* Feb. 1983. Much of the same information also appears in the pamphlet *Raising an Adopted Child,* which Berman wrote. Available from Public Affairs Committee, Inc., 381 Park Avenue South, New York, N.Y.
4. Lifton, p. 20.
5. Pat Tobin, "Blessing in a Back Street," in FACE booklet *Family Building Thru Adoption*.
6. Lifton, p. 206.
7. Krementz, pp. 79–80.
8. Children's Bureau of Delaware, *Ours Is a Solomon's Child*, p. 9.
9. H. David Kirk, *Shared Fate* (New York: The Free Press, 1964), pp. 30 and 35.
10. *Newsweek,* 12 Dec. 1983, pp. 78–85; and *Time,* 12 Dec. 1983, pp. 64 and 67.
11. Article in the 1982 newsletter of Holt International Children's Services.

12. *Woman's Day,* 13 Sept. 1983, p. 12.
13. Ruth Chamberlin, "Conference Review: Adoptees Talk about Transracial Adoption," *Adoptalk,* Oct. 1982. There have been several major studies of transracial adoption and the adoptees' adjustment and identity. You may want to look at Rita J. Simon and Howard J. Altstein, *Transracial Adoption* (New York: John Wiley & Sons, 1977) and *Transracial Adoption: A Follow-Up* (Lexington, Mass.: Lexington Books, 1981); Ruth G. McRoy, Louis A. Zurcher, Michael L. Lauderdale, and Rosalie N. Anderson, "Self-esteem and Racial Identity in Transracial and Inracial Adoptees," *Social Work* 27, no. 6 (Nov. 1982); Dong Soo Kim, "How They Fared in American Homes: A Follow-up Study of Adopted Korean Children in the United States," *Children Today,* Mar.–Apr. 1977; William Feigelman and Arnold R. Silverman, *Chosen Children* (New York: Praeger, 1983).
14. Holt International Children's Services, *Adoption—A Family Affair.*
15. Holt newsletter, 1982.
16. Holt newsletter, 1982.
17. Jayne Askin, *Search* (New York: Harper & Row), p. xiv.
18. Sorosky, Baran, and Pannor, p. 201.

Index